THE UNCONSCIOUS AT WORK

Why do our organizations so often seem to be less than the sum of their parts? What undermines effectiveness and morale, and gets in the way of achieving what we set out to do?

The Unconscious at Work, Second Edition draws on a body of thinking and practice which has developed over the past 70 years, often referred to as 'the Tavistock approach' or 'systems-psychodynamics'. All the contributors are practising consultants who draw on this framework, bringing it alive and making it useful to any reader – manager, leader or consultant, regardless of whether they have any prior familiarity with the underlying concepts – who is curious about what might be driving the puzzling or stressful situations they find in their workplace.

The First Edition was addressed to people working in 'the human services': health, social care and education. Since it was published in 1994, there has been growing interest in the business world, and in understanding more about the 'irrational' side of organizational life. Therefore, this Second Edition includes an entirely new section where the key ideas are revisited and illustrated with case studies from a wide range of business organizations, from large corporations to start-ups and family businesses.

The aim, however remains the same: to enlarge readers' existing sense-making 'tool-kits' so that they can look at themselves and their organizations with fresh eyes, deepening the emotional intelligence they bring to bear on the challenges they face and providing new possibilities for action. *The Unconscious at Work*, Second Edition is for managers, leaders, consultants, and anyone working in organizations who has been puzzled, disturbed or challenged by their experiences at work.

Anton Obholzer, BSc, MB, ChB, DPM, FRCPsych is a psychoanalyst, organizational consultant, and former CEO of the Tavistock and Portman NHS Foundation Trust. He is a senior member of faculty of the Advanced Management Programme of the INSEAD Global Leadership Centre in Paris.

Vega Zagier Roberts, MD is an independent consultant and coach, an associate consultant at Tavistock Consulting, and a faculty member on the Tavistock and Portman NHS Trust master's programme *Consulting and Leading in Organisations* and doctoral programme *Consultation and the Organisation*.

THE UNCONSCIOUS AT WORK

A Tavistock Approach to Making Sense of Organizational Life

Second Edition

Edited by
Anton Obholzer and
Vega Zagier Roberts

Routledge
Taylor & Francis Group

LONDON AND NEW YORK

Second Edition published 2019
by Routledge
2 Park Square, Milton Park, Abingdon, Oxon OX14 4RN

and by Routledge
52 Vanderbilt Avenue, New York, NY 10017

Routledge is an imprint of the Taylor & Francis Group, an informa business

First Edition published as *The Unconscious at Work: Individual and Organizational Stress in the Human Services* by Routledge, 1994

British Library Cataloguing-in-Publication Data
A catalogue record for this book is available from the British Library

Library of Congress Cataloging-in-Publication Data
Names: Obholzer, Anton, 1938– editor. | Roberts, Vega Zagier, 1948– editor.
    Tavistock Clinic "Consulting to Institutions" Workshop.
Title: The unconscious at work : a Tavistock approach to making sense of
    organizational life / edited by Anton Obholzer and Vega Zagier Roberts.
Description: 2nd Edition. | New York : Routledge, 2019. | Revised edition of
    The Unconscious at work, 1994. | Includes bibliographical references and index.
Identifiers: LCCN 2018046804 (print) | LCCN 2018049459 (ebook) |
    ISBN 9781351104166 (Master) | ISBN 9781351104159 (Adobe) |
    ISBN 9781351104142 (ePub3) | ISBN 9781351104135 (MobiPocket) |
    ISBN 9780815361343 (hardback : alk. paper) | ISBN 9780815361350 (pbk. : alk. paper) |
    ISBN 9781351104166 (ebk)
Subjects: LCSH: Human services personnel—Job stress. | Human services personnel—
    Psychology. | System theory. | Group relations training.
Classification: LCC HV40.35 (ebook) | LCC HV40.35 .U53 2019 (print) |
    DDC 361.301/9—dc23
LC record available at https://lccn.loc.gov/2018046804

ISBN: 978-0-8153-6134-3 (hbk)
ISBN: 978-0-8153-6135-0 (pbk)
ISBN: 978-1-351-10416-6 (ebk)

Typeset in Bembo by Apex CoVantage, LLC
Printed and bound by CPI Group (UK) Ltd, Croydon, CR0 4YY

To Eric Miller
With gratitude and affection

CONTENTS

FIGURES

ABOUT THE AUTHORS

The editors

Anton Obholzer, BSc, MB, ChB, DPM, FRCPsych, member of the British Psychoanalytic Society. Born in South Africa, Anton Obholzer came to the UK in the 1970s, working as a psychiatrist and psychoanalyst. He was Chair of the Tavistock Clinic from 1985 and then the first CEO of the Tavistock and Portman NHS Trust until 2002, and from 2005–2014 was Chair of its Board of Trustees. For the past 35 years he has balanced clinical work with management and leadership, as well as coaching and organizational consultancy in the public, voluntary and private sectors. He has designed and directed many group relations conferences, and has run organizational consultancy courses in Turin and Madrid. He was Visiting Professor at the Universities of Vienna, Graz and Innsbruck, and is a senior member of Faculty of the Advanced Management Programme of the INSEAD Global Leadership Centre in Paris.

Vega Zagier Roberts, M.D. is an independent consultant and coach, an Associate Consultant at Tavistock Consulting, and a faculty member on the Tavistock and Portman NHS Trust/University of Essex master's and doctoral programmes *Consulting and Leading in Organisations*. She has been a Fellow of the Tavistock Institute of Human Relations Action Research Training Programme, Organizational Behaviour Specialist in the Riverside NHS Trust, and Director of the Management and Leadership Programme at the Cassel Hospital. From 2005–2014 she was a Senior Organizational Analyst at the Grubb Institute of Behavioural Studies where she co-directed the master's programme *Organisation Analysis: Freedom to Make a Difference*.

Guest editor

Kay Trainor, BA, MA, DConsOrg is Principal Consultant at Tavistock Consulting at the Tavistock and Portman NHS Trust. She consults on and designs development programmes for a wide variety of organizations, including retail, media, business schools and NHS Trusts. She is Director of the Tavistock and Portman NHS Trust/ University of Essex master's programme *Consulting and Leading in Organisations: Psychodynamic and Systemic Approaches*, and has directed and worked on many group relations conferences, both in the UK and internationally.

The authors

Francesca Cardona, BA is an organizational consultant and coach. She is a practice tutor on the professional doctoral programme *Consultation and the Organisation* at the Tavistock and Portman NHS Foundation Trust and has coached senior managers from global organizations in London Business School programmes. She has extensive experience in international group relations conferences.

Nancy Cohn, PhD is a child and adult psychotherapist, recently retired from the NHS, where she developed and managed a multi-disciplinary psychological service at an acute hospital. She is now working for the British Red Cross providing consultation and support to staff and volunteers in the UK, as well as being available to support British citizens abroad in crisis situations.

Sheila Damon, MA, MSc, MSc, MSc, C. Psychol. is the Director of Mitchell Damon; a chartered psychologist consulting to individuals, teams and organizations; and an adjunct professor in McGill University's Desautels Faculty of Management. She was formerly a senior manager at the King's Fund and has been a board member in the university, public and charitable sectors.

Anna Dartington, BA, Dip. Soc. Admin. was a psychoanalytic psychotherapist and Senior Lecturer in Social Work in the Adolescent Department of the Tavistock Clinic, and a lecturer in Adult Counselling at Birkbeck College, University of London. She worked on Tavistock international group relations conferences and as an organizational and management consultant to groups and individuals. She died in 2007.

Matthieu Daum, MSc is director of Nexus, a French consultancy firm specialising in 'Working Together Differently'. He helps international clients adapt to tomorrow's world of leadership, strategic re-orientation, change management and diversity in the workplace. Matthieu is also Visiting Lecturer at ESSEC Business School, one of France's leading business schools.

William Halton, BA is an independent organizational consultant and executive coach. His former positions include faculty on the Advanced Personal Leadership programme, Henley Business School, and child and adult psychotherapist. He has contributed to *Working below the Surface* (Karnac 2004); *Social Defences Against Anxiety* (Karnac 2015) and *Couple Dynamics* (Karnac 2016).

James Krantz, PhD is an organizational consultant and researcher from New York, is a Principal of Worklab Consulting. He has taught on the faculties of the Wharton School and Yale's School of Management. Jim's writing focuses on the unconscious background of work life, the dilemmas of contemporary leadership and the socio-psychological challenges of new forms of work organization.

Chris Mawson, BSc, C. Psychol. is a training and supervising analyst of the British Psychoanalytical Society and works in private practice as a psychoanalyst. He is the editor of *The Complete Works of W.R. Bion* (Karnac 2014), and *Bion Today* (2010), in the New Library of Psychoanalysis series.

Ajit Menon, MA, MSc is an organizational consultant and coach in the financial services industry where he has consulted to banks, insurers, and wealth managers. He co-founded and leads Blacklight Advisory, a specialist change consultancy. Ajit lectured on organizational development at the London School of Economics and Political Sciences.

James Mosse, BA has worked as a manager in manufacturing industry, an institutional consultant in public and voluntary sector organization, a staff member on many group relations conferences, and a psychoanalytic psychotherapist in private practice and in the NHS.

Deirdre Moylan, BA, MA, Dip. Psych., TQAP. is a psychoanalyst and organizational consultant. Before retiring from the Health Service, she was Director of the Adolescent Department at the Tavistock Clinic and Co-director of Tavistock Consultancy Service; as well as Director of the MA and Co-director of the doctoral programme *Consultation and the Organisation*. She has worked on many group relations conferences nationally and internationally. After retiring, she studied fine art and now works as an artist in Ireland.

Peter Speck, BSc., MA, Dip. Pastoral Studies, DM has been a healthcare chaplain for over 30 years, visiting tutor at the Tavistock Clinic, staff member on group relations conferences and external examiner for the master's programme *Organizational Analysis* at UEL/Grubb Institute. He is currently Honorary Senior Lecturer (Palliative Care) at King's College London, and a researcher.

Jon Stokes, MA, C.Psychol, AFBPsS is a Senior Fellow at the Said Business School, a Member of St Anthony's College, Oxford University, and Director at Stokes & Jolly Ltd. Jon is a clinical psychologist, psychoanalytic psychotherapist, organizational consultant and leadership coach who has worked with a wide range of organizations in both public and private sectors.

FOREWORD

Jonathan Gosling

Thinking more deeply about managing

The unconscious is always at work – and at play; it is in many respects the climatic conditions within which we seek to manage our lives, our organizations and our politics. All of us manage, are managed, and depend on managed institutions.

This book offers a structured opportunity for enquiry into the detail, and with deeper appreciation, of the real work of management. This is more difficult than it might seem because we are very practised at talking about our jobs in managing as if it is something to be thrown away with light words – the Orwellian 'newspeak' that skates over the moral predicaments implicit in 'process improvement', 'down-sizing', 'efficiency gains' and so forth.

So, we must take time to listen carefully to our own experience and each other's experience, and from listening carefully comes insight and appreciation, and more importantly, curiosity – it's such an interesting job, managing and doing business. The real opportunity of this book is to grow more curious and more interested in what is involved in making things happen, in working with people to develop new opportunities and to solve very difficult problems when they arise, in order to create more value in the working lives of all of us, and to generate wealth for ourselves, our societies and for future generations.

This book is important also because it examines significant and sometimes para-doxical concepts; well thought-out, scientifically derived concepts from the world of scholars and clinicians are tested and it homes in on the daily practising life of managers.

How to make it valuable for you – as manager or managed

Each chapter is a whole unto itself – an opportunity to reframe the kinds of things one might notice at work or when thinking about how business is conducted.

The reader is urged to try out these new perspectives, test them against your own experience, and be alert to possible resonances (and discords). That way, you can do more than read *about* the unconscious, by working *with* it. Perhaps playfully, you can look forward to the week ahead to speculate about how you might start to manage a little differently . . .

So start each chapter with a lively curiosity and interest into what kinds of experience the author is talking about; in other words, allow yourself into the perspective from which these are important issues to deal with; read with your sympathy as well as your mind. Reflect and think back on your experience of managing the past week or two, and quietly remembering the problems you have had to deal with. Curiosity is the starting point.

In many ways this book is built on reflectiveness, and that's probably still the key to reading it. It's very difficult for a busy manager to imagine how much value can be found in quiet reflective reading. But the very special opportunity you have with this book is to structure your reflective reading and (probably) to discover how much you really know.

Nonetheless, bring your critical, analytical attention to each chapter. The term 'analysis' is inextricably linked to work with the unconscious for good reason. *Ana-Lysis* comes directly from the Greek 'loosen up', because it eases the tightly bound coherence of the accounts we are given, to reveal constituent elements and dynamic forces that could perhaps be put together in other ways. A financial analyst 'undoes' the reports and accounts put out by a company, to try to find out how they have been put together under what assumptions and to serve which interests. The authors of these chapters have done the same with organizational accounts – they loosen-up the stories we are told about organizational life – resistance to change, rogue behaviour, role confusion and so on – to find out what might lie beneath these appearances, and how else we might describe them. So, enjoy loosening up and re-tying with the authors.

Weaving organizational work

This metaphor of loosening and tying the threads of comprehension has been a consistent texture to my thinking about management, so allow me draw to it out here; to spread it over the couch before you lie back with this book.

What is managing? Imagine that managerial work is like weaving a beautiful piece of cloth from different shades, in particular five colours, each a distinctive mindset; five ways to think, to approach the world.

The first is reflectiveness. If we are not *reflective* we can't think about or learn from our experience, we bring no intelligence to the job. But reflection alone is the work of a recluse – not of a manager. You have to also be *active*, to drive to make things happen, to change, adapt and invent.

Then act and to reflect, act and reflect soon develops into a more thoughtful relationship between what I do and what I think and what happens. This is the beginning of an *analytic* mindset, which unties and reconstitutes the meaning of things, weighs and assesses each yarn.

Nothing gets done in this world without other people; it's only by collaborating with others that new possibilities (beyond mere visions) are discovered, especially in managing, which is all about relationships. The *collaborative* mindset is that inner urge to connect with other people, to create something valuable and new together and to discover opportunities that can only be made when two different people come together.

The fifth mindset is *worldliness*. This is not the same as global, which is when we see the whole world as one: important in business - in fact most discussion in business assumes everything is one and alike in capacity for exchange, but you don't get anything done on that level of abstraction. Really making a business work is when you understand how the world looks from where others are. This requires a generous spirit to put yourself in their shoes, to see the world from their point of view. This is the spirit or mindset of worldliness. There's another aspect – practical wisdom, that knowledge which comes from experience, many years of making things happen, working with people – sometimes you can't say why you think something is true, but you know it is, from your experience. This is worldly wisdom.

So we have five mindsets, reflective, active, analytic, collaborative and worldly. Weaving these five mindsets through the daily tasks is what we do when managing. If some come more easily than others, it is likely because they defend us against discomforting aspects of experience. Action crowds out the need to empathise collaboratively with others; reflection can become a way to avoid conflict that might follow from action, however necessary to progress; and earnest collaboration can be a way to avoid recognising worldly diversity in a team or partnership. The particular texture of management in any organization is an expression of both personal and cultural defences. This book might be approached as a way to lift the covers of organizational life, perhaps to see clearly what we always suspected was going on beneath.

I hope you will enjoy it, and find it fruitful.

Jonathan Gosling
Emeritus Professor of Leadership, University of Exeter
Lead Faculty, The Forward Institute

PREFACE TO THE SECOND EDITION

As human beings, we are all making sense of what we see and experience all the time. Every action we take is based on a hypothesis, even for such simple actions as turning up the thermostat when we feel cold or reaching for a glass of water when we are thirsty. When the action fails to produce the intended result, our initial hypothesis is disconfirmed and we have to develop others. For more complex situations, it is invaluable to develop multiple hypotheses, each of which opens up options for action (or a decision not to act just now). We each have default ways of making sense of our experience. Some of us use a psychological lens, others a political or economic or historical one. When one fails to lead to effective action, we may use another. However, often we stick to our first hypothesis, which may then become a theory – or even 'the truth' – about what is going on.

This aim of this book is to be useful, to encourage a spirit of curiosity by offering other lenses that may help you go beyond your 'native' way of looking at what is happening in the workplace, and thus to open up new options for actions. Or at least to suffer less from some of the irrationality (and sometimes destructiveness) of what is going on around and inside us.

When Miller and Rice first developed the idea of the primary task, they described it as 'a heuristic concept' (Miller and Rice 1967 p. 25), that is, one designed to support exploration and problem-solving. We see all the concepts in this book as heuristic concepts, not intended as definite explanations that exclude others but as tools for sense-making. Thus, the key question for the reader is not 'is this true?' but 'is this useful?'. All the contributors to this book are practising organizational consultants who would answer this question with a 'yes'. They draw on a body of thinking and practice which has developed over the past 70 years, sometimes referred to as 'systems-psychodynamics' or 'the Tavistock approach'.

Twenty-five years ago, we set out to produce a book that would make this body of thinking accessible to any reader interested in the undercurrents of organizational life. While there already existed a rich literature on the subject, most of it was fairly academic and many of the original texts were out of print. Since this book was first published, there have been many more excellent books published in 'the Tavistock tradition', but none occupies quite the same niche as an introduction to this approach to thinking about everyday experiences at work.

The contributors to the First Edition were members of the 'Consulting to Institutions Workshop', founded in 1980 by Anton Obholzer and chaired by him until his retirement from the Tavistock Clinic (by then the Tavistock and Portman NHS Trust) in 2002. The workshop met weekly throughout that time, with consultants from both inside and outside the clinic presenting current work for discussion. At the time, most worked entirely, or at least predominantly, in the public sector, and the sub-title of the First Edition, 'Individual and organizational stress in the human services', reflected this.

Since then, most of us have extended our consulting practice into the private sector, and many have been teaching in business schools, including the London Business School, IMD (International Institute for Management Development) in Switzerland, and INSEAD (Institut Européen d'Administration des Affaires) in France, that offer modules in psychologically informed approaches to organizational behaviour. At the same time, post-graduate programmes in leadership and consultancy based on systems-psychodynamic and group relations thinking were attracting increasing numbers of students from the corporate world. While many business sector leaders, managers, consultants and students found the book relevant, extrapolating from the public sector case studies to their own settings, others felt 'this is not my world, it has nothing to do with me'. The last six chapters aim to address this, taking up the key concepts from earlier parts of the book and illustrating them with a wide range of case studies ranging from retail and IT to the financial services and insurance industries.

Most of the original chapters remain intact. We have deleted four which were outdated, but have made only small changes to the others. While the world of 'the human services' has of course changed significantly, the original case studies continue to serve the purpose of bringing the conceptual base of the book to life and of enabling readers to apply it to their own situations. We have however reorganized the sections of the book to give it a logical flow and to integrate the new chapters.

Part I, 'Conceptual framework', together with the introduction by James Mosse, explores the theoretical strands of the Tavistock approach: psychoanalysis, open systems and group relations. It can be read first, but it can also serve as a resource for readers who prefer to start with chapters relevant to their own organizations and dilemmas and then find themselves wanting to know more about the concepts. It includes one new chapter (Chapter 6), which addresses some of the dynamics of changes in the public sector over the past 20 years, and explores 'organization-in-the-mind', which has become much more central to the Tavistock approach than it was in 1994.

The second part focuses on 'the human services'. Part IIa is about the impact of the nature of the work itself on staff and organizational functioning. The order of the chapters follows the life cycle, from services for babies and children, to services for elderly and dying clients. Part IIb addresses broader organizational issues, not specific to working with a particular client group, such as conflict and change.

Part III is entirely new. The focus of the six chapters moves from the individual to the group and organizational level, and then to the societal level, exploring how the dynamics at each level can affect managing and leading business organizations. Each chapter, and the section as a whole, can stand alone; any theoretical concepts are explained, even if they have already been discussed in preceding sections of the book. However, concepts are also cross-referenced to earlier chapters which provide more detail for readers who become curious and want to know more.

This book is not primarily about theory. Rather, it is about a way of thinking and being: being curious about what might be driving the puzzling or stressful situations we find ourselves in. Why do our organizations so often seem to be less than the sum or their parts? What undermines effectiveness and morale, and gets in the way of achieving what we most care about? The book seeks to enlarge our readers' existing tool-kits so that they can look at themselves and their organizations with fresh eyes, deepening the emotional intelligence they bring to bear on the challenges they face.

Anton Obholzer
Vega Zagier Roberts
July 2018

ACKNOWLEDGEMENTS

Acknowledgements for the First Edition

The title *The Unconscious at Work* was coined and first employed by Jon Stokes some years ago – we are indebted to him for its use. This book could not have been written without the constant and cheerful help of Sandra Masterson, who was responsible for typing and re-typing the manuscript, Vicky Davenport, who helped edit the work towards coherence, and Don Zagier and Jennifer Hicks, whose comments on successive drafts helped us keep our intended readership clearly in mind. Their support and enthusiasm for the project were invaluable. We would also like to thank Lotte Higginson, Ruth Sonntag, Lyndsay MacDonald, Margaret Walker and the staff of the Tavistock Joint Library, all members of the Consulting to Institutions Workshop both past and present, and many others.

Acknowledgements for the Second Edition

We would like to acknowledge Colin Quine for his generous permission to use diagrams from his unpublished working note 'Discovering purpose: exploring organizational meaning' (Grubb Institute 2006); Ruth Bourne for her careful copy-editing; David Cotson, Tim Dartington, David Freedman, Megan Meredith, Mannie Sher and Don Zagier for their comments on drafts of the new chapters; and Deborah Davidson for assisting us in updating some of the original ones. A special thanks goes to Amber Segal for her dedication in preparing the manuscript, and for her sharp eye for style and detail; and to Kay Trainor who joined us in editing Part III, and whose unwavering belief in the value of extending the scope of this book was key to making it happen.

A NOTE ON CONFIDENTIALITY

The examples used in this book have been selected because they are typical of situations that challenge us in our working lives. Readers may therefore recognise – or think they recognise – some of the individuals and organizations described. However, all names are fictitious, and identifying details have been altered to preserve the anonymity of those involved.

A NOTE ABOUT 'A TAVISTOCK APPROACH'

In this volume, 'a Tavistock approach' refers to a body of theory and practice developed over the past seven decades at the Tavistock Institute of Human Relations and at the Tavistock Clinic (now the Tavistock and Portman NHS Foundation Trust), and which in recent years has come to be referred to as 'systems-psychodynamics'. Within these institutions, there are many other approaches to understanding and working with individuals, groups and organizations, drawing on other theories and practices. However, the contributors to this book draw on a particular framework and tradition which we hope readers will find useful in making sense of their own experiences at work.

INTRODUCTION

Making sense of organizations – the institutional roots of the Tavistock approach

James Mosse

Most people spend their working lives as part of a group which is itself part of a larger institution or organization. In this book we explore the implications of thinking about such groupings as having not only directly observable structures and functions, but also an unconscious life comparable to that described by psychoanalysis in an individual. We suggest that organizations pursue unconscious tasks alongside their conscious ones, and that these affect both their efficiency and the degree of stress experienced by staff.

We view organizations as social systems to be studied using the established methodologies of the social sciences, but with an unconscious life to be studied psychoanalytically and we also believe that the social and the psychoanalytic perspectives must be deployed *together* if real change is to be effected in those aspects where structure and unconscious function overlap. This is because working only from the psychoanalytic perspective may heighten people's awareness of and sensitivity to unconscious processes, but it will not create the conditions in which such awareness can be used, and staff will therefore become ever more depressed and frustrated. Conversely, if only the social perspective is employed, a two-dimensional blueprint for structural change may be produced, but because no account is taken of the psychic determinants of the previous organizational structure, unconscious needs are unlikely to be met by the proposed new structure, and so it will probably fail.

While linking of the social and the unconscious has a history almost as long as that of the psychoanalytic conception of the unconscious itself, the thinking and manner of work described here is derived from specific traditions rooted in the Tavistock Institute of Human Relations. These in turn grew from the work of the Tavistock Institute of Medical Psychology (better known as the Tavistock Clinic). We will therefore start with an historical overview of the development of these two closely linked institutions and their intellectual traditions.

Historical overview

The Tavistock Clinic

The Tavistock Clinic was founded in 1920 by a number of professionals, who voluntarily gave at least six hours a week to pursue psychodynamic treatments reflecting their belief that the neurotic disorders labelled as 'shell-shock' that they had been treating in combatants during the First World War were not merely transitory phenomena related to the peculiar stresses of war, but were now endemic and pervasive in modern society. From the beginning, the aims of the clinic were fourfold: to offer *treatment,* partly as a means of *research* into possible social means of *prevention* of such difficulties, and then to *teach* their emerging skills to other professionals. Not only did the medical staff of this founding group include general physicians, neurologists and psychiatrists, but from the first there were also psychologists and social workers. Furthermore, some of these were also trained anthropologists, so there was always a combination of a medical with a social science perspective.

In 1938, the then Medical Director of the Clinic, J. R. Rees, was appointed Consulting Psychiatrist to the Army. The army was interested not only in curing individuals, but also in developing an understanding of and treatment for the stresses of military life in time of war. During the Second World War, 31 ex-Tavistock staff members entered the army, many of them as staff officers in influential positions, charged with developing particular aspects of this programme. The resulting innovations can be classified as follows:

- Command psychiatry: a reconnaissance process by senior psychiatrists who were engaged full-time in trying to identify critical problems.
- Social psychiatry: a policy science seeking to develop preventive interventions in large-scale social problems.
- Cultural psychiatry: a means of profiling and analysing the mentality of very large groups (initially the 'enemy nations').
- The therapeutic community as a means of psychiatric treatment in groups.
- The development with the military of new institutions to effect the policies derived from social psychiatry. The War Office Selection Boards were one instance of such practical developments.

The immediate post-war period

By the end of the war, a substantial number of the psychiatrists and social scientists who had been involved in the development of these innovative applications of social psychiatry to military life were determined to pursue their relevance in the post-war civilian world. A number of them returned to the Tavistock Clinic with the aim of using it as a vehicle to continue this kind of work. There followed detailed planning, intended to prepare the Tavistock to undertake its new self-appointed role. The documents produced included a discussion of 'The place of the Tavistock Clinic in British medicine and social science', the first item of which was 'The integration of social science with dynamic psychology – a) at the level of interpersonal relations between workers, b) at the conceptual level, c) in method-ology'. There were numerous references to a new discipline called 'sociatric work', and to the Tavistock's role in training people for it (Dicks 1970).

A substantial social agenda was being proposed, which was felt to require the transformation of the large pre-war voluntary and part-time staff group into a smaller core of salaried, full- or almost full-time staff members. Some existing staff were asked to leave, and other new members were recruited. Criteria included commitment to the redefined social mission, but also a willingness to undertake a personal psychoanalysis, if this had not already been done; there was a perception that psychoanalytic object relations theory had proved to be relevant in the social as well as the clinical field during the war. This element in the training of the new Tavistock staff was the subject of a special arrangement with the British Psycho-Analytical Society (BPS) and reflected the BPS's part in the widespread optimism and commitment to social change – 'winning the peace' – that was already driving the formation of the reborn Tavistock, and that had swept a Labour government to power in 1945.

The clinic explored a number of possible formal links with other institutions, both academic and clinical, which they hoped might further their agenda. For a variety of reasons, however, not much came of these. Meanwhile, the emer-gence of plans for the new National Health Service brought a clear problem. The therapeutic work could logically become a part of the NHS, but the research, development and training activities envisaged as part of the heightened social engagement stood outside the scope of the NHS. Indeed, once within the NHS, the clinic would be precluded from accepting many of the projects and sources of funding it was so keen to pursue. Preparations were therefore made to form the Tavistock Institute of Human Relations as a separate non-profit organization. This took place in September 1947, leaving the clinic free to enter the NHS in July 1948. As a part of the same strategic manoeuvring to ensure the long-term security of the social agenda, a new international learned journal, *Human Relations*, was launched jointly with Kurt Lewin's Research Center for Group Dynamics in the United States, and a new publishing imprint, Tavistock Publica-tions, was established.

The Tavistock Institute of Human Relations (TIHR)

By 1948, the British government was sufficiently worried about the low levels of productivity in the post-war economy to establish an Industrial Productivity Com-mittee. This included a Human Factors Panel, which was empowered to grant-aid research intended to improve productivity through better use of human resources. The fledgling TIHR applied for and secured funding for three projects. One was a training project for a group of six 'industrial fellows', to be seconded from industry for two years to learn about unconscious group processes in the workplace from their own experience. Each of them would take part in other TIHR research projects, and also participate in a therapy group to study their own unconscious group life. They would then return to their seconding organizations, and, by applying their newly gained experience, would help to change work practices in beneficial ways. This can be seen as one of the forerunners of the Group Relations Training Programme (see Chapter 5).

Another early project to receive a grant was a study by Eric Trist of work organization in the newly nationalised coal-mining industry. It was discovered that groups of workers supposedly doing similar jobs in separate coal mines in fact organized themselves very differently, and that this had significant effects on levels of productivity. This led to the concept of the self-regulating work group, and to the idea that differences in group organization reflect unconscious motives, which also affect the subjective experience of the work. It was through this project that the 'socio-technical system' came to be defined as an appropriate field of study (Trist et al. 1963). Organizations as socio-technical systems can be understood as the product of the interaction between a work task, its appropriate techniques and technology, and the social organization of the workers pursuing it. While originating from research in industry, this approach has subsequently been applied to the study of a wide range of organizations. In particular, Isabel Menzies' (1960) study to identify the causes of the high drop-out rate from nurse training was an early example of bringing the TIHR socio-technical model to bear on an institution where the technical system is largely human.

The last of these three original projects was a detailed study of the internal relations of a single manufacturing company. The aim was to identify ways of improving cooperation between all levels of staff, and then help the company to move towards implementing these. The project was undertaken by Elliott Jaques at the Glacier Metal Company, and led to extensive change in the culture and organization of the firm. However, though it was widely reported and studied, it was not much copied. One of Jaques' most significant contributions resulting from this project was the recognition that social systems in the workplace function to defend workers against unconscious anxieties inherent in the work. To the extent that such defences are unconscious, the social systems are likely to be rigid and therefore uncomfortable; but because of their role in keeping anxiety at bay, they may also be very resistant to change (Jaques 1951, 1953).

Most of the core theoretical influences on the work discussed in this book derive from these first three projects. The one major addition still to be introduced is that of open systems. From the first, systems theory was one of the imports from the social sciences that underpinned socio-psychological thinking. The particular application of open systems theory to the work of TIHR was substantially the contribution of A. K. Rice, later working together with Eric Miller. In essence, the open systems view sees an organization as having boundaries across which inputs are drawn in, processed in accordance with a primary task, and then passed out as outputs. While this may sound like a model best suited to understanding manufacturing processes, Miller and Rice (1967) applied it far more widely. They traced many of the difficulties faced by work groups to their problems in defining their primary task and in managing their boundaries (see Chapter 3).

TIHR personnel did not go in as experts who already knew what their clients must do to improve things: they went to study whatever they would find. The study was undertaken jointly *with* the clients, and, to a large extent, *by* them. TIHR staff then sought to contribute a way of construing their observations and experiences, which they believed would point to potentially helpful changes. Once introduced, the effects of the changes would themselves become the subject of further study, leading to further change. The role of the TIHR staff member was designated as 'participant observer', and the whole style of working was known as 'action research'. This was a continuation of the clinic's longstanding doctrine, 'No research without therapy, and no therapy without research' – though now applied to institutions rather than individuals (Dicks 1970). As government and charitable funding became more difficult to secure through the 1950s and 1960s, the TIHR shifted its focus from grant-aided research towards consultancy work directly commissioned by client organizations. Since then, TIHR staff have undertaken a large number of both research and consultancy projects combining perspectives both from the social sciences and from psychoanalysis, a body of theory and practice which has shaped many of the interventions described in this book. It has also influenced the training and consultancy activities of many organizations worldwide. Together, these two perspectives can provide us with tools not only for taking up a role as leader, manager or consultant, but also for thinking about our experiences as members of organizations, both at work and in many other areas of life. So what are these tools?

Tools for organizational leaders, managers and consultants[1]

From the social sciences

Anyone engaging with an organization is engaging with a social system. This system exists in the real world, and has a structure intended to relate to the effective discharge of its primary task. Both this structure and the technology of task performance must therefore be understood, as must the interface between them. This means understanding the organization's description of itself and its intended structure. However, regardless of what is claimed, it is important also to be able to observe for oneself what seems actually to go on and then to reflect upon the significance of what has been discerned, particularly where there seems to be a gap between the claim and what is observed or experienced. Exploring social structures has long been the province of the social sciences. Among the founders of the 'Tavistock approach' were anthropologists and sociologists, and subsequent developments have drawn on many other disciplines including economics, history and political science. In addition, we all – readers and authors – have wide and varied experience of institutional membership derived from both our working and private life. Families, schools, clubs, professional bodies and employing organizations are all institutions in this sense. A capacity to keep all these experiences alive and available for recall has many benefits. This includes helping one to stay thoughtful and on the margin of a group when necessary, rather than being sucked into shared assumptions about how things 'have' to be organized. For example, I have worked both as a manager in the manufacturing industry and as a psychotherapist in a multidisciplinary mental health team, and thus have experienced two very different sets of beliefs about delegation and decision-making. In industry, I heard suggestions for widespread consultation before reaching a decision described as 'analysis paralysis'. In the health service, on the other hand, I have seen a capacity for effective action described as 'manic', and detailed planning ridiculed as 'obsessional'. My own memory of both positions and my efforts to reconcile these differing views of how decisions 'must' be taken have been of considerable value in a wide range of situations, not least my consultancy work.

Being able to call on a diverse range of experience can also reduce the likelihood of being swept away by the institutional defences of a group of which one is a part by ensuring that no single role is too easily mobilised in isolation. For the consultant, it also reduces the risk of being seduced into the inappropriate role of 'expert', 'manager' or 'supervisor' (unless, of course, it is that kind of consultancy, but that is not what we are discussing here).

Social science aims to relate observable social structures to their functions in the external world. These are held to be, at least in principle, directly accessible to consciousness. Any organization having sufficient structural coherence and money to take the real-world action of hiring a consultant will support such an analysis. On its own, however, this can produce a two-dimensional blueprint rather than a three-dimensional working model. The so-described inanimate institution is also made up of living people who have unconscious and non-rational aims and needs, which they must serve simultaneously with the rational aims of the organization. The pure social scientist has neither the tools nor the theoretical framework for observing this third dimension.

From psychoanalysis

These tools and theories can be drawn from psychoanalysis. Freud writes that the analyst 'must turn his own unconscious like a receptive organ towards the transmitting unconscious of the patient' (1924 p. 115). It is axiomatic, and stands at the very heart of applied psychoanalytic work, that the instrument with which one explores unconscious processes is oneself – one's own experience of and feelings about the shared situation. If the self is to be the scientific instrument on which 'readings' are taken, then how is this instrument to be calibrated? The answer from psychoanalysis is unequivocal: through personal analysis. Anyone wishing to work as an analyst must first undertake an analysis of their own, through which they should be able to distinguish what comes from themselves – their own unresolved conflicts – and what belongs to the patient. They should also gain experientially based understanding of theoretical concepts described in the literature. But how do these views derived from the world of clinical psychoanalysis relate to the work and practice we are discussing here?

Organizational leaders and managers are likely not only to be caught up in the unconscious dynamics of the very organizations they are leading but in addition are likely by virtue of their leadership roles to be subject to particularly strong and entangling projections from staff. Anybody seeking to undertake the kind of organizational consultation described in this book will have similar experiences. How is one to 'catch' and reorient oneself within the powerful unconscious psychic currents that run through all groups, particularly when their unconscious defences are under scrutiny?

Though this book aims to develop the reader's capacity to discern, think about and understand such forces, really to engage with these ideas will almost certainly imply further *experiential* learning. This may initially come through membership of an organization undertaking a Tavistock-style consultation but it can (or perhaps even should) be further refined and developed by participation in Group Relations Conferences, personal role consultancy or even personal therapy.

Just as I suggested previously that there are dangers in applying ideas derived from social sciences in isolation, however, there are also two particular dangers in seeking to apply a purely psychoanalytic perspective to organizations.

The first is that it may lead to attempts to develop members' 'sensitivity' and insight into their own and the organization's psychological processes while ignoring the systemic elements that affect the work. In this case, instead of bringing about useful and needed change, their heightened sensitivity may only add to members' frustration and have a negative effect (Menzies Lyth 1990).

The second is the risk of attributing institutional problems to the individual pathology of one or more of its members (see Chapter 15) or of a pathologising of the behaviour and functioning of the organization and its individual members without giving due regard to the effectiveness with which the conscious real-world tasks are being pursued. For example, a staff group may be efficiently developing and delivering a highly successful website or app while simultaneously experiencing sufficient difficulties in the work to seek help from an external consultant. The real-world success may be undervalued or ignored by a consultant whose focus is on the psychological functioning and experiences of individuals. This difficulty may arise innocently, as an empathic response to the observable suffering of the staff, but it can also result from a tendency to disparage and discount the expertise of others working in cultures different from one's own. This is another area in which continuing mental access to a wide range of membership experiences may be a bulwark against being swept away by the shared assumptions of any one group, either those of the client institution, or of one's home-group whose assumptions the client is most powerfully challenging.

Maintaining an outside perspective

We all participate as members in a large number of different social systems of which our workplace is usually one of the most structured and demanding. Often we are acutely aware that our involvement is causing us distress, and yet for all our cries of 'If only *that* was different!' we cannot put our finger on quite what is wrong. For some reason, it seems terribly hard to use our powers of observation or our memories of how things were done elsewhere to bring about change. What prevents us from doing this is the main theme of this book. Our central hypothesis is that membership of an organization makes it harder to observe or understand that organization: we become caught up in the anxieties inherent in the work and in the characteristic institutional defences against those anxieties. This soon leads to shared, habitual ways of seeing, and a common failure to question 'holy writ'. Newcomers may be able to see more clearly, but have no licence to comment. By the time they do, they have either forgotten how to see, or have learned not to. They, too, require defending against anxieties, not least the anxiety of upsetting their new colleagues.

Like the readers, the authors bring to this book their experience in a range of roles but each of us has spent at least a part of our working life as an organizational consultant. By definition, consultants take a stance outside the daily life of the organizations they are working with. This makes it easier for them to observe, and to think about what they observe, without getting caught up in institutional defences. It may also make it easier for the organizations to license them to see and be heard (or to get rid of them if they don't like what they are being told).

Consultants also have at their disposal particular tools to make sense of what they see and feel. It is our tool-kit that we offer in this book. The 'tools' are explained in Part I; the other parts illustrate how they can be used. The tool-kit does not purport to be complete; other tools from other kits will be more appropriate in certain situations. Our hope is to offer readers some ways of thinking and managing themselves that may enable them to function more effectively and with less distress. We are not experts on how to do their work. Rather, we hope *our* skills lie in helping to liberate *their* expertise.

Note

1 Readers may find it useful to refer to the Appendix, 'The genealogy of systems-psychodynamics', which lays out the historical development of the concepts and tools used in this book.

PART I
Conceptual framework

1

SOME UNCONSCIOUS ASPECTS OF ORGANIZATIONAL LIFE

Contributions from psychoanalysis

William Halton

'None of your jokes today,' said an eight-year-old coming into the consulting room. Interpretations about the process of the unconscious may often seem like bad jokes to the recipient, if not frankly offensive. Although some elements of psychoanalysis have become part of everyday life, psychoanalysis as a treatment for individual emotional problems remains a minority experience. As a system of ideas it has adherents, sceptics and a multitude of indifferent passers-by.

Despite the fact that there is no exact parallel between individuals and institutions, psychoanalysis has contributed one way to approach thinking about what goes on in institutions. This approach does not claim to provide a comprehensive explanation or even a complete description. But looking at an institution through the spectrum of psychoanalytical concepts is a potentially creative activity which may help in understanding and dealing with certain issues. The psychoanalytical approach to consultation is not easy to describe. It involves understanding ideas developed in the context of individual therapy, as well as looking at institutions in terms of unconscious emotional processes. This may seem like a combination of the implausible with the even more implausible or it may become an illuminating juxtaposition.

The unconscious

As Freud and others discovered, there are hidden aspects of human mental life which, while remaining hidden, nevertheless influence conscious processes. In treating individuals, Freud found that there was often resistance to accepting the existence of the unconscious. However, he believed he could demonstrate its existence by drawing attention to dreams, slips of tongue, mistakes and so forth as evidence of meaningful mental life of which we are not aware. What was then required was interpretation of these symbolic expressions from the unconscious.

Ideas which have a valid meaning at the conscious level may at the same time carry an unconscious hidden meaning. For example, a staff group talking about their problems with the breakdown of the switchboard may at the same time be making an unconscious reference to a breakdown in interdepartmental communication. Or complaints about the distribution of car-park spaces may also be a symbolic communication about managers who have no room for staff concerns. The psychoanalytically oriented consultant takes up a listening position on the boundary between conscious and unconscious meanings, and works simultaneously with problems at both levels. It may be some time before the consultant can pick up and make sense of these hidden references to issues of which the group itself is not aware.

The avoidance of pain

Like individuals, institutions develop defences against difficult emotions which are too threatening or too painful to acknowledge. These emotions may be a response to external threats such as government policy or social change. They may arise from internal conflicts between management and employees or between groups and departments in competition for resources. They may also arise from the nature of the work and the particular client group, as described in detail in Part II of this book. Some institutional defences are healthy, in the sense that they enable the staff to cope with stress and develop through their work in the organization. But some institutional defences, like some individual defences, can obstruct contact with reality and in this way damage the staff and hinder the organization in fulfilling its task and in adapting to changing circumstances. Central among these defences is *denial*, which involves pushing certain thoughts, feelings and experiences out of conscious awareness because they have become too anxiety-provoking.

Institutions call in consultants when they can no longer solve problems. The consultant who undertakes to explore the nature of the underlying difficulty is likely to be seen as an object of both hope and fear. The conscious hope is that the problem will be brought to the surface, but at the same time, unconsciously, this is the very thing which institutions fear. As a result, the consultant's interpretations of the underlying unconscious processes may well meet with *resistance*, that is, an emotionally charged refusal to accept or even to hear what he or she says. The consultant may only gradually be able to evaluate the nature of the defences, reserving interpretation until the group is ready to face what it has been avoiding and to make use of the interpretation.

A symbolic communication may occur just at a point where the consultant's understanding of the hidden meaning coincides with the group's readiness to receive it. The following example illustrates a symbolic communication occurring in a group unable to accept the reality of a threat from an external source:

> The Manfred Eating Disorders Unit at Storsey Hospital was conducting a last-ditch campaign against closure, and had engaged the help of a consultant.

The campaign had been running for several months, with the staff working late and over weekends organizing a local petition and lobbying professional colleagues, local councillors and MPs. Public opinion was on the side of keeping the unit open; closure seemed unthinkable. New patients were still being admitted and no preparation had been made for transferring existing patients. Only the consultant did not share the excited mood and felt depressed after each meeting.

At one meeting the discussion strayed to the apparently irrelevant topic of the merits of euthanasia. The consultant heard this as an indirect expression of the anticipated relief which the completion of closure would bring, and said this to the group. Their first reaction was one of shock. However, over time the interpretation led to a more realistic attitude to the possibility of closure, which made it possible for the staff to begin to think and plan for the patients.

In this example, the staff had been responding to the threat of closure with angry and excited activity aimed at saving the unit. By relating only to the possibility of winning their fight for survival, they resisted and denied the possibility of closure, ignoring the reality of financial cuts which had already closed other local units. The motivation behind this resistance was not only the wish to save the unit for the benefit of patients; closure would also hurt their pride, cast doubts on the value of their work, and cause other emotional pain. But insofar as they had lost touch with reality, they had also failed in their responsibility to prepare patients for the possibility of closure. As an outsider, the consultant felt the depression which was so strikingly absent in the group; this was an important clue to what was being avoided. The euthanasia discussion indicated that previously denied feelings were moving towards the surface as a symbolic communication, and that the group was ready to acknowledge them.

The contribution of Melanie Klein

In play, children represent their different feelings through characters and animals either invented or derived from children's stories: the good fairy, the wicked witch, the jealous sister, the sly fox and so on. This process of dividing feelings into differentiated elements is called *splitting*. By splitting emotions, children gain relief from internal conflicts. The painful conflict between love and hate for the mother, for instance, can be relieved by splitting the mother-image into a good fairy and a bad witch. *Projection* often accompanies splitting, and involves locating feelings in others rather than in oneself. Thus the child attributes slyness to the fox or jealousy to the bad sister. Through play, these contradictory feelings and figures can be explored and resolved.

Through her psychoanalytic work with children in the early 1920s, Melanie Klein developed a conceptualisation of an unconscious inner world, present in everyone, peopled by different characters personifying differentiated parts of self or aspects of the external world. Early in childhood, splitting and projection are the predominant defences for avoiding pain; Klein referred to this as the *paranoid-schizoid position* ('paranoid' referring to badness being experienced as coming from outside oneself, and 'schizoid' referring to splitting). This is a normal stage of development; it occurs in early childhood and as a state of mind it can recur throughout life. Through play, normal maturation or psychoanalytic treatment, previously separated feelings such as love and hate, hope and despair, sadness and joy, acceptance and rejection can eventually be brought together into a more integrated whole. This stage of integration Klein called the *depressive position*, because giving up the comforting simplicity of self-idealisation, and facing the complexity of internal and external reality, inevitably stirs up painful feelings of guilt, concern and sadness. These feelings give rise to a desire to make reparation for injuries caused through previous hatred and aggression. This desire stimulates work and creativity, and is often one of the factors which leads to becoming a 'helping' professional (see also Chapter 13).

The paranoid-schizoid position

The discovery from child analysis that the different and possibly conflicting emotional aspects of an experience may be represented by different people or different 'characters' is used in institutional consultancy as a guide for understanding group processes. In play, the child is the originator of the projections and the play-figures are the recipients. In an institution, the client group can be regarded as the originator of projections with the staff group as the recipients. The staff members may come to represent different, and possibly conflicting, emotional aspects of the psychological state of the client group. For example, in an adolescent unit the different and possibly conflicting needs of the adolescent may be projected into different staff members. One member may come to represent the adolescent's need for independence while another may represent the need for limits. In an abortion clinic, one nurse may be in touch only with a mother's mourning for her lost baby, while another may be in touch only with the mother's relief. These projective processes serve the same purpose for the client as play does for the child: relief from the anxieties which can arise from trying to contain conflicting needs and conflicting emotions. It is hard to contain mourning and relief simultaneously, or to experience the wish for independence and the need for limits at the same time. The splitting and projection of these conflicting emotions into different members of the staff group is an inevitable part of institutional process.

Schizoid splitting is normally associated with the splitting off and projecting outwards of parts of the self perceived as bad, thereby creating external figures who are both hated and feared. In the helping professions, there is a tendency to deny feelings of hatred or rejection towards clients. These feelings may be more easily dealt with by projecting them onto other groups or outside agencies, who can then be criticised. The projection of feelings of badness outside the self helps to produce a state of illusory goodness and self-idealisation. This black-and-white mentality simplifies complex issues and may produce a rigid culture in which growth is inhibited.

> A student occupation protesting against the effects of government cuts was condemned by the college authorities as a ludicrous and irrational waste of resources. They were quoted in the press as saying: 'The question remains as to who was leading this disruption. We have had complaints from students suggesting that outsiders and non-students took active parts in proceedings in meetings and occupation action . . . there was no apparent agenda other than disruption.'

The implication was that inside the college there were good students and good managers. Outside there were bad people who contaminated and disrupted the institution, manipulating its members for destructive purposes. Splitting and projection exploits the natural boundary between insiders and outsiders which every institution has. In this example it led to a state of fragmentation because contact was lost between parts of the institution which belonged together inside its boundary. There was no dialogue possible between the conflicting points of view within the college, and so change and development were frustrated.

Sometimes the splitting process occurs between groups within the institution. Structural divisions into sections, departments, professions, disciplines and so forth are necessary for organizations to function effectively. However, these divisions become fertile ground for the splitting and projection of negative images. The gaps between departments or professions are available to be filled with many different emotions – denigration, competition, hatred, prejudice, paranoia. Each group feels that it represents something good and that other groups represent something inferior. Doctors are authoritarian, social workers talk too much, psychotherapists are precious, managers only think about money. Individual members of these groups are stereotyped like the characters playing these roles in children's games and stories. The less contact there is with other sections, the greater the scope for projection of this kind. Contact and meetings may be avoided in order unconsciously to preserve self-idealisation based on these projections. This results in the institution becoming stuck in a paranoid-schizoid projective system. Emotional disorder interferes with the functioning of an organization, particularly in relation to tasks which require cooperation or collective change (for further examples of these processes, see Chapters 9, 11, 17 and 18).

Envy

On occasion, difficulties in collaboration arise not so much from the desire to be an ideal carer or a more potent worker, but from a sense of being an inevitable loser in a competitive struggle. In the current climate of market values and shrinking budgets, the success of one part of the organization can be felt to be at the expense of another. The survival-anxiety of the less successful section stimulates an envious desire to spoil the other's success. This spoiling envy operates like a hidden spanner-in-the-works, either by withholding necessary cooperation or by active sabotage.

> A group of lecturers at Branston Polytechnic were organizing a money-raising short course out of term-time. They found it impossible to gain the cooperation of the catering department, who refused to provide tea and coffee for course participants. Then, on the first day of the course, despite the lecturers' having requested a delay, maintenance work was started on the toilet facilities, putting them out of action. Both the catering and maintenance departments were about to be closed down, their services to be taken over by private organizations following tendering. Their uncooperativeness led to considerable inconvenience for the participants, who blamed the course organizers and left the course very critical of the polytechnic as a whole.

Catering and maintenance staff felt devalued by the decision to 'sell off' their services, and envious of the academic staff's protected status. This kind of spoiling envy often gives rise to hostile splits between parts of an organization such that the enterprise as a whole is damaged.

Projective identification and countertransference

Although psychoanalysis is based on the idea that the behaviour of an individual is influenced by unconscious factors, the psychoanalytic view of institutional functioning regards an individual's personal unconscious as playing only a subsidiary role. Within organizations, it is often easier to ascribe a staff member's behaviour to personal problems than it is to discover the link with institutional dynamics. This link can be made using the psychoanalytic concept of *projective identification*. This term refers to an unconscious inter-personal interaction in which the recipients of a projection react to it in such a way that their own feelings are affected: they unconsciously identify with the projected feelings. For example, when the staff of the Manfred Eating Disorders Unit projected their depression about closure into the consultant, he felt this depression as if it were his own. The state of mind in which other people's feelings are experienced as one's own is called the *countertransference*.

Projective identification frequently leads to the recipient's acting out the countertransference deriving from the projected feelings. For example, the staff of an adolescent unit may begin to relate to each other as if they were adolescents themselves, or may act in adolescent ways such as breaking the rules and otherwise challenging authority figures. Such behaviour indicates that projective identification is at work, but the true source of their feelings and behaviour is likely to remain obscure until staff achieve a conscious realisation that they have become trapped in a countertransference response to a projective process (this is discussed in more detail in Chapter 2, and further illustrated in Chapter 8).

It is also through the mechanism of projective identification that one group on behalf of another group, or one member of a group on behalf of the other members, can come to serve as a kind of 'sponge' for all the anger or all the depression or all the guilt in the staff group. The angry member may then be launched at management by the group, or a depressed member may be unconsciously manoeuvred into breaking down and leaving. This individual not only expresses or carries something for the group, but may be used to export something which the rest of the group then need not feel in themselves (see Chapter 15). Similarly, a group may carry something for another group or for the institution as a whole (see Chapter 11). If there is something which a group cannot bear at all, like the depression about the closure of the Manfred Unit, it may call in a consultant to carry that feeling on its behalf.

The depressive position

When we recognise that our painful feelings come from projections, it is a natural response to 'return' these feelings to their source: 'These are *your* feelings, not mine'. This readily gives rise to blaming, and contributes to the ricocheting of projections back and forth across groups and organizations. However, if we can tolerate the feelings long enough to reflect on them, and *contain* the anxieties they stir up, it may be possible to bring about change. At times when we cannot do this, another person may temporarily contain our feelings for us. This concept of a person as a 'container' comes from the psychoanalytic work of Bion (1967). He likened it to the function of the mother whose ability to receive and understand the emotional states of her baby makes them more bearable (this is discussed further in Chapters 2 and 8).

Certainly, both psychoanalysts and psychoanalytical consultants aim to identify the projective processes at work and trace the projections to their source, but this in itself is not enough. What was previously unbearable – and therefore projected – needs to be made bearable. It is painful for the individual or group or institution to have to take back less acceptable aspects of the self which had previously been experienced as belonging to others: for example, that legitimate criticisms may arise from within a college, and not simply as intrusions by malicious outsiders; or that no psychiatric unit is so ideal that it cannot be closed; or that in adolescents the need for independence and the need for limits are equally valid concerns and should be held in a complementary tension; or that abortion gives rise to both mourning and relief; or that good managers and good caretakers are both necessary to make a healthy organization; or that authorities who implement cuts and students who protest may both care about the education system.

The consultant's willingness and ability to contain or hold on to the projected feelings stirred up by these ambiguities until the group is ready to use an interpretation are crucial. Otherwise the interpretation will be experienced as yet another attack. However, when the timing is right, some of the projections can be 're-owned', splitting decreases, and there is a reduction in the polarisation and antagonism among staff members themselves. This promotes integration and coop-eration within and between groups or, in psychoanalytic terms, a shift from the paranoid-schizoid to the depressive position.

In a group functioning in the depressive position, every point of view will be valued and a full range of emotional responses will be available to it through its members. The group will be more able to encompass the emotional complexity of the work in which they all share, and no one member will be left to carry his or her fragment in isolation. Furthermore, in order to contain the tendency towards split-ting in the client group, the staff group must be able to hold together the conflict-ing elements projected into them, discussing and thinking them through instead of being drawn into acting them out. This requires being aware of the particular stresses involved in their work, as well as recognising its limitations. The lessen-ing of conflict may then open the way to better working practices and greater job satisfaction, as staff process and integrate their collective work experience. How-ever, the depressive position is never attained once and for all. Whenever survival or self-esteem are threatened, there is a tendency to return to a more paranoid-schizoid way of functioning.

Conclusion

Psychoanalytical concepts make a particular contribution to thinking about institu-tional processes, though contributions from other conceptual frameworks are also necessary to understand institutional functioning. Psychoanalysis is concerned with understanding the inner world with its dynamic processes of fragmentation and integration; key concepts include denial of internal and external reality, splitting, projection and idealisation.

Psychoanalytically oriented consultants extend these concepts to understand-ing unconscious institutional anxieties and the defences against them. Besides concepts, they bring from psychoanalysis a certain stance or frame of mind: to search for understanding without being judgemental either of their clients or of themselves. This enables them to make themselves available to receive and process projections from the institution. The feelings experienced by the consultant or, indeed, by any member of an institution, while interacting with it, constitute the basic countertransference response on which the understanding of unconscious institutional processes is based.

At its best, such understanding can create a space in the organization in which staff members can stand back and think about the emotional processes in which they are involved in ways that reduce stress and conflict, and can inform change and development. The ideas discussed in this and subsequent chapters can be used to develop a capacity for self-consultation: for observing and reflecting on the impact unconscious group and organizational processes have on us all, and our own contribution to these processes as we take up our various roles.

2

THE DANGERS OF CONTAGION

Deirdre Moylan

It is sometimes impossible for people in distress to put into words those aspects of their experience for which they want help. They do not know much consciously about what is troubling them; they only know they are suffering. They may turn up at the therapist's consulting room saying, 'I feel bad. I get depressed. Something is wrong with me'. Institutions sometimes seek consultation in the same way, saying what can be translated as, 'There's something wrong here, but we don't know what it is. It doesn't feel good to work here anymore'. Attempts made by the consultant to clarify the nature of the problem may be strenuously resisted; the wish, as is often the case with individual clients in therapy, is to have the problems eliminated, not clarified. It is evident that the individual or the institution is suffering, but from what? More information is needed.

To discover what is wrong, one needs to listen carefully to their story. It is not just the content of what is presented that gives information, but also the way it is presented, and the mood as the information is conveyed.

> A young woman, Joanna, told me a story of a traumatic childhood event. On one occasion, the atmosphere was one of horror, dismay and disgust. I felt I was with a small, frightened little girl who did not know what was going on. On another occasion, the story was told again and the emotional tone was quite different: there was an air of triumph, contempt for the alleged abuser. This time I felt I was sitting in the presence not of a little girl, but of a judge. On a third occasion, the details of the story were quite exciting, and I felt privileged to be the one entrusted with this information.

The words are the same, the story is the same: what is different is the experience. The different ways in which the story is told offer glimpses of the different levels of meaning that this particular event has for Joanna. These are conveyed not by the words she uses, which may be identical each time, but by creating an experience. So, on the first occasion I felt horrified and desperately sorry for her suffering. The second time, I felt little sympathy, and even somehow guilty, as if I were the one who had committed the offence. I felt dirty and uncomfortable, and wanted to get away. By contrast, on the third occasion I felt rather special, and wanted to hear more. Three very different experiences for the listener, which reflect accurately three different aspects of the experience for Joanna, each requiring understanding. If only the frightened girl gets attention, the story may have to be told again and again until the guilty, uncomfortable girl who feels dirty, or the excited little girl who feels special, can be understood. To start with, however, Joanna was not able to put these difficult and complex feelings into words. Instead, she conveyed exactly what it was like to be there by recreating the experience. Between us, we relived it in the session, painfully piecing it together, and putting it into words that could be thought about, so that the whole experience, in all its complexity for Joanna, could be understood.

The ability to recreate experiences in this way is an important method of communication. It is by no means limited to the psychotherapeutic situation, but is a form of communication we all use, part of our human experience. For small babies, for example, it is usually the only means at their disposal for communicating their needs. Adults tend to get agitated when a baby is crying; they know something of the distress of the baby because they are experiencing it too. This may lead them to want the baby to be quiet, or to try to alleviate the distress. In psychoanalytic terms, this communicative process is called *projective identification* (see Chapter 1): the baby projects the feelings it cannot manage into the mother, so that – through feeling them herself – she can process them on the baby's behalf.

Learning to listen

However, merely sending a message is not enough. Communication also requires that there is someone who is able to hear and correctly understand the message. Too often, we are only able to hear what we expect to hear. Alternatively, we hear what we are comfortable with, and screen out the rest. In listening to a story like Joanna's, for example, we may be able to hear only the distress of the molested child, and not the communications about excitement or triumph, which we find more disturbing. The painful story is therefore not fully understood by either, and so gets repeated endlessly. What needs attention is the listener's *own* experiences, or *countertransference* (see Chapter 1), as the story is told. This conveys the essence of the trauma, how painful it was to be there, and can make it possible to discover the exact nature of the pain. The capacity to hear the message accurately requires the ability to pay attention to all aspects of one's experience, and depends on many things. For example, the mother of the crying baby may or may not be able to respond accurately to the communication, to hear the difference between a cry for food, and one of fear or loneliness. If she is tired or preoccupied, her capacity to hear – and therefore her ability to respond appropriately and to 'contain' the baby's distress – may be impaired.

We can see similar processes in operation in many other situations. Thoughts and feelings are often stirred up by our contacts with others. Sometimes these are ignored, perhaps because we find them too disturbing. At other times we pay attention, and they can greatly influence our subsequent behaviour. For example, while listening to a charming sales representative, a potential buyer has a brief image of the salesman back at his office, laughing with his colleagues. The image might alert the buyer to recheck the credentials of both salesman and product, in case the laughter is at the gullible customer. On the other hand, if the idea of oneself as the victim of a confidence trickster is too disturbing, the troublesome image may be ignored.

A fundamental part of the training of psychoanalytic psychotherapists is to learn to attend to the material that patients bring on a number of different levels, including attending to the feelings it evokes in themselves. This is just as important in working with groups and institutions. We can 'hear' and learn a great deal if we are able to attend to atmosphere and to our own feelings, and not just to what is actually being said.

> I was told that the staff of the Daniel Finch Drug Dependency Clinic were finding it a difficult place to work, and I was asked if I would offer consultation. I arranged a first appointment to meet with the staff to find out more specifically what it was that they wanted help with. My most powerful memory of this first encounter is of my horror because it felt like there were dozens of people in the room, all looking at, and to, me to do something about the problems they were having. What could I do for these hordes of people? The door opened and a few more came in – and then again. How many more of them were there? I sat frozen in my chair. I did a surreptitious head count. Sixteen. I had two reactions simultaneously. One was, 'Oh! Is that all? Sixteen is a manageable number.' The other was, 'How can I alone work with 16 people?' But I remembered I was not quite alone: I worked in a clinic which had a wealth of experience. In this way, I reminded myself that I had a context, which reminded me of my role. Also, I reminded myself that I had worked with larger groups than this in the past, so that my feeling of being overwhelmed by numbers was probably telling me something important about the staff's experience. This enabled me to proceed with the task I was there to undertake, which was to find out what this group of people were looking for when they asked for a consultant.

It takes much longer to describe these first moments than to experience them, but they are worth close attention. They provided an enormous amount of information about the unit, which had been conveyed with great efficiency in the first seconds of the consultation. The atmosphere of a horde conveyed graphically one aspect of what it was like to work within this clinic: my experience mirrored the staff's experience of feeling overwhelmed by the huge numbers of people waiting for treatment. They were trying to deal with a large and demanding clientele at a time when staff quotas were being decreased and demands increased; patient numbers were multiplying and pressure was growing because of AIDS- and HIV-related problems.

Actual figures emerged much later to confirm this first impression of being swamped with clients. Over the previous year, the team had seen about 30 new referrals every month. The average weekly caseload for full-time members of staff was 26. The reality of this in terms of the amount of pressure on each worker, the number of case histories to remember, the level of pain witnessed, the projections and countertransference to be managed, all added up to a monumental task. Indeed, the sense of being overwhelmed emerged as one of the chief stresses of working in this clinic.

One might speculate that the opening moments of a first encounter with a new group will always contain some of this sort of anxiety. I will contrast it, therefore, with another beginning.

> Some nurses had requested a group in which to think about their difficulties working on Sheehan Ward, part of a prestigious and specialised unit offering a particular form of cancer treatment. When I arrived on the ward for the first meeting, arrangements for which had been made well in advance, nobody seemed to be expecting me. When I introduced myself there was puzzlement, followed by recognition. I was then shown to a small room and was told I would be joined shortly by the group of nurses involved. There was a television blaring loudly, and a blackboard bore a large notice saying, 'Support group with Dedrie Maybler today at 2.30'. Only the time was correct, but even this clearly had little impact since no one had arrived. I felt quite uncomfortable: no one seemed to know who I was or what I was there for, despite the preliminary negotiations. Eventually, some nurses drifted in, talking among themselves. They made coffee, ignoring both me and the loud television, as if I had become invisible. I began to feel angry and impotent – I did not know what to say. What I experienced in a dramatic and painful way in these opening minutes later turned out to reflect one of the major concerns of this group. It was not until several sessions later, after the following story had been told, that I was able to understand it.
>
> One of the nurses, Mary, spoke very movingly about how pained and guilty she felt going into the room of Ulrich, a patient who did not speak English. Such patients were not unusual on this ward. She described how awful she felt undertaking a treatment procedure while ignoring the young man's obvious distress and fear because she was not able to talk to him about it. She quickly did her work, left the room, and avoided Ulrich if she possibly could, although she was aware he was frightened and lonely, and did not know what was happening to him. Her experience was of helplessness because she was unable to use her usual skills to inform or reassure the patient.

Like Ulrich, Mary was unable to communicate; like him she felt frightened and impotent, and sometimes angry that she had to tolerate this painful experience she had not expected. She also felt guilty that she was not meeting her own high standards of care and concern.

It seemed that Mary's experience must have been very close to Ulrich's, who – in the absence of a common language – could communicate only with the primitive, unconscious language of projective identification. Ulrich projected his feelings into Mary, who then had to deal with being filled with powerful and painful feelings of impotence, fear, anger and guilt after each contact with him. Mary's wish to do her job to the best of her ability made her particularly likely to have this experience, because she had a strong wish to communicate with Ulrich. In fact, Mary was doing a reasonable job in the circumstances, and the quality of the medical aspects of her work was not diminished. Being helped to understand the unconscious communication going on between her and her patient enabled Mary to feel less overwhelmed by strong emotion when with him, and to understand that she was experiencing what it was like to be a patient on this ward, the feelings of anger and helplessness about having cancer, and the strong desire to run away from it. With this kind of understanding, it can become more bearable to face the situations which stir up the painful feelings, instead of having to avoid them.

Looking back at the beginning of this consultation, we can see how my own experiences mirrored some of the painful aspects of being a patient or a staff member on this ward – in particular, my sense of isolation and impotence, my inability to speak, and my feeling that nobody knew who I was or wanted to communicate with me. Although the difficulties were emphasised with patients who spoke little English, they were also present when all apparently spoke the same tongue. After all, what explanation in any language is adequate for illness, pain or premature death, or when a 15-year-old girl's hair has fallen out following chemotherapy? The staff of the ward inevitably experienced helplessness in the face of fatal disease, and difficulty in communicating bad news.

It is therefore not surprising that my initial experience of these feelings was so intense. It was by remembering my own experience that I could understand Mary's impulse to leave Ulrich quickly and have no further contact with him. By staying with instead of avoiding their uncomfortable feelings, it gradually became possible for the staff to understand what they were about, and to tolerate better the reality of working on a ward with cancer patients, where sometimes there is the pleasure of a successful cure, and sometimes the distressing helplessness of watching a patient die.

Projective identification and institutional stress

These examples have been given in order to illustrate two points. The first is the helpful nature of projective identification, if it can be understood as a communication. One task of the consultant to an institution is to help staff learn to understand and interpret this communication. The second point is to emphasise the difficulties with which the staff have to cope, not least because they are constantly barraged by clients' projections. They need to have adequate and helpful defences of their own; otherwise they are likely to succumb to despair, illness or withdrawal, and to get entangled with the clients in projective identification processes that are not understood and therefore cannot be worked with. The more distressed the client group, the more these unconscious communications are likely to predominate. When there is a lot of pain involved, a natural reaction is to attempt to avoid it, as we saw with Mary, or with the example of the crying baby. Staff groups will tend to avoid understanding or dealing with what is projected into them in this way, and deal with their unprocessed emotions by themselves relying on projective identification as a means of getting rid of what feels too painful. When this predominates, it becomes very difficult for the group to find other ways of coping; it is almost impossible to think clearly, to locate the source of problems, and to find appropriate and creative solutions. In this situation, staff burn-out is also much more likely to become a problem.

I was asked to provide consultation for the Daniel Finch Drug Dependency Clinic at a time when the staff had become demoralised. There was a threat of redundancies, but many were also leaving because of a prevailing sense of hopelessness about the unit. It was difficult for them to find adequate and helpful defences in the service of undertaking their demanding job. Why was their work so difficult? One reason was that, as an everyday aspect of their job, the staff were experiencing and processing painful countertransference feelings similar to those I described occurring in myself at the beginnings of their consultations – but often without being consciously aware that this was what was going on. Very distressed clients constantly project painful experiences into the staff. Without understanding why they felt so hopeless and demoralised, the only recourse for the staff was to leave the clinic, or to attempt to get rid of the pain by avoiding knowledge of it in themselves. A few examples will follow.

Drug addicts frequently live with an internal world full of chaos and uncertainty. Drugs are often used to escape from the experience of this terrible turmoil. Reality becomes distorted, while they convince themselves that, for example, the drug has a beneficial effect on their lives, that it saves them from loneliness, despair and so on. The reality of the damage that the drug does along with the damaging lifestyle needed to maintain the addiction cannot be tolerated for long. Knowledge of the internal and external chaos is defended against by an assault on truth and reality, which in turn adds to the internal chaos. Those who work with drug addicts are also subjected to this assault on truth and reality; they have to make professional decisions, while living with uncertainty about what is really going on. For instance, they constantly have to make decisions about repeating a patient's prescription for methadone, a drug used to replace heroin while the patient builds up a healthier lifestyle away from the criminal world of illegal drug acquisition.

Jonathan, a recent referral to the Daniel Finch Clinic, told his key-worker Paul that he needed an extra methadone prescription because he had been mugged and his prescription stolen. Was this the whole truth, or a distorted version of the truth? Was Jonathan mugged or did he turn a blind eye while his girlfriend pocketed the drug? Or had he already filled the prescription and sold the methadone on the black market? If Paul gave the new prescription, would he just have been conned? If he did not give it, was he heaping further injury on someone who was already suffering? Would it then be his fault if, as he threatened, Jonathan committed a crime to obtain money to buy the heroin he needed, since he no longer had his methadone? By now Paul was experiencing doubt, uncertainty, guilt, anger and internal chaos; in fact, his state of mind for the moment mirrored that of the client.

To remain aware of this state of mind, to try to understand it and function professionally at the same time, is very difficult. Small wonder, then, that the staff need to develop defences in order to cope. Some defences are necessary and can serve development, creativity and growth. However, there is a strong pull in these circumstances to use the same defences as the clients. Caught up in projective identification with the clients, the workers can, and do, find themselves operating in similar ways.

One member of the group, Harry, spent considerable time in one of our meetings talking about plans for the future of the unit, and projects he would undertake in the coming year. Others joined in the discussion, which was lively and stimulating. Meanwhile, I found myself feeling confused. I thought Harry had given in his notice, and would be leaving the unit shortly. I was full of doubt. Was it my imagination that he was leaving, and if so, why would I imagine such a thing? I was tempted to say nothing and let the discussion run on, but something felt wrong and I decided to express my doubts.

Notice the similarity of my state of mind to the state of uncertainty and confusion described earlier. Like the staff, I was asking myself if I could trust my own memory, my own instinct that something was wrong – just as they had to ask themselves constantly if they could trust their own memories and their instincts. The state of mind of the patient was mirrored in the staff, which was then mirrored in the consultant.

I asked Harry if he was leaving the unit shortly. He looked surprised, and agreed he was – in fact, within a couple of weeks. He then thought about the way he and the others had been talking. He had not forgotten he was leaving, but said it felt like it would not happen for a long time; it was as if he had no sense of the reality of time. Then he remembered one of his long-term clients, Ian. When he heard Harry was leaving, Ian was very upset. Eventually he was able to ask when it would happen, and was told it would be in three months' time. 'Three months!' said Ian, 'But that's forever!' And the sense of upset disappeared. Ian had completely obliterated the reality that time would pass, that three months would go by, and that Harry would then leave.

In the staff group, Harry and the group were living out the same defence, planning work as if Harry were never going to leave. All of them were caught up in a protective identification with the client, using the same defence of denial of reality. By understanding what was happening, we were able to see that this denial served to protect the group for the moment from the pain of the impending separation and loss. The reality, however, was that the separation would take place, and the team needed to prepare themselves for the loss of a highly valued colleague. Harry, too, needed to prepare himself for the loss of a job and colleagues he had enjoyed. Only when reality was faced could the future be considered; for example, the question of how to recruit a suitable replacement for Harry could now be thought about. By being more in touch with his own reluctance to deal with the painful realities of leaving, Harry was also able to understand better his client's fear that to face his own pain about the loss of his key worker would be intolerable. Work could now begin with Ian too, to prepare him for what would happen, and to plan more realistically for his future therapy.

Here we see how protective identification can be used as a defence against facing a reality that feels unbearable. The same defence was being used by the patient and the staff, and, for a while, by me when I was tempted to avoid the problem also. In situations like this, it is as if the whole system gets caught up in something contagious, a state of mind that is passed rapidly from one person to another until everyone is afflicted and no one any longer retains the capacity to face the pain of reality.

One of the tasks of the consultant is to use his or her own feelings to understand the staff's experiences, and to help them recognise how they become caught up in projective identification with their clients. By noticing and reflecting on their experiences, rather than avoiding them, the staff can free space for thinking about task-appropriate ways of going about their work.

For instance, when I first began consulting to the Daniel Finch Clinic, the staff tended to blame all their difficulties on incompetent management, upon whom they seemed angrily dependent. They were not able to deal directly with the managers about whom there was so much complaint, or to take decisions for themselves, projecting all the feelings of helplessness and incompetence arising from the work itself into the management group outside the unit. When they began to recognise this, they could start to separate their own emotional responses from those of their drug-dependent clients, and their inappropriate dependency on management lessened considerably. Complaints or questions were taken up actively with managers, rather than being left as a source of helplessness and resentment. Workers also took on more self-management, negotiating among themselves and with other units in the wider organization to improve their service. Being less caught up in projective identification with their clients, they were able to function in a more creative, satisfying and efficient way.

Conclusion

This kind of understanding is not limited to consultants. Managers or other members of a team can learn to stand back from their experiences and to use their feelings to understand what is going on. By knowing about ways in which the institution can become 'infected' by the difficulties and defences of their particular client group, staff are more likely to be aware when this is happening, and to use their feelings to tackle their problems in a direct and appropriate way, rather than resorting to avoidance or despair.

Although the examples in this chapter have been of organizations both of which deal with very ill patients, the processes described are evident in all organizations, whatever their task and whatever their client group. The other chapters in this part describe other settings, each with its own particular unconscious pressures to which staff are subjected, and its own unconscious organizational defence systems. Awareness of these opens up the possibility of choice. Instead of denial and projection, there is room for thoughtful and creative interest in the problems of the institution, and for developing conscious strategies that support healthy growth and development.

3

THE UNCONSCIOUS AT WORK IN GROUPS AND TEAMS

Contributions from the work of Wilfred Bion

Jon Stokes

Our experiences of being and working in groups are often powerful and over-whelming. We experience the tension between the wish to join together and the wish to be separate; between the need for togetherness and belonging and the need for an independent identity. Many of the puzzling phenomena of group life stem from this, and it is often difficult to recognise the more frequent reality of mutual interdependence. No man is an island, and yet we wish to believe we are indepen-dent of forces of which we may not be conscious, either from outside ourselves or from within. At times we are aware of these pulls within ourselves; at other times they overwhelm us and become the source of irrational group behaviour. While most obvious in crowds and large meetings, these same forces also influence smaller groups, such as teams and committees. This chapter will focus on groups at work, and how they are affected by unconscious processes.

The psychoanalytic study of unconscious processes in groups begins with Freud's *Group Psychology and the Analysis of the Ego* (1921). Essentially, Freud argued that the members of a group, particularly large groups such as crowds at political rallies, follow their leader because he or she personifies certain ideals of their own. The leader shows the group how to clarify and act on its goals. At the same time, the group members may project their own capacities for thinking, decision-making and taking author-ity on to the person of the leader and thereby become disabled. Rather than using their personal authority in the role of follower, the members of a group can become pathologically dependent, easily swayed one way or another by their idealisation of the leader. Criticism and challenge of the leader, which are an essential part of healthy group life, become impossible (this is further discussed in Chapter 5).

Wilfred Bion and basic assumptions in groups

A major contributor to our understanding of unconscious processes in groups was the psychoanalyst Wilfred Bion, who made a detailed study of the processes in small groups in the army during World War II, and later at the Tavistock Clinic. On the basis of these, he developed a framework for analysing some of the more irrational features of unconscious group life. His later work on psychosis, thinking and mental development (Bion 1967, 1977) has also contributed much to our understanding of groups and organizational processes and is referred to elsewhere in this book (see Chapters 1, 8, 13 and 19). Bion himself wrote little further on groups as such, preferring to concentrate on the internal world of the individual. In fact, as he himself argues, the group and the psychoanalytic pair of psychoanalyst and analysand actually provide two different 'vertices' on human mental life and behaviour. Each is distinct but not mutually incompatible, just as, for example, physics and chemistry provide distinct levels of understanding of the material world. Indeed, the whole matter of the relationship between the individual and the group is a central theme throughout both Bion's work and his life (Armstrong 1992 and Menzies Lyth 1983 – for a further understanding of Bion's work see Anderson 1992; Meltzer 1978; and Symington 1986: Chapters 26 and 27). This chapter concentrates solely on some of the implications for understanding groups and teams based on the ideas contained in Bion's *Experiences in Groups* (1961).

Bion distinguished two main tendencies in the life of a group: the tendency towards work on the primary task (see Chapter 4) or *work-group mentality,* and a second, often unconscious, tendency to avoid work on the primary task, which he termed 'basic assumption mentality'. These opposing tendencies can be thought of as the wish to face and work *with* reality, and the wish to evade it when it is painful or causes psychological conflict within or between group members.

> The staff of a day centre spent a great deal of time arguing about whether or not the clients should have access to an electric kettle to make drinks with. Some were strongly of the opinion that this was too dangerous, while others were equally adamant that the centre should provide as normal an environment as possible. While there was a real policy issue, the argument was also an expression of the difficulty the staff were having with their angry and violent feelings towards their clients, who were behaving in ways that frustrated the staff's wish that they 'get better'. The fear of the clients scalding themselves also contained a less conscious and unspoken wish to punish them. However, it was too painful for the staff to face these feelings. Instead, each time the ostensible problem was near to solution, some new objection would be raised, with the result that the group was in danger of spending the whole of its weekly team meeting on the matter of the kettle. An interpretation of this problem by the consultant enabled a deeper discussion of the ambivalent feelings, and a return to the group's work task: the exploration of working relations and practices in the centre.

In work-group mentality, members are intent on carrying out a specifiable task and want to assess their effectiveness in doing it. By contrast, in basic assumption mentality, the group's behaviour is directed at attempting to meet the unconscious needs of its members by reducing anxiety and internal conflicts.

The three basic assumptions

How groups do this varies. According to Bion, much of the irrational and apparently chaotic behaviour we see in groups can be viewed as springing from *basic assumptions* common to all their members. He distinguished three basic assumptions, each giving rise to a particular complex of feelings, thoughts and behaviour: *basic assumption dependency*, *basic assumption fight–flight* and *basic assumption pairing*.

Basic assumption dependency (baD)

A group dominated by baD behaves as if its primary task is solely to provide for the satisfaction of the needs and wishes of its members. The leader is expected to look after, protect and sustain the members of the group, to make them feel good, and not to face them with the demands of the group's real purpose. The leader serves as a focus for a pathological form of dependency which inhibits growth and development. For example, instead of addressing the difficult items on the agenda, a committee may endlessly postpone them to the next meeting. Any attempts to change the organization are resisted, since this induces a fear of being uncared for. The leader may be absent or even dead, provided the illusion that he or she contains the solution can be sustained. Debates within the organization may then be not so much about how to tackle present difficulties as about what the absent leader would have said or thought.

Basic assumption fight–flight (baF)

The assumption here is that there is a danger or 'enemy', which should either be attacked or fled from. However, as Bion puts it, the group is prepared to do either indifferently. Members look to the leader to devise some appropriate action; their task is merely to follow. For instance, instead of considering how best to organize its work, a team may spend most of the time in meetings worrying about rumours of organizational change. This provides a spurious sense of togetherness, while also serving to avoid facing the difficulties of the work itself. Alternatively, such a group may spend its time protesting angrily, without actually planning any specific action to deal with the perceived threat to its service.

Basic assumption pairing (baP)

BaP is based on the collective and unconscious belief that, whatever the actual problems and needs of the group, a future event will solve them. The group behaves as if pairing or coupling between two members within the group, or perhaps between the leader of the group and some external person, will bring about salvation. The group is focused entirely on the future, but as a defence against the difficulties of the present. As Bion puts it, there is a conviction that the coming season will be more agreeable. In the case of a work team, this may take the form of an idea that improved premises would provide an answer to the group's problems, or that all will be well after the next annual study day. The group is in fact not interested in working practically towards this future, but only in sustaining a vague sense of hope as a way out of its current difficulties. Typically, decisions are either not taken or left extremely vague. After the meeting, members are inevitably left with a sense of disappointment and failure, which is quickly superseded by a hope that the next meeting will be better. Indeed, one might use the term 'Ba Hope' rather than 'Ba Pairing' as a more accurate description of this mental state.

Recognising basic assumption activity

The meetings of a group of psychologists to which I consulted would often start with a discussion of their frustration at decisions not having been implemented. At one meeting, the main topic for a considerable time was the previous meeting, whether it had been a good meeting or a bad meeting – it being entirely unclear what this meant. When I pointed this out, there followed a lengthy debate about the relative merits of various chairs, seating arrangements, and, finally, rooms in which to hold the meeting. Various improved ways of organizing the meeting were proposed, but no decision was reached. I suggested there was a fear of discussing matters of real concern to the members present, perhaps a fear of conflict. At this point it emerged that there was indeed considerable controversy about a proposed appointment, some favouring one method, others another. Eventually a decision was almost reached, only to be resisted on the grounds that one significant member of the team was absent.

When under the sway of a basic assumption, a group appears to be meeting as if for some hard-to-specify purpose upon which the members seem intently set. Group members lose their critical faculties and individual abilities, and the group as a whole has the appearance of having some ill-defined but passionately involving mission. Apparently trivial matters are discussed as if they were matters of life or death, which is how they may well feel to the members of the group, since the underlying anxieties are about psychological survival.

In this state of mind, the group seems to lose awareness of the passing of time, and is apparently willing to continue endlessly with trivial matters. On the other hand, there is little capacity to bear frustration, and quick solutions are favoured. In both cases, members have lost their capacity to stay in touch with reality and its demands. Other external realities are also ignored or denied. For example, instead of seeking information, the group closes itself off from the outside world and retreats into paranoia. A questioning attitude is impossible; any who dare to do so are regarded as either foolish, mad or heretical. A new idea or formulation which might offer a way forward is likely to be too terrifying to consider because it involves questioning cherished assumptions, and loss of the familiar and predictable which is felt to be potentially catastrophic. At the prospect of any change, the group is gripped anew by panic, and the struggle for understanding is avoided. All this prevents both adaptive processes and development (Turquet 1974). Effective work, which involves tolerating frustration, facing reality, recognising differences among group members and learning from experience, will be seriously impeded.

Leadership and followership in basic assumption groups

True leadership requires the identification of some problem requiring attention and action, and the promotion of activities to produce a solution. In basic assumption mentality, however, there is a collusive interdependence between the leader and the led, whereby the leader will be followed only as long as he or she fulfils the basic assumption task of the group. The leader in baD is restricted to providing for members' needs to be cared for. The baF leader must identify an enemy either within or outside the group, and lead the attack or flight. In baP, the leader must foster hope that the future will be better, while preventing actual change taking place. The leader who fails to behave in these ways will be ignored, and eventually the group will turn to an alternative leader. Thus the basic assumption leader is essentially a creation or puppet of the group, who is manipulated to fulfil its wishes and to evade difficult realities.

A leader or manager who is being pulled into basic assumption leadership is likely to experience feelings related to the particular nature of the group's unconscious demands. In baD there is a feeling of heaviness and resistance to change, and a preoccupation with status and hierarchy as the basis for decisions. In baF, the experience is of aggression and suspicion, and a preoccupation with the fine details of rules and procedures. In baP, the preoccupation is with alternative futures; the group may ask the leader to meet with some external authority to find a solution, full of insubstantial hopes for the outcome.

Members of such groups are both happy and unhappy. They are happy in that their roles are simple, and they are relieved of anxiety and responsibility. At the same time, they are unhappy insofar as their skills, individuality and capacity for rational thought are sacrificed, as are the satisfactions that come from working effectively. As a result, the members of such groups tend to feel continually in conflict about staying or leaving, somehow never able to make up their minds which they wish to do for any length of time. Since the group now contains split-off and projected capacities of its members, leaving would be experienced as losing these disowned parts. In work-group mentality, on the other hand, members are able to mobilise their capacity for cooperation and to value the different contributions each can make. They choose to follow a leader in order to achieve the group's task, rather than doing so in an automatic way determined by their personal needs.

The multidisciplinary team

I wish now to look at the effects of the interplay between work-group mentality and basic assumption mentality functioning in a particular situation – the multidisciplinary team. Such teams are to be found in both public and private sector settings. For example, a health centre may be staffed by several doctors, a team of nurses, social workers, counsellors, a team of midwives and a number of administrative staff. In industry, management teams will consist of individuals from production, marketing, sales, audit, personnel and so on. In universities and schools, teams consist of staff teaching a range of subjects, the heads of different departments, together with administrators and others.

Teams such as these often have difficulty developing a coherent and shared common purpose, since their members come from different trainings with different values, priorities and preoccupations. Often, too, team members are accountable to different superiors, who may not be part of the team (see Chapter 17). This is an important and yet often ignored reality which leads to the illusion that the team is in a position to make certain policy decisions which, in fact, it is not. Considerable time can be wasted on discussions which cannot result in decisions, instead of exploring ways the actual decision-makers can be influenced in the desired direction.

The meetings of such teams typically have a rather vague title such as 'staff meeting' or 'planning meeting'. Their main purpose may well be simply for those present to 'meet' in order to give a sense of artificial togetherness and cohesion as a refuge from the pressures of work. The use of the word 'team' here is somewhat misleading: there may be little actual day-to-day work in common. Indeed, because of a lack of clarity about the primary task (see Chapter 4), confusion, frustration and bad feeling may actually be engendered by such meetings, interfering with work. The real decisions about work practices are often made elsewhere – over coffee, in corridors, in private groups, between meetings but not in them. Furthermore, such decisions as are taken may well not be implemented, because it is rare for anyone in the group to have the authority to ensure they are carried out.

Task-oriented teams have a defined common purpose and a membership determined by the requirements of the task. Thus, in a multidisciplinary team, each member would have a specific contribution to make. Often, the reality is more like a collection of individuals agreeing to be a group when it suits them, while threatening to disband whenever there is serious internal conflict. It is as if participation were a voluntary choice, rather than that there is a task in which they must cooperate in order to achieve. The spurious sense of togetherness is used to obscure these problems and as a defence against possible conflicts. Even the conflicts themselves may be used to avoid more fundamental anxieties about the work by preventing commitment to decisions and change.

Basic assumptions in different professions

So far I have referred to basic assumptions as defensive or regressive manifestations of group life. However, Bion (1961) also refers to what he termed the 'sophisticated use of basic assumption mentality', an important but lesser-known part of his theory. Here, Bion suggests that a group may utilise the basic assumption mentalities in a sophisticated way, by mobilising the emotions of one basic assumption in the constructive pursuit of the primary task.

An example of such sophisticated and specialised use of baD can be found in a well-run hospital ward. An atmosphere of efficiency and calm is used to mobilise baD, encouraging patients to give themselves over to the nurses or doctors in a trusting, dependent way. BaF is utilised by an army to keep on the alert, and, when required, to go into battle without disabling consideration for personal safety. In social work, baF supports the task of fighting or fleeing from family, social and environmental conditions or injustices which are harmful to the client. BaP finds a sophisticated use in the therapeutic situation, where the pairing between a staff member and a patient can provide a background sense of hope in order to sustain the setbacks inevitable in any treatment.

In trying to understand some of the difficulties of multidisciplinary work, it is helpful to understand the different sophisticated uses of basic assumption mentality adopted by the various professions or disciplines that make up a team. Fights for supremacy in a multidisciplinary team can then be viewed as the inevitable psychological clash between the sophisticated use of the three basic assumptions. Each carries with it a different set of values and a different set of views about the nature of the problem, its cure, what constitutes progress, and whether this is best achieved by a relationship between professional and client involving dependency, fight–flight or pairing. Furthermore, individuals are drawn to one profession or another partly because of their unconscious pre-disposition or *valency* for one basic assumption rather than another. As a result, they are particularly likely to contribute to the interdisciplinary group processes without questioning them (see Chapter 13).

Put another way, one of the difficulties in making a team out of different professions is that each profession operates through the deliberate harnessing of different sophisticated forms of the basic assumptions in order to further the task. There is consequently conflict when they meet, since the emotional motivations involved in each profession differ. However, conflict need not preclude collaboration on a task, provided there is a process of clarifying shared goals and the means of achieving these. However, difficulties in carrying out the task for which the team is in existence can lead to a breakdown in the sophisticated use of the various basic assumptions, and instead *aberrant* forms of each emerge. Examining these can illuminate some of the frequently encountered workplace tensions in teamwork.

For instance, medical training involves an institutionalised, prolonged dependency of junior doctors on their seniors over many years, from which the medical consultant eventually emerges and then defends his new independence. This can degenerate into an insistence on freedom for its own sake. The doctor may then operate from a counterdependent state of mind, denying the mutual interdependency of teamwork and the actual dependency on the institutional setting of hospital or clinic. This can extend to other professionals, each arguing for their own area of independence, with rivalry and embittered conflict impeding thought and work on establishing shared overall objectives for the team.

By contrast, the training of therapists – whether of psychological, occupational, speech or other varieties – tends to idealise the pairing between therapist and client as the pre-eminent medium for change. Aberrant baP can lead to collusion in supporting this activity, while refusing to examine whether or not it is in fact helping, or how it relates to the team's primary task. Indeed, therapist and client may remain endlessly 'glued' together as if the generation of hope about the future were by itself a cure.

In social work, the sophisticated use of baF in the productive fight against social or family injustices can degenerate into a particular kind of litigious demand that justice be done, and on 'getting our rights'. Responsibility for improvement is felt to rest not at all with the individual, but solely with the community. Projecting responsibility in this way then disables the client and social worker from devising together any effective course of action: it is only others that must change.

In the commercial sector, basic assumption mentality can similarly be used in both sophisticated and defensive (anti-task) ways. For example, in the airline industry, passengers are encouraged into a basic assumption dependency state of mind (baD) in order to allow their lives to be temporarily managed by others. In this regressed state of mind disappointment, such as the late arrival of an aeroplane, can generate infantile panic and rage. The investment banking industry is shaped by the basic assumption of fight–flight (baF) which may result in dysfunctional competition within the bank rather than with those outside. Marketing and advertising utilise basic assumption pairing (baP), which might be better labelled 'basic assumption Hope', and operate in the service of generating positive expectations about a product or service, sometimes resulting in the manic production of ineffective campaigns.

These are examples where the capacity for the sophisticated use of basic assumption activity has degenerated, and the professional's action and thought becomes dominated by its aberrant forms. Each then produces a particular group culture. Aberrant baD gives rise to a *culture of subordination* where authority derives entirely from position in the hierarchy, requiring unquestioning obedience. Aberrant baP produces a *culture of collusion*, supporting pairs of members in avoiding truth rather than seeking it. There is attention to the group's mission, but not to the means of achieving it. Aberrant baF results in a *culture of paranoia and aggressive competitiveness*, where the group is preoccupied not only by an external enemy but also by 'the enemy within'. Rules and regulations proliferate to control both the internal and the external 'bad objects'. Here it is the means which are explicit and the ends which are vague.

Conclusion

In a group taken over by basic assumption mentality, the formation and continuance of the group becomes an end in itself. Leaders and members of groups dominated by basic assumption activity are likely to lose their ability to think and act effectively: continuance of the group becomes an end in itself, as members become more absorbed with their relationship to the group than with their work task. In this chapter, we have seen how the functioning of teams can be promoted by the sophisticated use of a basic assumption in the service of work, or impeded and distracted by their inappropriate or aberrant use.

An understanding of these phenomena of group life, perhaps best obtained through the kind of group relations training programmes described in Chapter 5, can greatly assist both the members and managers of multidisciplinary teams, committees and other working groups.

4

THE ORGANIZATION OF WORK

Contributions from open systems theory

Vega Zagier Roberts

A living organizm can survive only by exchanging materials with its environment, that is, by being an *open system*. It takes in materials such as food or sunshine or oxygen, and transforms these into what is required for survival, excreting what is not used as waste. This requires certain properties, notably an external *boundary*, a membrane or skin which serves to separate what is inside from what is outside, and across which these exchanges can occur. This boundary must be solid enough to prevent leakage and to protect the organizm from disintegrating, but permeable enough to allow the flow of materials in both directions. If the boundary becomes impermeable, the organizm becomes a *closed system* and it will die. Furthermore, exchanges with the environment need to be regulated in some way, so that only certain materials enter, and only certain others leave to return to the outer environment.

In complex organizms, there will be a number of such open systems operating simultaneously, each performing its own specialised function. The activities of these different sub-systems need to be coordinated so as to serve the needs of the organizm as a whole, and complex superordinate systems are evolved to provide this coordinating function, which includes prioritising the activities of certain sub-systems over others in times of crisis. In the human body, for example, blood flow to the brain will be preserved at the expense of blood flow to the limbs when there is an insufficient supply of oxygen.

The work of Kurt Lewin (1947) in applying these ideas to human systems was extended and developed at the Tavistock Institute of Human Relations in the 1950s, notably by Rice and Miller. Their organizational model provides a framework for studying the relationships between the parts and the whole in organizations, and also between the organization and the environment (Miller and Rice 1967).

Organizations as open systems

An organization as an open system can be schematically represented as in Figure 4.1. The box in the centre represents the system of activities required to perform the task of converting the inputs into outputs. Around it there is a boundary separating the inside from the outside, across which the organization's exchanges with the environment take place. These exchanges need to be regulated in such a way that the system can achieve its task, and therefore there needs to be *management of the boundary*, represented by M. For example, an automobile factory takes in or imports raw materials such as steel, and converts them into products or outputs which it exports. This throughput defines its task, namely producing cars.

Obviously, most enterprises are much more complex than shown in Figure 4.1, with many different kinds of inputs and outputs, and a variety of task-systems. The factory, for instance, also takes in information from the environment and uses it to produce financial plans and marketing strategies. It is likely to have different departments such as production, marketing, personnel, and so on, all of which need to be coordinated. Furthermore, the tasks of these sub-systems may at times conflict or compete. How to allocate resources and how to prioritise among the organization's different activities is determined by its *primary task*, defined by Rice (1963) as the task it must perform if it is to survive.

This is not as simple as it might first appear. Different groups within the organization may have different definitions of the primary task. For example, the primary task of an automobile factory would seem to be to produce automobiles, and that is how the assembly-line workers are likely to define it. Members of other departments may see it as remaining at the forefront of new technology, or in terms of sales figures. Consequently, the decision to stop producing high-performance cars or to use parts manufactured by another company will be experienced very differently by different members of the organization. If the factory is the principal employer in the local community, its primary task may be regarded by some as providing employment, and the decision to reduce the labour force may well precipitate intractable conflict. Where the primary task is defined too narrowly, or in terms of its members' needs, the survival of the organization can become precarious.

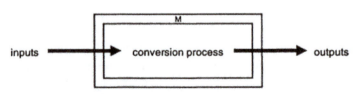

FIGURE 4.1 Schematic representation of an organization as an open system[1]

Task and anti-task in the human services

In institutions which exist to change or help people, the difficulties in defining the primary task precisely and realistically are even greater. They usually have multiple tasks, all of them important and even essential. For example, teaching hospitals must treat patients, train staff and do research; prisons are required to be custodial, punitive and also rehabilitative. There are often conflicting assumptions both inside and outside the organization about which task has priority, and some objectives may even be incompatible. Furthermore, it can be inherently difficult to define aims in other than general terms, such as health, or education, or welfare. This problem is exacerbated by the current dramatic pace of social change and the accompanying changes in the assumptions underlying such terms.

The concept of the primary task can seem to be an oversimplification, given the complexities with which most organizations have to contend. However, it can provide an invaluable starting-point for thinking about what is going on in a group or organization. Miller and Rice described it as 'a heuristic concept', that is, a tool 'which allows us to explore the ordering of multiple activities . . . [and] to construct and compare different organizational models of an enterprise based on different definitions of its primary task' (1967 p. 62). It is not a matter of saying that an enterprise *should* have a primary task, but rather that at any given time it *has* one which it must perform if it is to survive. As conditions change, the primary task may shift, either temporarily, at times of crisis, or permanently. When changing conditions lead to a permanent change in the primary task, either explicitly or implicitly, this can affect 'the ordering of multiple activities' in ways which have major implications for everyone involved.

Gordon Lawrence (1977) developed this idea of the primary task as a tool for examining organizational behaviour by proposing that people within an enterprise pursue different kinds of primary tasks. The *normative primary task* is the formal or official task, the operationalisation of the broad aims of the organization, and is usually defined by the chief stakeholders. The *existential primary task* is the task people within the enterprise believe they are carrying out, the meaning or interpretation they put on their roles and activities. The *phenomenal primary task* is the task that can be inferred from people's behaviour, and of which they may not be consciously aware. Analysis of the primary task in these terms can highlight discrepancies between what an organization or group says it sets out to do and what is actually happening. It can thus serve as a tool for individuals and groups within an enterprise, as well as for consultants, to clarify and understand how the activities, roles and experiences of individuals and sub-systems relate to each other and to the enterprise as a whole.

The confusion in helping institutions and in the society they serve about what their primary task is (or should be) often results in inadequate task definitions, which provide little guidance to staff or managers about what they should be doing, or how to do it, or whether they are doing it effectively (Menzies Lyth 1979).

This is a major source of the individual, group and institutional difficulties described in this book. Turquet (1974) warned that when a group does not seek to know its primary task, both by definition and by feasibility, there is likely to emerge either dismemberment of the group, or the emergence of some other primary task unrelated to the one for which it was originally called into being. This *anti-task* is typical of groups under the sway of basic assumptions, as described in Chapter 3, whereas the primary task corresponds to the overt work-oriented purpose of Bion's sophisticated work group. Both are about survival. The primary task relates to survival in relation to the demands of the external environment, while basic assumption activity is driven by the demands of the internal environment and anxieties about psychological survival. In the examples which follow, we will see how lack either of task definition, or of feasibility, or both, can lead to anti-task activity as a defence against anxiety.

Vague task definition

One of the commonest ways of dealing with the problems outlined previously is to define organizational aims in very broad and general terms.

> The Tappenly Drug Dependency Unit was originally set up as a methadone clinic, staffed by nurses and doctors, to help clients reduce and eventually abstain from abusing heroin. In the 1970s, a psychologist and a social worker joined the team, and the orientation began to shift towards a more holistic approach, with attention to addicts' psychosocial as well as their medical needs. In the 1980s, concerns about HIV infection shifted the emphasis in drug work across the country away from emphasis on abstinence *per se* towards 'harm reduction'. Counsellors were hired to join the multidisciplinary team and long-term support to help clients stabilise their lifestyle became the predominant form of treatment. The stated aim of the unit became 'to provide a comprehensive service to residents of Tappenly with drug-related problems'.
>
> Over a two-year period, the team almost doubled in size, yet the waiting list continued to grow longer. The staff felt the only solution was to recruit yet more staff, despite evidence that this shortened the waiting list only briefly, until the new workers had full caseloads. Instead of hiring more staff, the managers suggested that the team review and revise their working methods and curtail the amount of counselling offered to clients, which the team experienced as devaluing and undermining their good work. They continued to struggle to provide as much counselling as was needed to as many clients as possible, repressing their anxiety about the people on the waiting list who were getting no support at all. When the hospital management finally intervened actively in the crisis by imposing a limit on the number of counselling sessions any one client could have, team members felt outraged, betrayed and demoralised.

The statement of their aims, which the team had written in such a way that any and all of their activities were covered, was of no help in determining how best to deal with drug problems in Tappenly. The team behaved as if their task were to provide as much help as was needed to everyone who needed it. As the demands on the unit increased in both scope and numbers, this became impossible. In turn, this created a great deal of stress for the staff: both the conscious stress of ever-growing caseloads, and the unconscious stress of failing to help the many addicts on the waiting list. Their only recourse was to blame the shortcomings of the service on the managers' refusal to provide them with sufficient resources.

Defining methods instead of aims

Another common way of dealing with the difficulties in defining the aims of helping organizations is to define their methods rather than what these methods are intended to achieve.

Pathways, a service for young people aged 16 to 24 in a deprived inner-city area, defined its aim as 'to provide free information, advice and counselling to young people in difficulty, especially those suffering from the results of social deprivation and prejudice'. This service had two parts: social workers gave advice and information about housing and benefit rights, equal opportunities, career training and other community resources; volunteer counsellors and therapists provided support for psychological problems.

There was constant conflict between the two groups, ostensibly about how the premises were used. The social workers ran the advice and information service as a drop-in centre, encouraging clients to stay around to meet each other informally. This made for a good deal of noise and sometimes so much crowding that it was hard to get through the door. The counselling service was based on an appointment system, with clients being encouraged to arrive and leave promptly, and the counsellors complained that the noise interfered with their work, which required a quiet and reassuringly calm atmosphere. The ill feeling could be dealt with only informally, since there were no staff meetings at which all workers met together.

Consultants, called in to help with an organizational review, noticed how each group spoke disparagingly about the other, but in fact were largely ignorant and even misinformed about each other's training, skills and ways of working. The social workers worried that the counsellors encouraged futile navel-gazing which might well undermine the clients' capacity to fight for their rights, while the counsellors considered that the emphasis on resisting social injustice prevented the young people from taking responsibility for their own lives and fostered an expectation of being taken care of. As a result, there was no cross-referral between the two services. New clients whose first contact was to drop in would meet a social worker. If, on the other hand, the first contact were by telephone, they would be more likely to be allocated to a counsellor.

It seemed to the consultants that neither view was accurate and that the two groups were doing potentially complementary work. They therefore worked with the organization as a whole on developing a definition of their primary task towards which both sets of activities would contribute. Meeting together as a single staff group enabled workers to develop more understanding and respect for each other's work, and to focus on the question of what the organization was trying to achieve, rather than on which method of work was superior. This not only improved relations among the staff, but was also of benefit to clients, who began to be cross-referred when appropriate, and thus to have access to the specific help they needed.

By splitting up the task of supporting young people in developing the resources – both internal and external – necessary for taking up an adult role in society, and by defining its methods rather than its aims, Pathways defended itself from anxieties about failing to remedy some of its clients' problems. Instead there was conflict and rivalry among staff which interfered with effective work. Furthermore, the aims as originally stated could do nothing to resolve the conflicting assumptions about the cause of the clients' difficulties.

Avoiding conflict over priorities

Another way of avoiding dealing with disagreements within an organization is to define the task in a way that fails to give priority to one system of activities over another.

Early Days Nursery School defined its task as 'providing quality care and education for under-fives'. Staffed by both nursery nurses and nursery teachers, it had a high ratio of staff to children, and an excellent reputation, particularly for its standard of teaching. When funding was suddenly severely reduced, there was great uncertainty and conflict about how to use the now limited resources. Should the higher-paid teachers be replaced by more nursery nurses? Or should the ratio of staff to children be reduced? Or should they spend less on equipment, or move to smaller premises in an effort to maintain the standard of teaching at all costs? Different people had quite different ideas about priorities, and latent disagreements about what constituted quality care and education, and what resources were required to produce these, erupted, largely as painful personal attacks.

At this point, it seems useful to make a distinction between the terms 'aim' and 'primary task', which are to some extent used interchangeably in this and subsequent chapters. More precisely, aims are broadly outlined statements of the intended direction of an enterprise, while primary task refers to the way in which the system proposes to engage with these aims. Thus, Pathways might say that its aim was to provide opportunities for the development of under-fives. One way of engaging with this would be to facilitate the children's transition from home to primary school. In open systems terms, the inputs in this case would be children under five who were not yet ready for school, and the outputs would be school-ready five-year-olds. This would then open a crucial debate within the nursery about what Pathways regarded as the most important features of school-readiness, which in turn would assist it in making decisions about 'the ordering of multiple activities'.

Failing to relate to a changing environment

When the external environment into which an organization exports its products changes, it may become necessary for it to revise its primary task. Failure to do so will cause stress and compromise the organization's effectiveness.

> Putlake High School had long been considered an outstanding school, with a reputation for innovative programmes, including work experience, personal and career counselling, and an individual tutorial system. When funding cuts and restructuring of the county's educational system threatened these programmes, there was a steep decline in staff morale and an external consultant was invited to work with the teachers on how to cope with the recent changes.
>
> On her first visit, the consultant was struck by the quiet everywhere; there was little contact between teachers and pupils outside the classroom, and there were no telephones in the staff rooms. In fact, it was quite hard to find anyone to speak to, or to reach staff members by telephone. Interviews with individual teachers revealed their great anxiety about what would happen to their pupils when they left, and despair about their efforts to equip the pupils with skills they would not be able to use, given the high local unemployment. The teachers were cynical about their task, seeing it as 'keeping the kids off the streets for an extra year or two' and 'keeping unemployment figures down'.

Here the staff were continuing to work at the now outdated task of preparing their students for the world of work. To cope with their guilt and anxiety, they avoided contact both with the students and with the outside world, clustering together to whisper complaints about their managers. Most had been at the school for over ten years; it was as if the primary task of the school had become to provide the staff with secure jobs in a citadel cut off and protected from the terrifying world outside the school. It had become a closed system, existing primarily to meet the needs of its members: transactions across its boundaries with potential employers, former students and parents were kept to a minimum. Internal boundaries, too, notably those between staff and managers, and between staff and pupils, had become rigid, defending the staff from anxieties and information that they could no longer manage.

Task and anti-task boundaries

Where there are problems with the definition of the primary task, there are likely also to be problems with boundaries, so that instead of facilitating task performance, they serve defensive functions. In the last example, the boundary around Putlake High School had become relatively impermeable, so that the necessary exchanges with the environment no longer took place. In the next example, boundaries were located and managed in such a way that they failed to relate the parts to each other and to the overall enterprise.

Cannon Fields, the Community Mental Health Centre (CMHC) for North-west Wresham, was one of three such centres – the others serving Northeast and South Wresham – set up to provide mental health services in the community as part of a plan to close wards at Wresham Psychiatric Hospital. The team, most of whom had previously worked at the hospital, were very committed to creating a service where clients would flourish, developing social and independent living skills which would give them a better quality of life as well as preventing breakdown and hospitalisation. They regarded the hospital as rigid, oppressive and suppressive of individuality, and based their programme planning on the intention to be as different from it as possible. The clients could come and go freely, choosing whether or not to attend formal therapeutic activities. Similarly, staff could work as they chose, with individuals or groups, chronic or acute patients. It was difficult to set any limits or enforce any decisions, lest this curtail individual freedom, evoking the spectre of the 'bad old days' on the wards.

The aim of Cannon Fields was defined as 'offering a comprehensive community-based mental health service to residents of Northwest Wresham with emotional and psychiatric problems, and to prevent admission to hospital'. As a result, admission of anyone in their catchment area to Wresham Hospital was experienced by the staff as a failure, which they tended to blame on bad management, inadequate resources or incompetence on the part of general practitioners, casualty room staff and other professionals.

Relations between the centre and the hospital's C ward, to which North-west Wresham residents were admitted when they needed in-patient care, were antagonistic. Cannon Fields staff considered attending ward rounds at the hospital a disagreeable chore, and left as soon as the round was over, as if contact might contaminate them with something they had been lucky to escape. They spoke of ward staff with pity, but also with contempt, and the ward staff regarded them as stand-offish and unhelpful.

The wording of the aims statement of Cannon Fields placed a boundary between it and the hospital. The first part defined Cannon Fields in terms of being what the hospital was not, namely community-based, rather than indicating what it might be trying to do. The second part, 'to prevent admission to hospital', on the one hand was too narrow a definition, and on the other hand set an impossible task. Together, the two parts supported the staff ideal of being a superior alternative to hospital care, as different and separate from it as possible. The team behaved *as if* the task it existed to perform were to do away with the need for a hospital altogether.

This as-if task was supported by the management structure. Community psychiatric care was managed as a system quite separate from, and even in competition with, the hospital-based psychiatric service (see Figure 4.2(a)). Subsequently, the management structure was altered to correspond to the three catchment areas (see Figure 4.2(b)). The new boundaries matched and supported the task of providing a comprehensive mental health service, comprising both inpatient and community services, to each catchment area. Patients could then be more readily seen as a shared responsibility, whether they were at any given moment in the hospital or in the community, and the rivalry between the hospital and community lessened. Ward rounds became a central activity for the staff of Cannon Fields as well as of C ward, involving their working together at assessing the needs of their joint clients.

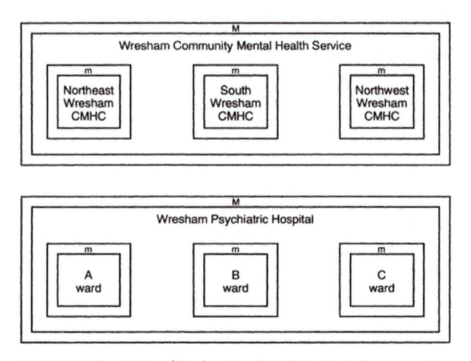

FIGURE 4.2(a)   Organization of Wresham Mental Health Services before restructuring

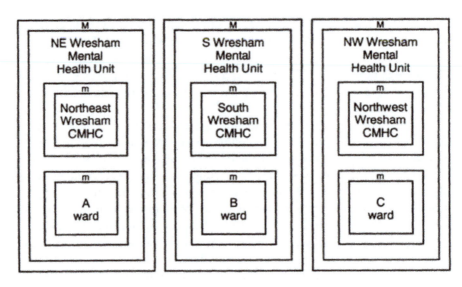

FIGURE 4.2(b) Organization of Wresham Mental Health Services after restructuring

Management at the boundary

The management of boundaries is absolutely crucial to effective organizational functioning. Boundaries need both to separate and to relate what is inside and what is outside. Where an enterprise consists of multiple task-systems, there is a boundary around the system as a whole, as well as one around each of the subsidiary systems, and each of these boundaries needs to be managed so that all the parts function in a coordinated way in relation to the overall primary task (Miller and Rice 1967).

Whereas most organizational charts place managers above those they manage, the open systems model locates them *at the boundary* of the systems they manage (see Figure 4.3). It is only from this position that they can carry out their function of relating what is inside to what is outside the system. This includes being clear about the primary task, attending to the flow of information across the boundary, ensuring that the system has the resources it needs to perform its task, and monitoring that this task continues to relate to the requirements of the wider system and to the external environment.

The manager who loses this boundary position, either by being drawn too far into the system, or by being too cut off, can no longer manage effectively. This is also the case for each individual in an organization. Even those who are not in designated management roles need to manage the boundary between their own inner world – their wishes, needs and resources – and external reality, in order to take up their roles (Grubb Institute 1991).

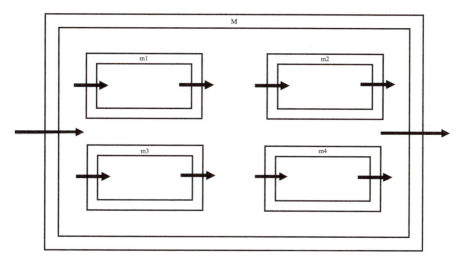

FIGURE 4.3 Management of multiple systems of activity within an organization

Note: The smaller boxes represent discrete task-systems, each with a boundary managed by m1, m2, etc. The larger box represents the overall enterprise, managed by M. In conventional organizational terms, M is the line manager of the four ms.

Conclusion

In trying to make sense of the often very confusing processes in institutions, it is useful to start with the question, 'What is the primary task?' This often proves surprisingly difficult to answer, as many of the examples in this chapter have illustrated. However, using the model depicted in Figure 4.1 (p. 38) can help to identify the dominant throughput. In a human service enterprise, this dominant throughput is likely to be people, who enter the system in one state and – as a result of the 'conversion' or 'transformation' process within – leave in a different state. Thus, defining the primary task requires thinking first about what this intended or desired 'different state' is, and then about how the system (group, department or organization) proposes to bring this about.

The next question is, 'How does our way of working relate to this task?' If it does not, it can be helpful to ask 'What are we behaving *as if* we were here to do?' Identifying this as-if task can provide clues about the underlying anxieties, defences and conflicts which have given rise to the dysfunctional task definition and to the associated dysfunctional boundaries. These are questions not only for managers and consultants, but also for the individual worker. To be personally effective in our work roles, we need to be clear about the task we have to do; to be able to mobilise sufficient resources, internal and external, to achieve it; and to have some understanding of how our own task relates both to the task of the system in which we are working and to the task of the institution as a whole. These questions pave the way for asking 'How well are we doing?' and for beginning to think about how we might engage differently with the task in hand.

We have seen many examples in this chapter of groups and organizations whose primary task lacked definition or feasibility or both. When managers fail to maintain their position at the boundary, they are likely to get caught up in unconscious group and institutional processes, and will not be able to ask the questions that need to be asked. They will then be unable to do what needs to be done to restore to the system the capacity for effective work.

Note

1 The figures in this chapter are adapted from Miller and Rice (1967).

5

AUTHORITY, POWER AND LEADERSHIP

Contributions from group relations training

Anton Obholzer

It is self-evident that clarity in matters of authority, leadership and organizational structure is essential for the competent functioning of any organization. Yet confusion abounds. Why should this be so? What are the factors contributing to the perpetuation of this state? In this chapter we shall look at these core concepts, their derivation and interrelationships, and the individual and organizational factors that commonly lead to the appearance and persistence of institutional anti-task phenomena. The way these concepts are used throughout this book is grounded in a model of group relations training described at the end of this chapter.

Authority

Authority refers to the right to make an ultimate decision, and in an organization it refers to the right to make decisions which are binding on others.

Authority from 'above'

Formal authority is a quality that is derived from one's role in a system and is exercised on its behalf. For example, the director of a company derives authority from the board of the company. The board makes the appointment, holds the director responsible for outcomes, and also has the power to sack him or her. The board, in turn, is elected by, and derives its authority from, the shareholders of the company. Thus, authority derives from a system of delegation, in this case from the shareholders to the board, and from the board to the director. Usually there is a constitution or other formal system which lays down terms of office and other mechanisms for delegating authority. These are human-made systems, agreed through common consent. If the system becomes outdated and is no longer held by common consent, it has to be changed to take the new factors into account.

However, not all systems are so clear-cut in hierarchical terms. For example, in voluntary organizations there are often a number of 'stakeholders' – funders, management committee members, clients, staff, professional groups, referring agencies and so on – which may all, in different ways, claim ownership of the organization. Some of these will hold different views on where authority ultimately comes from (or should come from), to whom it is delegated, and to what extent.

Authority from 'below'

Members who voluntarily join an organization are, by definition, sanctioning the system. By the act of joining, they are, at least implicitly, delegating some of their personal authority to those in authority, and so is doing confirming the system.

Authority does not, however, derive only from an external structure as outlined latterly. It also has internal components which may be explicit and conscious, or unconscious and therefore not available to be worked with. These internal components include the nature and extent of the ambivalence affecting the delegation of authority to those in charge. For example a chief executive might have full authority delegated to him or her by the authorising body, but there may have been no dialogue or consultation with the working membership of the organization regarding the appointment. In this case, the latter may accept the concept of management and sanction the authority of the role, but not that of the person in role. The withholding of authority from below, in the form of not sanctioning, means that full authority cannot be obtained, and there is an increased risk of undermining and sabotage.

Of course, 'full authority' is a myth. What is needed might be called 'full-enough' authority, to coin a term derived from Winnicott's (1971) concept of 'good-enough' mothering. This would imply a state of authority in which there would be an ongoing acknowledgement by persons in authority, but also and equally of the limitations of that authority. An integral part of this state of mind would be an ongoing monitoring of authority-enhancing and of authority-sapping processes in the institution.

> A head teacher learned that an informal meeting had been called at school, after school hours, in which the teachers attending planned to discuss the new curriculum. As this had previously been decided at a policy meeting chaired by him, he now faced some difficult questions. Was this to be interpreted as evidence of staff initiative, of their taking their authority to extend the debate, and thus enhancing the head's aims? Or was it to be interpreted as an undermining of authority and formal decision-making structures?

The head's understanding of the meaning of the proposed meeting would probably determine not only what action he would take, but also its outcome.

Authority from within

Apart from the delegation of authority from above and sanctioning from below, there is the vital issue of the authorisation or confirmation of authority from within individuals. This largely depends on the nature of their relationship with the figures in their inner world (see Chapter 1), in particular past authority figures. The attitude of such 'in-the-mind' authority figures is crucial in affecting how, to what extent and with what competence external institutional roles are taken up. For example, an individual might be appointed to a position of authority, sanctioned from below, yet be unable to exercise authority competently on account of an undermining of self-in-role by inner world figures. Such 'barracking' by inner world figures is a key element in the process of self-doubt, and, if constant and evident, is likely to prevent external authorisation in the first place.

> An accountant who was perceived by both his peers and seniors as very competent, having gone through all the correct processes, was promoted to director of finance, a move approved by his colleagues. Once that promotion had taken place, his work seemed to falter. He had lost his membership of the office club, and in himself felt he was not really up to the job, and that his former peers were now making snide comments. There was no evidence in reality that this was going on. However, snide remarks were an integral part of his relationship with his father; as a child, he had been at both the giving and receiving end of this process.

The opposite dynamic also exists, with inner world figures playing into a state of psychopathological omnipotence, which makes for an inflated picture of the self as regards being in authority, and is likely to produce authoritarian attitudes and behaviour.

> A doctor, appointed at an early age to a consultant post, became increasingly pompous, arrogant and hard to bear by staff and patients alike. His incapacity to listen, to learn from his own or others' experience, and thus to modify his behaviour, arose from an inner world constellation in which he was mother's only child, her adored companion who could do no wrong. Transferred to outer world behaviour, the consequences were disastrous.

There is an important difference between the terms 'authoritative' and 'authoritarian'. 'Authoritative' is a depressive position state of mind (see Chapter 1) in which the persons managing authority are in touch both with the roots and sanctioning of their authority, and with their limitations. 'Authoritarian', by contrast, refers to a paranoid-schizoid state of mind, manifested by being cut off from roots of authority and processes of sanction, the whole being fuelled by an omnipotent inner world process. The difference is between being in touch with oneself and one's surroundings, and being out of touch with both, attempting to deal with this unrecognised shortcoming by increased use of power to achieve one's ends.

Good-enough authority, at its best, is a state of mind arising from a continuous mix of authorisation from the sponsoring organization or structure, sanctioning from within the organization, and connection with inner world authority figures.

Power

Power refers to the ability to act upon others or upon organizational structure. Unlike authority, it is an attribute of persons rather than roles, and it can arise from both internal and external sources. Externally, power comes from what the individual controls – such as money, privileges, job references, promotion and the like – and from the sanctions one can impose on others. It also derives from the nature of one's social and political connections: how many individuals of prominence can be summoned to one's aid in role. Internally, power comes from individuals' knowledge and experience, strength of personality, and their state of mind regarding their role: how powerful they feel and how they therefore present themselves to others.

In all these, the perceived power or powerlessness counts more than the actual, both of which depend on the inner world connectedness mentioned previously. For example, powerlessness is often a state of mind related to problems with taking up authority. At times there is an interplay between this state of mind and an actual lack of external resources that could otherwise be used to bolster power. However, an individual in a state of demoralisation or depression may well have adequate external resources to effect some change, but feel unable to do so on account of an undermining state of mind. In this case, power is projected, perceived as located outside the self, leaving the individual with a sense of powerlessness. By contrast, someone who attracts projected power is much more likely to take – and to be allowed to take – a leadership role. The nature of the projections will affect whether that person is hated and feared, or loved and admired (Grubb Institute 1991).

Power, authority and language

The terms 'authority' and 'power' are often used interchangeably, leading to confusion. They are different, although related, and in organizations both are necessary. Authority without power leads to a weakened, demoralised management. Power without authority leads to an authoritarian regime. It is the judicious mix and balance of the two that makes for effective on-task management in a well-run organization.

The title given to the person in authority in an organization generally gives some indication of the authority/power ratio. Thus 'dictator' makes it clear that the essential component is power. 'Director', 'manager' or 'chairman' generally imply a mix of authority and power. By contrast, 'coordinator', a title often given to the most senior manager in voluntary sector agencies, suggests that the person can only take decisions if everyone agrees to them – an unlikely phenomenon and that there is very little power and capacity to exert sanctions. The choice of such a title may well express ambivalence in the organization about the amount of authority and power it is prepared to give its office-bearer. In addition, the type and length of appointment can radically affect how the post is perceived in terms of power and authority. For example, there is a considerable difference between being appointed general manager and acting manager, or between being given a fixed-term or permanent contract.

Clarity of structure and of the constitution make it possible to assess whether or not the system of authorisation is functioning, and what steps would need to be taken to withdraw authorisation, should that be decided. This is, of course, not possible in authoritarian regimes, where the constitution either does not exist or else is subverted, and rule or management is on the basis of power rather than of law. Furthermore, there needs to be a match between authority and power, and responsibility. Responsibility for outcomes involves being answerable or account-able to someone, either in the organization or else in one's own mind as part of an inner world value system. A sense of responsibility without having adequate authority and power to achieve outcomes often leads to work-related stress and eventually burn-out.

In assessing the nature and functioning of an organization, whether as a member or as an outside consultant, the time used in clarifying the nature, source and rout-ing of authority, the power available, and the names describing various organiza-tional functions, is time well spent.

Leadership

'Leadership' and 'management' are also terms that are often used interchangeably. It is true that they have a 'headship' function in common, but 'management' gen-erally refers to a form of conduct by those in authority that is intended to keep the organization functioning and on-task, while 'leadership' also implies looking to the future, pursuing an ideal or goal. Furthermore, leadership by definition implies followership, while management does so to a much lesser degree.

The story of Judith and Holophernes in the Apocrypha is an extreme example of leadership, with consequent risks to the followership. When Judith cut off the head of Holophernes, the leader of the Assyrians, and displayed it to the Assyrian army, they behaved as if they had all lost their own heads and were then easily routed by the Israelites. If the Assyrian army had had less of a leadership cult and more emphasis on management, Holophernes could have been quickly replaced and the outcome would have been quite different. Similar difficulties can often be observed after the departure of a charismatic leader in present-day institutions. Followers are left in disarray, and at the same time may withhold followership from the person appointed as a replacement, disabling this person from both leading and managing.

Leadership, followership and envy

Task performance requires active participation on the part of the followers as well as of the leader. A passive, accepting, *basic assumption* state of followership (see Chapter 4), such as one might find in a demoralised organization, is quite different from a state of mind of exercising one's own authority to take up the followership role in relation to the task. The latter implies clarity about the organization's task, and about where one's role fits in with others.

In order to manage oneself in role, the fundamental question is 'How can I mobilise my resources and potential to contribute to the task?' This requires recognition of where one's role ends and another person's begins, the scope and limits of one's own authority, and a readiness to sanction that of others. Rivalry, jealousy and envy often interfere with the process of taking up either a leadership or a followership role. Staff rivalry is a ubiquitous phenomenon. In a misguided attempt to avoid fanning rivalry and envy, managers may try to manage from a position of equality, or, more commonly, pseudo-equality, often presented as 'democracy'. The term is used as if everyone has equal authority. The hope is that rivalry, jealousy and envy will thereby be avoided; the reality is the undermining of the manager's authority, capacity to hold an overall perspective and ability to lead.

Although there is a substantial body of work on envy in intra- and interpersonal relationships, there is little written about its manifestation in institutions. Yet it is clear that envy in institutional processes is one of the key destructive phenomena, particularly in relation to figures in authority. Envy results in a destructive attack on the person in authority, with resultant spoiling of the work arising under the aegis of that person's authority. Typically, the envious attack on the leader is led by the member of staff with the highest naturally occurring quantum of rivalry and envy. This person is unconsciously set up, by means of projective identification (see Chapters 1 and 15) to express not only his or her own destructive envy, but also that of other group members. The dynamic for the institution is then one in which leader and attacker are pushed into a deadlocked fight, while the remainder of the staff take on the role of distressed and helpless onlookers.

In professional settings, the envious attack may take the form of a debate about 'general principles', or 'technical issues' or 'technique', and is presented as if it were in the pursuit of progress, if not of ultimate truth. It is often only with time that the envious, attacking, destructive nature of this process is revealed. The beauty of this particular defensive institutional constellation is that it not only gratifies unconscious wishes but also attacks the pursuit of the primary task, and this reduces the amount of pain arising from the work of the organization. Such anti-task phenomena are often presented as the most progressive, anti-hierarchical, anti-authoritarian, anti-sexist, anti-ageist, anti-racist way of going about the work of the organization. At times, these ideological arguments are little more than a rationalisation for the defensive processes associated with envy; at other times they are serious on-task comments about an organization in urgent need of reform. It is essential that there be enough thinking space in the organization for these differentiations to be worked on, and for the resulting understanding to be implemented.

On-task leadership

Leadership and management share a boundary-regulating function (see Chapter 4), which requires relating what is inside and what is outside the organization. Like the two-faced Roman god Janus, the leader must always be looking both inwards and outwards, a difficult position which carries the risk of being criticised by people both inside and outside the system for neglecting their interests. Concentrating solely on one or the other is a more comfortable position but it undermines the role of the leader, and thus the strength of the institution's representation in the outer world.

In addition to the boundary-management function, leadership is directly related to the pursuit of the aims and of the primary task of the organization (the distinction between aim and primary task is discussed on p. 42). Without the concept of primary task, whether called that or something else (according to the language of the organization), it is not possible either to have a marker against which the direction and functioning of the organization can be monitored, or to effect the necessary adjustments to this course and functioning. Such monitoring and adjustment are essential functions of leadership, and the leader's authority to carry them out derives ultimately from the primary task. It is only through a consistent and clear monitoring of the primary task that it is possible to develop and maintain on-task leadership, to avoid the abuse of power, and to keep at a relative minimum the occurrence and spread of basic assumption activity in the organization (see Chapter 3). This also implies that, as the primary task changes, so leadership and followership roles may need to change. For example, in an operating team the head surgeon is usually the leader, but if the patient stops breathing during an operation, the anaesthetist needs to take over the leadership until the breathing is restored (Turquet 1974).

The group relations training model

Many of the key concepts referred to in this chapter either originate from, or have been developed and refined through, the experiential study of group and organizational processes in group relations conferences. Central among these is the Leicester Conference, first run by the Tavistock Institute of Human Relations in conjunction with Leicester University in 1957. Since then, in addition to more than 40 Leicester conferences, there have been numerous other group relations training events of varying length and design in the United Kingdom, the United States and many other countries, adapted from the original model and expanding its application (see Appendix). The basic conceptual framework of the Leicester model corresponds to that described in the three foregoing chapters, combining open systems theory, Bion's work on groups, and later developments from psychoanalysis (Miller 1990a, 1990b). However, the influence of these conferences on the understanding of groups and organizational behaviour, and on the practice of organizational consultancy, has less to do with theory than with learning from the conference experience itself.

At the core of all group relations training models is the idea of the individual participant learning from here-and-now experience. Conferences are designed to be temporary learning institutions, giving participants the opportunity to learn from their own experience about group and organizational processes, and their own part in these. Events are planned to be educational and not therapeutic, although personal change may well occur as a 'side effect'. Basic to this work is Bion's concept of *valency* – the innate tendency of individuals to relate to groups and to respond to group pressures in their own highly specific way (see Chapter 4). It is important for individuals to know the nature of their own valency, a group and organizational version of the need to know oneself, in order to be prepared for both the resultant personal strengths and weaknesses as manifested in group situations.

Depending on the nature of the design, and the focus of the event, individuals also have the opportunity to study the nature of intragroup processes in groups of different sizes, and to participate in intergroup activities to learn about intergroup processes. In all these events, members can take up a variety of roles and thus learn about the processes of giving and taking authority, working with tasks and roles, bidding for and exercising leadership, and so on.

In moving from one event to another (that is, from one grouping to another with different memberships and tasks), members also have the opportunity to experience their fellow members in a variety of roles, often behaving quite differently according to the roles they are engaged in and the group process in which they are enmeshed. Similarly, they experience the different behaviour of the conference staff in new roles and settings. Thus they can learn about role and task, and how these affect behaviour and feelings. The process of crossing boundaries, as members move from one grouping or event to another, makes available learning which is applicable to organizational settings and to the management of change and of multiple roles.

Consultancy from experienced conference staff is usually available to help members think about what is happening. In most models, there are also times set aside specifically to give participants the opportunity to review their experiences of the various conference events, and to work out how to apply their learning to their 'back-home' situation (Rice 1965). The membership of these 'application' events is usually made up of participants from different organizations and professional backgrounds, and often also from different countries and cultures. This provides opportunities for members to be witnesses to different styles of perceiving and working at problems, whether from leadership or followership perspectives.

Central to the learning process is the repeated discovery of the presence of irrational and unconscious processes that interfere with attempts to manage oneself, the group, task and roles in a conscious and rational way. Such insights, when experienced in the pure culture of a training event, make for powerful learning from experience. The hope is that, as a result of their greater awareness of unconscious processes and their own part in them, members will return to their 'back-home' work-settings better able to exercise their own authority and to manage themselves in role (Miller 1990a).

Conclusion

Clarity about the sources from which authority is derived is important, not least so that at a time of crisis further confirmation of authority, possibly with additional powers, can be sought. Similarly, an awareness of the importance of sanction from below can lead to more dialogue between managers and the workforce. Finally, careful monitoring of one's connectedness with one's own inner world authority figures is also important if 'shooting oneself in the foot' is to be avoided or kept to a minimum.

Effective leadership requires not only an authoritative state of mind to monitor the functioning of the organization against the benchmark of the primary task. A leader also needs the power to initiate and implement changes as required by a change in social or institutional circumstances, or even, in the light of these factors, to change the primary task of the organization. As part of this process, a system of accountability needs to exist, as does a mechanism for the delegation of authority, an in-house network that allows for the flow of both authority and feedback. By such means, it becomes possible to delegate aspects of the primary task to individuals or teams within the structure, and to call them to account for the nature of their functioning in relation to the overall task of the organization.

6

CHANGING THE STORIES WE ARE 'IN'

Power, purpose and organization-in-the-mind

Vega Zagier Roberts

Over the two decades since this book was first published, there has been an increasingly pervasive discourse among providers across the public sector about shrinking resources and how we can no longer do well what needs to be done. Stories of neglected patients, cancelled operations, failing schools, and children suffering abuse and neglect are the daily fodder of the media. People leading and managing services feel trammelled by impossible targets imposed on them, and oppressed by their inner sense of being unable to fulfil the aims that drew them into their professions. The stories they tell themselves (and each other), while they may to some extent alleviate pain and stress, can also lock them into feeling even more hopeless and helpless – what Lerner (1986) called 'surplus powerlessness'. While not denying the very real differentials in power that exist both in organizations and in society, he argues we can misinterpret and even distort our experiences in ways that lead to our losing touch with the power we do have.

In this chapter we will look at two ways that can help to shift this discourse. One is through retrieving purpose – the 'why' of services – which can often get lost under the pressures of the 'what' (outputs and targets) and the 'how' (methods and protocols). The other is through using organization-in-the-mind, a concept developed at the Grubb Institute of Behavioural Studies as a way of bringing into view the internal images that drive, or – as illustrated further on – can sometimes contradict the stories we are telling ourselves.

Getting trapped in the stories we are 'in'

When a story is told often enough, it can become hard to entertain the possibility that there might be other ways of telling the story. When the familiar version is shared by most of the people around us, this becomes even harder: we can become prisoners of a shared mind-set. Breaking out of it requires courage and leadership, as the following story illustrates.

> A mental health service was going through a major reorganization. It had been set up some ten years previously with a vision for a new way of working in the community with people with severe and enduring mental illness, offering a range of services in community venues like church halls and community centres, responsive to local needs and constantly evolving as these needs changed. This had initially been a huge challenge for staff accustomed to working to fixed schedules from fixed bases, and some left quite early on; those who stayed and those who joined later developed immense enthusiasm for the new client-centred way of working, and the service had received much praise.
>
> As the years went by, what had been innovative, anti-institutional practice became institutionalised in its turn. Now the staff were being asked to stop 'doing for' their clients, and instead to support them to develop user-led services, with funds and decisions in the hands of users and professionals taking the role of enablers of this process.
>
> At a service away-day early in the reorganization process, each person was invited to say briefly 'where they were' in relation to the change, and each talked about their anger and unhappiness at the dismantling of their cherished and much-acclaimed service. The manager's opening words came as a shock when she said, 'I like the story we are in,' and the consultant facilitating the day had a moment of near-panic at the risk the manager was taking by saying this.
>
> Up to that point, the 'story' in the service was the very familiar one of feeling at the mercy of the powers-that-be, themselves jumping to meet the requirements of the latest policy fad, without regard for the excellence of the service, the needs of the users, or the views of the committed staff who knew them best. Like the rest of her team, the manager had initially shared the outrage and consternation of her staff, but over many weeks of reflection had come to realize that the proposed new approach was actually closer than the old one to the beliefs and values that had brought her into mental health work in the first place. As she talked about this inner journey, a number of people began to see something new, something which connected the current plan both with the original vision for the service to be user-centred, and even further back, to their own deepest professional ideals such as empowerment and social justice. In other words, this was not (just) the old story of dismantling and restructuring to cut costs or meet targets, but potentially a revitalising new chapter that embodied a transformed picture of what community-based support for this user group could be.

Despondency, resentful compliance with directives, cynicism about the mindlessness of politicians and policy-makers, and the sense of an ever-darkening cloud are prevalent across the public sector. And yet, when one speaks with individuals, their passion for their work often surfaces very quickly. It is as if it is a 'closet passion' that cannot be acknowledged in public, or perhaps even to oneself.

One obvious hypothesis is that at times of heightened survival anxiety, the tendency of human groups to resort to defensive 'us-and-them' splitting is amplified to meet the need for the security of belonging and shared meaning-making. This can make it feel very risky to express, or even to think, differently from others who comprise our 'us'. But this seems insufficient to account for the intensity of the phenomenon, which feels more akin to what Gordon Lawrence (1995) calls a *totalitarian state of mind*. Speaking of the corporate world, he notes that, in many contemporary organizations, the desperate need for stability and security leads to massive projections of authority and power 'upward', leaving people with a sense of helpless dependency and fear that, in turn, leads to a false-self compliance with an authoritarian management. We suggest that we are also seeing a parallel phenomenon of dependency on and false-self compliance with the peer group. The moment of gut-wrenching anxiety the consultant experienced when the manager said 'I like the story we are in' suggests a counter-transference sense of the danger of speaking (and thinking) with one's own voice, independently of one's 'tribe'.

So a particular kind of conversation comes to dominate the workplace, of course shaped by our organization-in-the-mind (which we will discuss further on), but more importantly, shaping it, to the point where we can become disconnected from what we really feel and believe.

Some dynamics of the target-culture

In an attempt to bring galloping costs and a rising sense of chaos under control, and to respond to the demands of the electorate for greater accountability, a target-culture has come to dominate our public sector services, with punishments attached to not achieving these. Targets can of course be very useful: a clear 'must do' can and often does shift attention to gaps in services or to outmoded practices. For example, a psychotherapy department was warned it would be closed down unless it developed ways of engaging more with the ethnic minority communities in the borough. After an initial defensive reaction, the department transformed the way they reached and worked with their local population. However, targets often have some very negative consequences including corruption, cynicism, alienation and abdication of authority (totalitarian state of mind).

Examples of corruption are rife. Wheels are cut off trolleys in emergency departments, turning them into 'beds' to meet the target of discharging patients from A&E within four hours. Schools put children forward for public examinations in subjects where they are most likely to do well, in order to climb the league tables. Social workers are told client assessments should identify only needs which the local authority can meet, as 'unmet needs' are punished. Some GP practices have a 'one symptom only per appointment' rule in order to accelerate throughput, even though all doctors and most patients know that multiple symptoms may well be connected. As if what matters – the only thing that matters – is the target.

This engenders cynicism in the workforce (not to mention the public!), who withdraw psychologically from seeing themselves as part of this corrupt system, while complying in a dissociated way with the corrupt practices. The totalitarian state of mind becomes a defence against feeling guilt for being complicit. Power is projected upwards, enabling staff to maintain some semblance of fidelity to their professional ego-ideal, and to take a kind of moral high-ground – that only 'we' are caring, while 'they' . . .

Lawrence suggests that the totalitarian state of mind serves as a social defence system against 'the tragic', that is, against coming face-to-face with the human condition. For people working in the 'helping' services, it also serves as a defence against the anxiety they might feel if they were 'allowed' to do the work as they feel it ought to be done and the results were – as is so often the case – disappointing.

One might further speculate that working with the ill and dying, the distressed and disabled, the poor and the disadvantaged, contributes not only to collectively 'seeing' the darkest sides of society, but also to repressing our passions, excitement, pleasure and even joy in our work, keeping these feelings private, even from ourselves, to ward off envy and guilt. Gutmann and his colleagues (1999) describe a vicious cycle where guilt for not matching up to our ego-ideal leads to envy and anger at others whom we blame for our falling short of perfection. This vicious cycle can then get in the way of experiencing desire, which is the source of the energy and passion that fuel all creative endeavours.

All of this affects the stories that we tell ourselves, the conversations that we have with each other, and therefore the organizational cultures that we create.

From task to purpose

The classic definition of the primary task (see Chapter 4) relates to the dominant conversion process which turns inputs into outputs. Intended outputs are all too readily translated into targets, which then risk becoming 'things in themselves' rather than means to an end, eroding our sense of being engaged in a meaningful enterprise. We can depict the primary task of a human service organization as in Figure 6.1, where the triangle links three questions: who? what? and how? These are the business of management.[1]

What is missing is the 'why?' – the purpose of our system or organization. As Quine puts it:

> Purpose is a way of summing up the essence of an organization as a whole – what it is seeking to do and what it is contributing to its context(s) . . . a way of understanding why an organization exists in terms of what difference it makes to whom.

> *(Quine 2006 p. 1)*

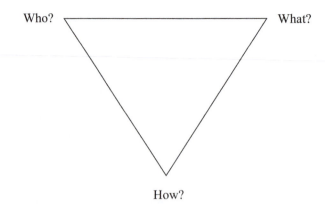

FIGURE 6.1 Primary task/management triangle

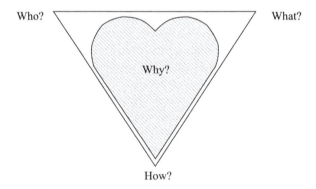

FIGURE 6.2 Purpose/leadership triangle

Thus, a statement of organizational purpose goes beyond the inputs–outputs dimension of a primary task definition to identify outcomes, namely, the impact the organization seeks to have in the wider context and what difference it aims to make. This could be said to include a 'so that' clause: 'We do X in order to produce or achieve Y (outputs), *so that* Z (outcomes/impact)'. This is the business of leadership.

Putting the 'why' – purpose – at the centre, as in Figure 6.2, can help us connect to 'the heart of the matter', putting new heart into our work.

Imagine three gold-miners in the depths of a mine. The first is condemned to ten years hard labour and counts down the days to the end of his sentence. The second comes from a mining family, proud of his competence and of being part of an excellent and productive team of miners. The third tells himself a different story: the gold the team are mining is their contribution to building the beautiful local cathedral. His labour and fatigue have a meaning which connects him not only to the system (the team of miners) but also to the wider context.

A beautiful example of this was portrayed in the 2017 film *The Post*, a true-life drama of the role of *The Washington Post* in publishing the leaked Pentagon papers that revealed truths which the government had been hiding about the Vietnam War. There is a moment in the film when the newspaper's owner is faced with deciding whether or not to ignore a court-ruling forbidding publication of the papers. Harking back to the founding purpose of the newspaper, to serve the governed rather than those who govern, enabled her to give the go-ahead, despite the risk that she and her closest colleagues might be sent to jail and that the newspaper might be shut down. The Chief Justice of the Supreme Court supported her decision, invoking freedom of the press as one of the nation's founding principles.

Purpose-based leadership

Clearly, purpose cannot be defined once and for all, since it is about what the context needs of a particular organization *now*. Shapiro (2000) proposes that a key function of leadership is to find and articulate the link to society, with its changing meanings, values and needs. In this sense, leadership can of course be exercised at any hierarchical level, by whoever is most in touch with these connections at a given time and can authorise themselves to speak to it. For those in designated leadership positions, it is essential to keep purpose in view.

> The head of a school for children with severe and profound learning difficulties (SPLD) came for coaching totally pre-occupied with management issues such as underperforming staff, recruitment and retention. She gave the impression of a harried housewife, and found the coach's question about the purpose of her school puzzling. Wasn't it simply 'to provide good teaching'? When asked what became of the children when they left at 19, she responded matter-of-factly that the majority did poorly, often becoming housebound, institutionalised or, in many cases, dying. Apparently this tragedy at the heart of the work was common to SPLD schools up and down the country.
>
> Then the school had an exceptionally successful inspection, receiving much praise for its outstanding teaching and care for the children. It was just after this that she was at last able to put into words her sense of the school's purpose: 'to give the children chances so that we discover what they are capable of'. For the first time, there was no harried housewife in the room, but someone excited and passionate about possibility. This had brought her to work in a school where 50% A–C grades[2] were never going to happen, and where therefore she had greater freedom than in a mainstream school to do what she had always believed all schools should be for.
>
> This was a turning point. As she shifted her attention from task to purpose, she delegated more and more of the day-to-day management to her deputy in order to focus her energy on the pupils' transition into adult life. For example, she found funding and premises to set up an intermediate facility where 16- to 19-year-olds could stay one or two nights a week, learning life

skills such as cooking and living with their peers. She also worked intensively with local employers and care agencies, inspiring them to collaborate with her to make the transition out of school life more successful. Her staff, previously so passive and demoralised, seemed to find a new energy and authority, developing all kinds of projects of their own to further the life-chances of the young people.

One might understand this story as a shift to 'the tragic position' Lawrence (1995) refers to, where there is simultaneously a capacity to tolerate the tragedy of the human condition and also – without lapsing into manic omnipotence – to resist assuming that things must necessarily remain as they are. The degree of disability of the children was profound, and many would continue to deteriorate and die from progressive conditions, but the limits of the possible could be tested, explored and enlarged.

As the sense of purpose emerges into sharper focus, and different levels of answer to the 'why' question come together, our internal picture of 'what business we are in' can become more coherent and meaningful. Getting (back) in touch with purpose releases energy previously locked into surviving, and can free people to transform their roles and work-systems.

Organization-in-the-mind (OITM)

Although the term 'OITM' was coined by Turquet in the 1960s, it was not until the 1990s that it became a widely used concept and tool for practitioners of the 'Tavistock approach'; in the First Edition of this book, it was mentioned only once (see Chapter 14). As developed at the Grubb Institute of Behavioural Studies:

> It is a model internal to oneself, part of one's inner world, relying upon the inner experiences of my interactions, relations and the activities I engage in, which give rise to images, emotions, values and responses in me, which may consequently be influencing my own management and leadership . . . [it helps me] to become alert to what is happening to me and around me.
>
> 'Organization-in-the-mind' is about what is happening inside my own head – it is my reality – and has to be distinguished from any other reality 'out there'. It is the idea of the organization which, through experience and imagining, forms in my inner psychic space and which then influences how I interact with my environment.
>
> *(Hutton, Bazalgette and Reed 1997 p. 114)*[3]

Clearly, our OITM is affected by our personal history and experience. But it is also shaped by our professional training which – among other things – teaches us to see the world in a particular way, paying more attention to some kinds of evidence than to others. Colleagues within a professional setting may then reinforce each other's assumptions and build up collective stories which in turn influence the particular shape of our OITM.

As Rock and Schwartz point out: 'Expectations shape reality . . . People's *mental maps*, their theories, expectations, and attitudes, play a central role in human perception' (Rock and Schwartz 2006). They describe how, when the brain gets an unexpected message, when there is a perceived difference between expectation and reality, it detects an 'error'. This shows up with imaging technology as dramatic bursts of light due to rapid intense neural firing in the more primitive parts of the brain (the amygdala and the orbital frontal cortex) which are closely connected to our fear circuitry. This draws metabolic energy away from the parts of the cortex that support higher intellectual functions.

This intense neural firing is generally experienced as negative, as the 'new' jars with existing patterns (though sometimes it can give a surge of energy – delight – when we have a new insight). So it comes as no surprise to find that there is a tendency to push the new back out of awareness, taking us back to status quo. Even when new learning is pleasurable, it is quickly forgotten: it takes energy and repeated re-focusing of attention over time for the new way of perceiving and interpreting to stick. However, if we work at this re-focusing of attention, then gradually new neural pathways develop. Thus, people as they train in a particular speciality actually come to perceive and interpret experience in particular ways: this becomes the default position; anything else becomes the error message.

A picture can be worth a thousand words

One way of shifting self-perpetuating stories is to use organization-in-the-mind drawings. Large sheets of paper and pens of many colours are provided. The client is invited to close their eyes, to let images and feelings about their workplace surface, and then to draw their work-system, in its context, with themselves in it.[4] Both client and coach share their associations to the picture, but without interpreting its meaning. This technique can also be used in groups; in this situation, each person offers their associations, with the person who drew the picture going last and saying where they see themselves in the picture.

In the following examples, the titles reflect the story each person was telling themselves at the time of making their drawing.

The task ahead is too big for me

A doctor in a developing country had been head-hunted to reform clinical services in the capital's top hospital. He felt overwhelmed at the magnitude of the task ahead of him and anticipated having an awful time, with his colleagues resenting and resisting his ideas for change. His drawing was of a very small square in the middle of a large sheet of otherwise blank paper. The square was filled with orange flames, in the centre of which was a tiny blue dot representing himself. While the coach's immediate association to the fire was about passion, his was that he felt enclosed in a cage, consumed by the heat of conflict.

Following her hunch about passion, the coach asked about his vision for the hospital. With great energy and without a moment's hesitation, he described his vision of a hospital where what mattered above all for everyone working there was the patients' experience. The hospital was excellent technically, but he thought the patients' experience there was very poor. So the coach then asked him to draw the future he envisioned. Instead of starting a new drawing, he simply drew a much larger square around the first one, as if his picture of the future was 'bigger' but not different. Of the many colours available, he used only blue for the outline of the squares and the dot representing himself, and orange for the flames. There was nothing else in the picture: no representations of staff or patients, no other systems, and nothing about the external context. It was as if he were alone in his task of transforming the system, unable to see and use resources there might be in the system, just as he had not been able to use the paper and pens that were available. Small wonder that he felt at risk of being consumed by his own fire.

It's impossible to change anything here

Over several sessions, the head of a university department had been describing how tired and gloomy she felt, endlessly encountering blocks, constraints and resistance. When her drawing was put up on the wall, she was stunned to see how vibrant it was, full of life and colour, with something like fountains or fireworks in the middle and bright stars of different sizes above; there was certainly nothing dark or gloomy in it. Asked where she was in the drawing, she pointed to one of the smallest stars, 'afraid to be too big'.

This opened up a new story about her in her workplace, and started her on a path towards taking up a bigger role which eventually led to her having significant impact in her field, well beyond the boundaries of her department and organization.

My manager cares only about targets[5]

Gerald was a senior manager of a social services department who felt his line manager, Keith, ignored his successes and constantly stopped his initiatives from going forward. The culture of the organization had changed radically from being mission-driven to being target-focused and for Gerald and his team, Keith embodied everything they hated about the changes: meetings with him focused almost entirely on how to achieve the government-imposed targets. In the first coaching session, Gerald remarked, 'I am more interested in making things happen than in targets', as if these two things were necessarily mutually exclusive.

Gerald's picture showed him and his team at the hub of what looked like a wheel, the spokes being lines between the team and the external stakeholders. The lines looked like spears flying inward and outward, as if Gerald's OITM were of an isolated group under siege. Neither Keith nor any other parts of the organization were in the picture: might Gerald be 'killing them off', just as he had felt Keith was killing him off?

He arrived at the next session very worried about a meeting with Keith scheduled for the next day, unsure whether or not to present his latest project. He could imagine only two scenarios: either he would share his ideas and Keith would crush them; or he would keep them to himself and the plan would get undone later. When the coach suggested involving Keith in some brainstorming, Gerald was sceptical but agreed to try. Afterwards, he described the meeting with amazement. Keith had covered the blank sheet with ideas in many colours. He had been full of an energy Gerald had never seen before. The final shape of the initiative was very little different from what Gerald had wanted to do in the first place, but this time Keith was backing it whole-heartedly. Not only did Gerald now have his manager's support, but also he had discovered a new side to him, a genuine passion for the 'real work' of the organization.

Over the next few months, Gerald shifted his energy from protecting himself and his team from the rest of the organization to having conversations with Keith and with other departmental managers about the vision and purpose of the work they were doing, and how they could work at these within the current context. Gradually a number of people began to recover a sense of meaning which had got submerged by the tsunami of recent government directives.

Gerald's drawing suggested that he had been in touch with what was inside (the work of his team) and with the external world (the needs of clients and the community), but he had obliterated the rest of the organization. As a result, he had restricted his role to fighting for the good of the clients and protecting his team's autonomy, ignoring the performance targets. This put the survival of the whole directorate at risk, and in the longer term therefore also threatened its capacity to continue to benefit clients. Bringing the missing bits of the organization into view was a crucial first step. As Gerald worked at redefining the core purpose of his own subsystem and how it connected with that of other parts of the organization, his organization-in-the-mind changed and it became possible for new stories to emerge, not only in Gerald's team but in other parts of the organization. Gerald was able to exercise leadership beyond his own team by engaging with others to forge some essential connections which had been lost as a result of the anxieties stirred up by the rising level of government control.

Conclusion: from change to transformation

One way of defining the difference between change and transformation is that change is about how to get from A to B, whereas transformation is about altering A (J. P. Pinho Figueirido personal communication January 2009).

A useful first step can be to bring into view new interpretations of our lived reality and of the key challenges that need to be addressed. This requires learning to hear and use the different perceptions and interpretations of people who are not (like) 'us', who have a different way of making sense of the world, and who are telling different stories about what is happening and what needs to happen next.

One of the best pieces of advice ever offered to leaders is Shapiro's (2001) admonition always to ask ourselves 'how are they right?', even – or especially – when they are most obviously 'wrong'. Not only does it shift us from a paranoid-schizoid position 'either-or' state of mind towards a depressive position 'both-and-also' one, and remind us that the views of the people we most disagree with can be valuable resources, but it is wonderfully easy to remember.

The large-system interventions designed by Isaacs draw on a similar principle. He calls these 'dialogues' to distinguish them from debate (etymologically 'to beat down') and discussion (etymologically 'to cut through').

> Dialogue can be initially defined as a sustained collective inquiry into the processes, assumptions, and certainties that compose everyday experience . . . [bringing] people into a setting where they, at their choice, can become conscious of the very process by which they form tacit assumptions and solidify beliefs . . . [and] become willing to loosen the 'grip of certainty' about all views, including their own . . .
>
> *(Isaacs 1993 p. 25)*

We also need to learn to listen differently to ourselves, to let stifled inner voices emerge, so as to be less prey to joining in with dominant and dominating (but inevitably partial) stories around us. And to recognise that the stories are interconnected: the more 'we' decry 'their' version of events, the more self-perpetuating 'our' stories become.

If we go back to the service manager's words 'I like the story we are in', perhaps the key issue is not so much about liking or not liking the story we are in, but about finding a way to be more present in the current story, in the reality of the here-and-now, rather than editing a story that shields us from facing our part in creating it, or losing ourselves in longing for a different one.

Notes

1 Figures 6.1 and 6.2 are taken from Quine (2006) and are reprinted by kind permission of the author.
2 The UK government target for pupil attainment in the national examinations taken at age 16 (end of compulsory education).

3 This is the definition I am using in this chapter. However, OITM is more than just a mental image: it is also what is created inside us by the organization and that we resonate with (like an aeolian harp that produces sound without a player when a current of air makes its strings vibrate). This way of thinking about OITM has been explored in depth by Armstrong (2005).

4 Different practitioners use slightly different approaches. Here I give the one used with the clients in the examples which follow.

5 An earlier version of this case study was published in Roberts, V. Z. and Brunning, H. (2007) 'Psychodynamic and systems-psychodynamics coaching' in Palmer, S. and Whybrow, A. (eds) *Handbook of Coaching Psychology.* Abingdon: Routledge. Reused here by permission of Taylor & Francis, LLC.

PART II

The unconscious at work in human service organizations

7

ATTENDING TO EMOTIONAL ISSUES ON A SPECIAL CARE BABY UNIT

Nancy Cohn

As a child psychotherapist covering a large area outside London, I came to be involved with a special care baby unit following a conversation with the consultant paediatrician responsible for the ward. She had told me she felt the staff were under particular stress because of the nature of their work, and wondered if I could do anything to help. Apart from wanting to be of help to the staff, I had my own reasons for wanting to work on the unit. I had observed that a number of children referred to the child guidance clinic in which I worked had begun life on such units, and I wanted to understand what those early experiences were like.

Overcoming suspicion

The consultant paediatrician had suggested I meet with the director of nursing services, Ms Larkin, to discuss the idea. Following this meeting, I was sent to see the senior nursing officer for paediatrics, who agreed there was a great deal of stress on the ward. She took me there and introduced me to Wendy, the nursing sister in charge, explaining briefly that I might be of some help, and she then left. My introduction to the ward felt somewhat awkward and abrupt. Might not Wendy and her staff regard my arrival as an unwelcome invasion? My presence had been initiated by managers without consultation with the people I was being sent to help. This probably contributed to the way in which I was originally seen on the ward and the degree of suspicion I had to deal with.

Initially, I went weekly to the ward on a regular day and at a regular time. Each time it was necessary for me to introduce myself all over again and explain why I was there. Because of shift systems, I was always unsure whom I would meet – and in the beginning I often faced an almost entirely new group of staff. Each time I would say to them that it had been thought that working on this type of ward was very stressful for staff and that it might be helpful for them to be able to talk about it. Some staff would say yes, they were under a tremendous amount of stress, but it was clear they felt uneasy about my presence. Other staff reacted in an openly hostile and persecuted way: when I walked on to the ward, they would turn away, as if they were hoping I would not approach them. They would try to look busy or talk together in a way that indicated I was not welcome. They seemed to fear that I was in some way finding them wanting, or even reporting back to managers, perhaps because I was part of the same organization and employed by the same authority. Another factor could have been the feeling among nurses, and perhaps all medical staff, that they should be able to cope with their emotions, and that discussing (or even having) them meant they were not coping. In that sense, my presence felt like criticism.

I found that my not being a nurse and not being able to enter into the work of the ward, or even to know in detail what the nurses did, was useful. It enabled me to ask basic questions, which sometimes led on to their thinking about aspects of the work which had formerly not been noticed. For instance, one day I saw a nurse massaging a baby's chest with an adapted electric toothbrush to clear the congestion in his lungs. In response to my asking if the baby liked it, the nurse became more aware that the baby was indeed enjoying this, and she then seemed to enjoy the procedure more herself. The nurses had many thoughts and feelings about what they were doing with the babies, to the babies and for the babies; my interest seemed to offer them a chance to explore these.

At this stage, I did not feel my presence was particularly welcomed, but it did not seem inhibiting either. Our talks continued in this casual way for some time. Either we sat around the desk in the nursing station, or I would walk around and approach nurses as they were working, asking them how things were or what they were doing. I spent a lot of time observing them at work, trying to keep out of the way while being close enough for anyone who wanted to talk to do so easily.

Then there was a turning-point. I had mentioned to Wendy that I would be interested in meeting the consultant paediatricians, and after about eight weeks she said she would be introducing me to Dr Miller when he came on his ward round that day. As the doctor and his entourage came past, Wendy stopped them and introduced me as 'the child psychotherapist coming to the ward'. Dr Miller looked somewhat surprised and wondered whether the babies were not a bit young for me to be working with. Wendy immediately replied, 'Oh, she's not here for *them*; she's here for *us* – because of the stress of our job.' This seemed to mark a degree of acceptance of me by Wendy, and, in turn, by her staff.

Doing something by doing nothing

In contrast to the constant activity on the ward, I was sure it sometimes seemed unhelpful to the nurses for me to be standing around when what they needed was another pair of hands. I often felt tempted to find something practical to do, and thought this was very likely how they felt – that looking after the emotional and psychological needs of the parents and babies might not seem like 'real' work to them either. They appeared to feel guilty if they were just being with the babies or mothers, rather than 'doing something'. There were so many urgent, practical, necessary procedures that needed to be followed that it was easy to see how emotional needs could be regarded as almost irrelevant. The primary task of the ward, after all, was the infants' survival. It seemed there were many nurses who would have liked to sit and talk with the parents more, hold the babies, hold the parents by means of their words, but these instincts were often overridden. Yet when they were not able to have contact with the families on an emotional as well as a physical level, the nurses could become mechanical, and sometimes appeared hard.

One example of this is the way they dealt with babies dying. Very ill babies were often sent to London, so deaths on the ward were not so frequent as they were elsewhere; however, they did occur regularly. One day when I came on the ward, I was told about an infant who had recently died. One of the nurses said it had been a particularly distressing experience: she had wanted to make the death as bearable for the parents as she possibly could, and felt she had failed to do so. I asked what happened when a baby died on the ward, and a discussion followed about the procedure. The baby would first be put into the sluice room, and then taken down to the mortuary where the parents could see their child. In the mortuary, there was a cot for children but it was far too large for babies.

It turned out that none of the staff individually were happy with this procedure, but they had never discussed it before. They told me they would have liked the parents to be able to spend some time with their baby on the ward before the body was moved. After our discussion, they decided to get a Moses basket. The parents could then sit in one of the side rooms with the baby, spending as much time as they needed. When I came back to the ward two weeks later, they proudly showed me the basket, which they had lined with pretty bedding. They felt they would be able to handle the next death in a different way, which in fact they did. The nurses could now think much more about making a place for grief on the ward, rather than getting rid of it.

Some time after this, a few of the nurses approached me to say they wanted to offer counselling to bereaved parents whom they had been involved with on the ward, as very little was done for the parents after a baby died. With agreement from Wendy, we arranged to have a series of sessions on bereavement using discussion and role-play. As a result, a new system was set up for supporting parents after the death of babies who had been on the unit. In addition to sending condolence cards and attending the babies' funerals, as they had already been doing, staff now also wrote letters to the parents three and six weeks after the death of their baby, offering visits and counselling, and telling them about a memorial book held in the hospital chapel. I made myself available for discussions with the staff following their visits to the parents.

Individual stress

As I became familiar to them, staff began to approach me more easily to talk about particular issues and difficult feelings. One day when I arrived on the ward, Sally came up to me and said she had been lying awake at two o'clock in the morning thinking, 'Thank goodness Nancy will be coming tomorrow.' This was a real surprise for me, as I had not realised that I was becoming important to them, and the extent to which I was now seen as someone who might be able to help them to think about the difficulties they were having.

Sally was under tremendous strain and feeling very anxious about her performance on the ward. She was in a highly charged emotional state, partly because she was undergoing treatment for infertility, and she was often tearful. She told me she was starting to make mistakes and was very worried about the possible consequences. After our discussion, Sally talked to her nursing officer and eventually moved to another ward, having decided not to work with small babies at that time. She also took a few weeks off work and organized some counselling through her GP.

Many of her colleagues had been encouraging her to stay on the ward, feeling it would be good for her to be around babies. They were unaware, as she was, of her anger, hostility and envy towards the mothers who had just had babies, and even towards the babies themselves. However, she was enough in touch with this part of herself to worry that it was affecting her work on the ward, and to realise it could put the babies she was looking after in some danger. After talking with me, Sally felt less as if she were giving up on the babies, and more as if she were looking after them, as well as herself, by having a brief break from work and then going to another kind of ward where the nature of the work would be less disturbing to her. Sally has since told me how valuable the counselling was in helping her to come to terms with some very painful issues which she had been unaware were troubling her. Following this, she conceived without medical intervention.

Interpersonal stress

A major area of concern over the years had been to do with staff relationships, both among the nurses and between them and the doctors. When staff feel hopeless or helpless in their attempts to help a baby, they often experience a tremendous amount of anger and frustration. Because this is often unrecognised and denied, and because staff need to protect their patients, their negative feelings erupt instead in relation to each other. There is also a conflict inherent in the kind of work they do which often goes unrecognised, namely reconciling having to do a painful procedure on a baby with wanting to be a caring and kind individual. Having to inflict pain on a baby, the nurses sometimes unconsciously blamed the doctors who prescribed the treatment but did not have to carry it out. Thus the frustration, anger and pain of the work tended to get displaced into conflicts over other issues.

As I became more accepted I was asked to help with some of these conflicts. For example, for a period of time all the anger seemed to be focused on Wendy. Things reached a point where complaints were flying in every direction, and Wendy was feeling persecuted and anxious. At this point, she got in touch with me, explained the situation and asked if I could help. She wanted to understand what she might be doing to provoke all this bad feeling, and I agreed to help her begin to think about this. I explained that I thought the problem probably had at least partly to do with the nature of the role she was in, and arranged to meet individually with her for a number of sessions to explore what might be going on. Later that same week, the director of nursing services telephoned me to ask if I could do something about the difficulties on the special baby care unit. She told me the atmosphere on the ward was very negative, with a lot of conflict and complaints. She was surprised to hear I had been approached directly by Wendy, and that we had already begun to do some work on this issue.

As a result of the discussions with Wendy, I felt that her staff were projecting into her some of the unbearable feelings stirred up by their work with suffering babies and sometimes disappointed or angry parents, especially feelings of guilt and inadequacy. I therefore suggested that we meet together with the senior staff nurses immediately under her in the ward hierarchy to explore these issues and to share the responsibility. It became possible for everyone to see how feelings that seemed to be directed at one or another individual might be to do with that person, but often had more to do with other issues: the work itself, frustration with the health authority, difficult relationships with their own parents or authority figures, and so on. Once the senior staff were more cohesive, we decided to meet with all the staff to discuss the difficulties they had been having with each other and with Wendy. Both Wendy and I now felt confident there would be some support for her from the senior staff, who had previously been allying themselves with the junior staff. They had more understanding of the processes going on within the ward, and could now help to move the group towards thoughtful discussion, rather than blaming and complaining.

These meetings were initially used as a chance to air feelings. It became clear that having discussions about people behind their backs was not helpful to the smooth running of the ward. Many staff talked about going home in a bad mood, and they agreed to try to speak more directly with each other about feelings as they happened, or as soon after as possible, rather than hanging on to these feelings and risking taking them out on the patients, their families or each other.

We also talked about their difficulties with the doctors, who did not attend these meetings or otherwise use me. This was unfortunate, particularly for the junior doctors, who were under tremendous pressure when they came on the ward. They usually had little or no experience of working with small babies, and yet were expected to know what to do and to get on with it. This whole situation was fraught with anxiety for them and for the nurses – and also, of course, for the babies. The nurses talked about having to watch inexperienced doctors trying to do complicated procedures, so that these sometimes lasted for hours instead of minutes. The structure of the relationship between doctors and nurses did not allow the far more experienced nurses to advise doctors on the best ways to do a particular procedure, leading to tremendous stress for all concerned, not least the babies who were 'worked on' for an inordinate length of time. As I could find no way to work directly with the doctors, all I could do was to try to help the nurses contain their anger and distress, and to think about ways they could support the junior doctors more effectively.

Making links

Because of my work in the child guidance clinic, I was particularly interested in understanding what problems might occur in bonding when mothers and babies are not able to be together immediately following the birth. There might be things which could be done to encourage better relationships between the mothers and their babies. A referral came to me which enabled me to learn in a vivid way about the experience of one mother and her baby on the ward.

Mrs Pearce was referred by her health visitor, who was extremely concerned about what seemed to be a lack of bonding between Mrs Pearce and her two-month-old daughter, Amy. Mrs Pearce had admitted she was hitting Amy regularly, and there was real concern for the baby's safety. Mrs Pearce, too, was desperate for help. Mother and child had been on the special care baby unit, although I had not met them or heard anything about them at the time. I found it worrying that Mrs Pearce's feelings towards Amy and the serious difficulties in their relationship had apparently not been picked up while they were there. The staff remembered her as a capable, coping mother, and had not had any special concerns about her. As I continued working with Mrs Pearce, it seemed to me that a big part of the problem was that, because Amy had so nearly died, now that she was out of danger Mrs Pearce was furious with her.

This still left the question whether there was anything the ward staff might have looked for or done differently. We used this opportunity on the ward to discuss ways we could try to identify where difficulties between mothers and babies might arise. This discussion would not have happened had I not been working in two different parts of the organization, since it is unlikely the staff would ever have heard what happened after Amy left the ward. Indeed, this story is a clear illustration of how things can go wrong when there is no way to link what happens or what is known in different parts of a large organization.

Conclusion

I was originally invited on the ward because of the stress of the job. This is surely an understatement about what is inevitably involved in working with such raw and vulnerable babies. The staff must to some degree distance themselves from the babies and from their own pain in order to perform their tasks. The intense feelings evoked by being exposed to these infants must not be underestimated. An acceptance by managers and the staff that feelings can and need to be expressed is essential.

In thinking back on my work with this unit over a period of about eight years, I can see that I was used in a wide variety of ways to address these feelings. Sometimes I was involved with individuals, where my role was in helping them to separate out personal difficulties from professional ones, and to direct them, where appropriate, to find the right kind of help. At other times I worked with the staff as a group, exploring their relationships and how these helped or hindered the task. Always my function was to facilitate an awareness of the emotional issues on the ward: the inevitable grief, pain, helplessness and sometimes hopelessness. Greater awareness and understanding of these feelings, and allowing for their expression, led to better working practices and to a happier ward.

8

CONTAINING ANXIETY IN WORK WITH DAMAGED CHILDREN

Chris Mawson

There are mental pains to be borne in working at any task, and these have to be dealt with by us as individuals, each with a personal history of having developed ways of managing or evading situations of anxiety, pain, fear and depression. Collectively, in our institutions, we have also learned to do this, installing defences against the painful realities of the work into our ways of arranging our tasks, rules and procedures. It is incumbent on us to try in whatever way we can to explore these aspects of our working practices, in order that our ways of coping do not grossly interfere, subvert or even pervert our efforts.

To understand the worlds of work occupied by ourselves and others, we need to be aware of the particular kinds of pain and difficulty encountered in everyday work situations. As Obholzer has observed:

> In looking at institutional processes it is obviously very helpful to have some inkling of what the underlying anxieties inherent in the work of the institution are . . . .. Given a knowledge of the nature of the task and work of an institution it is possible to have, in advance, a helpful, fairly specific understanding of what the underlying anxieties are likely to be, even though one might not know the 'institution specific' nature of the defences.
>
> *(Obholzer 1987 p. 203)*

Working with damaged children

Thus, when I was asked to consult to a child health team in a large teaching hospital, I anticipated certain difficulties. I knew they were involved in the assessment, long-term treatment and support of very young children who had been physically or mentally damaged from birth or soon after, and I expected from the outset to encounter considerable mental pain both in myself and in members of the team

stemming from the workers' close contact with these damaged children. I anticipated, as was indeed the case, that the workers would frequently feel depressed,
despairing of being able to make a worthwhile difference in the children's lives.
I also expected that they would sometimes feel intensely persecuted by these
feelings, even to the extent of experiencing at some level a measure of hostility
towards the children themselves. It was likely that such intensely guilt-inducing
feelings would often be deflected outwards and away from the work, in all
probability finding their way into other parts of the institution, where they
might well have adverse effects on working arrangements and interprofessional
relationships.

In order to gain a real understanding of the team's experience of their work,
I knew I would need to immerse myself in these experiences over a long period,
as they shared them with me and with one another in our regular meetings. The
following vignette, from one of my first meetings with the team, illustrates something of these problems.

> Marie, a young physiotherapist in the Walsingham Child Health Team,
> described her visits to the home of a small child with a deformed hand.
> Each time she went, she knew her treatment would cause the child intense
> pain. It was clearly saddening for Marie to see the child freeze and turn away
> from her as soon as she set foot in the family home. She began to adopt a
> brusque and matter-of-fact manner with both child and mother, at times
> being quite aware that she was being cold and impermeable, but for the most
> part conscious only of a heavy sense of persecution and dread whenever she
> visited. She felt ashamed and defensive whenever she discussed the child and
> her treatment with other members of the team, and came to feel that this
> one case was casting a shadow over her enjoyment of her work. To protect
> herself against her guilt, she tried to tell herself that she was only adopting an
> appropriately professional distance, and that the occasional reproaches from
> the child's mother were really evidence of the mother's inappropriate need
> for closeness with Marie.
>
> When this was explored in one of the first meetings the team had with
> me, there was a powerful reaction against opening up the issue of profes-
> sional distance, and great resistance to the idea that it can be used to defend
> us against painful feelings in our work. It was as though the whole group
> felt attacked by me, and for much of the meeting I felt as if I were a sadistic
> person forcing an unwanted and painful treatment on them. They told me
> forcefully that they did not want me to make the pain of their work more
> acute, even if this was only a temporary effect.
>
> It was clearly important for Marie to feel that her colleagues from other
> disciplines, particularly those whose role did not involve physical contact
> with the child, realised Marie's sense of hurt and rejection when faced with
> a child who was afraid of her, who did not perceive her as a healer or helper
> but as a cruel and sadistic figure who came into her home only to cause her

pain. Initially it was very painful for Marie to talk about experiences which caused her so much shame and guilt. The wish in the team was to treat it as Marie's problem, which added to her stress and interfered with the whole team's learning from her experience.

Once the team became able to discuss these kinds of experiences in a setting where anxiety and guilt over feeling inadequate could be contained and understood, it was possible for us to see the sad irony that becoming defensively hard and impenetrable had in fact made it much more likely that the child would perceive the physiotherapist as sadistic. To work well with such children, and to be clear and supportive to their parents and families, professionals cannot afford to defend themselves by erecting these sorts of barriers.

Providing a safe forum

Before such difficult feelings can be openly explored in a group, particularly when the members work together on a day-to-day basis, it is necessary to provide conditions of safety, respect and tolerance, so that anxiety and insecurity can be contained and examined productively. It is essential that a bounded space is created within which participants can begin to tolerate bringing more of their feelings than they are used to doing in other work activities, in an atmosphere which encourages openness and self-examination. Holding group meetings on the same day and at the same time each week helps strengthen this sense of containment, as does ending the meetings on time. It is not punctuality for its own sake that is important, but it is almost invariably disturbing for group members to feel that their emotions dictate the 'shape' and structure of the meeting, as well as its atmosphere and content.

The basic disposition of the consultant is important, too. The sense of security in the group is greatly encouraged by the consultant's restraint from judging and blaming, and 'knowing' too much too soon, or seeming to believe in quick solutions. It also helps if the membership of such a group is not constantly changing. The group often depends upon the consultant to stand up for the value of struggling for understanding, rather than rushing into the solving of concrete problems to get rid of uncomfortable feelings. They often find it useful to have such discussions in the presence of a consultant who is not a part of the organization, but this is not always the case.

Whether or not there is an external consultant, it is necessary for members to learn not just to listen to the content of what is brought to the discussion, but also to allow the emotional impact of the communications to work on and inside themselves. When primitive anxieties are stirred up, there is a natural tendency to try to rid ourselves of the uncomfortable and unwanted thoughts and feelings, locating them in others inside or outside the group, as described in Chapter 2. For example, recall how in the illustration given earlier I was temporarily experienced by the group as cruel, forcing on them an unwanted painful experience by looking at the issues in detail. When I was told that they were unsure they wanted such a painful 'treatment' if it made the pain of their work more acute, it was almost word-for-word what the parents had said to Marie. For a while, I had in turn felt in relation to the staff much as she must have felt with her young patient, saddened and guilty that my work was being experienced as cruelty. I had gone away from the meetings feeling somewhat persecuted, and had been tempted to defend myself by withdrawing from their reproaches and putting up something of a barrier, while telling myself that this was merely appropriate professional reserve. It was listening to my own feelings in this way that helped me to see how similar all this was to Marie's predicament. It was therefore possible not only to hear her feelings, but also to recognise from first-hand experience how such feelings are defended against, not only by her but also by the entire group in the institution. Understanding gained in this way can sometimes be put back to the group, or by the worker to the client, and, if timed sensitively, tends to carry a great sense of conviction.

In describing difficult work situations, members of the group will not only be communicating information, but will also be conveying states of mind which are often very disturbing and painful. From infancy we evolve the expectation that we can gain some relief from these pressures by seeking a 'container' for the painful feelings and the part of ourselves that experiences them. Partly, we unconsciously try to rid ourselves of them, but there is also the hope that the recipient of the projected distress might be able to bear what we cannot, and, by articulating thoughts that we have found unthinkable, contribute to developing in us a capacity to think, and to hold on to anxiety ourselves (these complex processes, termed 'projective identification', are discussed in detail in Chapter 2. See also Bion 1967; Klein 1959).

Shouldering inadequacy

In many work situations, the chief anxiety which needs to be contained is the experience of inadequacy. The following example is drawn from my consultation to the staff of the Tom Sawyer Adolescent Unit, who were complaining about a difficult group of adolescents.

> After several weeks of feeling increasingly useless as a consultant, inadequate and quite irrelevant to the needs of this hard-pressed group, I was told haughtily by one member that they would be better off without me. They would do better to organize a union meeting or an encounter group. I felt ridiculed, devalued and somewhat provoked. Another member of the team complained that I invariably took every opportunity to divert them from their real task. A third, speaking in falsely concerned tones and with knitted brows, asked why people like me were so intent on causing confusion by always looking

more deeply into things. They were, after all, just honest workers whose only wish was to be left alone to get on with a difficult job, with little or no support. Yet another wondered why I bothered with them, and whether I was some kind of masochist.

Just when I had taken about as much as I could without losing my temper, another staff member, who up to that point had remained silent, said how despairing she had been feeling in her work lately, and how devalued. She felt her efforts had been under attack by some of the adolescent clients and their families. Another then added that it seemed their work was frequently undermined by the administrative staff who were supposed to be supporting them. It emerged that the whole team had been criticised recently by management for their handling of a difficult and sensitive situation in the unit.

It was at this point that I was able to make sense of my own feelings and the way I had been made to feel by the group. I could then put into words the team's deep sense that they and their work were under attack. In turn, they had needed to make me feel unwanted, ineffectual and under attack, partly to get rid of their own feelings, but also to show me what it felt like for them; this may have been the only way they were able to let me know. It extended to their trying to get me to give up on them, or else to retaliate. Just as they sometimes spoke of going home wondering whether they should resign, or whether or not to appear at work the next day, they had spent a month testing whether I would have the tenacity (or was it masochism?) to keep coming back to them. Another previously silent member confirmed this, saying she had secretly hoped that I would be able to keep going and not 'pack it in'. She also had wondered whether I had anyone to whom I could turn when the going got tough.

This led to a change of emotional climate in the meetings. It became possible to reflect on what had been taking place in the room and to make useful links to the current problems both in the team and in the wider institution. For example, it was possible to consider the predicament of some of the team's patients and families who, in extreme distress, often seemed to use the same projective mechanisms for alleviating their anxieties as the team had been doing with me. The feelings of the staff mirrored those of the parents, who had repeatedly been made to feel useless and impotent. When such feelings of inadequacy are unbearable the temptation to 'pack it in' can be too strong to resist, and this is precisely what had happened with many of the children there. Their presence on a psychiatric ward felt to them (and also to their parents) as evidence that the job of parenting them had become overwhelming and had been 'packed in'. The children had made the staff feel much as they had made their parents feel, and in turn the staff had made me bear the impact of these violent and demoralising feelings. Furthermore, the question of whether I had my own sources of support could then be linked with the team's desperate need to find support and understanding in the face of such projections from their patients, so they would neither have to become masochistic nor have to 'pack it in' and resign.

The group came to feel that it had not so much been me who had been diverting them from their task, but that they had unconsciously been preventing me from doing my work with them. Their sense of having acted with some collective nastiness towards me made them feel guilty, but there was also the reality of what we had weathered and thus discovered together. This was of far greater value than any amount of abstract discussion or lectures – the latter having been suggested by them when free discussion had felt so bad and worthless. They had been able to experience someone who had obviously been buffeted by their attacks, but who had been able to contain feelings without hitting back or abandoning them. This demonstration of using reflection to manage feelings and reach understanding carried great conviction and helped them to move forward. At the next meeting it was possible for them to connect their fear that I would give up on them with their patients' anxieties that the staff would stop caring for them if they were too negative and unrewarding. They were also able to acknowledge their own fear that they would become too full of hurt and anger to continue their work, and that they really were at risk of abandoning their already traumatised clients. This had been mirrored in my impulses to explode or leave them, which I had managed to contain before acting on them.

Another common anxiety met by hospital workers is related to their inadequacy in the face of death; this is especially painful when it is a child or baby that has died. There is grief about the death itself, but also the feeling of having failed to save a life. The following example is taken from my consultation to the Walsingham Child Health Team:

As we were arranging the chairs into a circle a booming voice could be heard just outside the door – which was still open because there were five more minutes before our starting-time – saying 'Is this a séance?' The voice belonged to Dr Royce, a senior consultant paediatrician who did not attend the meetings, despite having been invited many times. There was no apparent reaction, as though nobody had heard this comment. However, when the meeting began, it seemed to me unusually sluggish and halfhearted, with team members looking at one another for an instant and then breaking off eye contact. There were then a few remarks complaining about the lack of participation by medical colleagues, and why they didn't value the meetings.

As I listened, I wondered what negative feelings about our work were being attributed to the 'absent profession'. I recalled similar remarks in the past about doctors' non-attendance: an often-shared attitude on the ward was that those who did not attend the meetings were commendably busy, while those who did had too much time on their hands. I also remembered that this had been a week in which the condition of several children on the ward had worsened, and a baby had died. There had been quite a sub-dued atmosphere before everyone had arranged their chairs, and nobody had made coffee today, which was unusual. I found myself thinking again about Dr Royce's jokey putdown. A séance is an attempt to contact the dead, and it suggests an unwillingness to face loss. Bearing all this in mind I decided to take up Dr Royce's remark, saying I had been surprised that not only had nobody commented on it, but there appeared to have been a concerted effort to act as though it had not been said. I wondered if they felt that their pain and loss could easily be denigrated.

Alison, a physiotherapist who tended to permit herself closer emotional contact with the children than most of the others, then spoke of the dif-ficulties in expressing feelings of grief in the hospital. Joan, an occupational therapist, spoke of her relief when a senior paediatrician had wept at the child's bedside. Alison remarked that nurses were labelled 'emotionally over-involved' if they grieved, and others chimed in with complaints about the 'stiff upper lip' culture. There were a number of issues here, but what I chose to address was the way in which the group preferred at that moment to think of this repressive culture as belonging to the nurses, rather than as something in themselves. Only when the members could face their own 'stiff upper lips', and their conscious and unconscious equivalents of Dr Royce's mock-ery, would they be able to carry through the necessary work of mourning for the baby, and for the many experiences of failure and limitation represented by that loss.

This was a moving and productive discussion, but in spite of the obvious shared relief, I was left feeling doubtful about whether the lessons learned would be generalised and applied elsewhere. Perhaps it was only in that par-ticular setting that professional defences could be lowered and such painful experiences explored.

Conclusion: conditions for growth and development

This raises a question about the potential for growth and development in groups, and how it can be supported. When painful work situations, such as those described here and in other chapters, are worked through again and again, it becomes pos-sible for some degree of individual change to take place. Institutional practices can be scrutinised and sometimes changed, though this is rarely without difficulty and resistance. The 'change in emotional climate' mentioned previously refers to shifts in the group from a highly defensive and mistrustful attitude towards one of regret verging on depression, as they recognised how efforts to protect themselves had led to treating others badly. The experiences I have described in this chapter stand out for me, not only because of the discomfort, but also because they are such vivid examples of the shift from a *paranoid-schizoid* position to one in which there was a preponderance of *depressive anxiety* (see Chapter 1). In the former position, the fear is of attack and annihilation, blame and punishment. Primitive defences against paranoid anxiety, if carried too far and with too much emotional violence, lead to the severance of contact with reality. For example, staff may deny the reality of the degree of damage, and of the limitations of what they can offer: the Walsingham team often felt under pressure to engender false hopes about the degree of improvement which could be expected.

The shift in emotional climate does not, however, result in freedom from anxiety. Instead, our fears of what others are doing to us are replaced by a fear of what we have done to others. This is the basis of genuine concern, but guilt and facing one's insufficiency are painful to bear. If these anxieties are not contained – and we therefore cannot bear them – there is likely to be a return to more primitive defences, to the detriment of our work and mental health, as was the case in the example of the staff grieving over the baby's death, where denial and mocking took the place of sadness and loss until the feelings could be worked through in the group discussions.

I have tried to demonstrate how important it is for staff involved in painful and stressful work to be given space to think about the anxieties stirred up by the work and the effects of these anxieties on them. The cost of not having this is considerable, both to clients and to workers. As well as offering much needed support, consultation can offer the opportunity for insight and change in the group and wider institution, *if* the pains and difficulties can be tolerated.

9

FRAGMENTATION AND INTEGRATION IN A SCHOOL FOR CHILDREN WITH PHYSICAL DISABILITIES[1]

Anton Obholzer

There are several ways of assessing, or attempting to assess, the functioning of an institution and whether it is performing its assigned task satisfactorily or not. In the case of an industrial organization, parameters such as productivity or the amount of profit generated are generally regarded as good indicators of the state of the organization. In human service organizations, it is much harder to ascertain effectiveness and functioning, although certain criteria apply here, too, such as the degree of staff turnover and the amount of illness or absenteeism. As a consultant, however, I often have no access to such information, and I have therefore become preoccupied with finding other criteria by which to assess the state of the organization. Over time, I have found that some of the same criteria that are useful in assessing an individual's psychological functioning can be usefully employed in the assessment of institutions. Central to this is the degree of integration, internal and external, on which satisfaction from work and relationships depend. To illustrate this, I will describe my work with a school for children with physical disabilities, as it shifted gradually from fragmentation towards integration.

The first phase

Goodman School served a wide catchment area, and places at the school were allocated on the basis of educational, social and medical assessment. The school had approximately 80 children on its books, ranging from under three to 18 years old, most with severe physical disabilities, cerebral palsy being the most common cause. Apart from the head teacher, there were ten full-time and six part-time teachers, as well as two nursery assistants. There were also five physiotherapists, a full-time nursing sister and her auxiliary, a part-time speech therapist and five general attendants. The school also drew on the services of outside staff, including a social worker, a school psychologist and myself.

My original appointment to the school as a consultant child psychiatrist was for one afternoon (three and a half hours) fortnightly. The post had been in existence for some years, and I had had several predecessors. However, there was no job description, only a vague assumption that the school should have access to the services of a child psychiatrist. From the first, I thought that, given the shortage of my time and the large numbers of people involved, it would probably be most economical and effective for me to consult to the staff group with regard to their work with the children, rather than working directly with individual children. However, it soon became clear that this was not feasible. For a start, there were no formal staff meetings. Such meetings as did take place were called at irregular intervals, usually at lunch time, and were, according to hearsay, poorly attended, regarded as 'teachers' meetings', and used essentially to distribute administrative information.

In the entrance hall to the school there was, and still is, a prominent notice on display: 'All visitors to report to the office'. This was ostensibly to prevent unauthorised and curious visitors and parents from wandering about the school. It also, however, captured the spirit of the institution, and I for one was treated for a long time with suspicion as to my motive for being in the school at all.

On my first visit, I therefore found myself in the office being interviewed by Mrs Ryman, the head of the school, an eminently reasonable thing to do from her point of view, particularly as she had had no say in my appointment. She was very vague about my role, and there is little doubt that I was seen not as helpful, but as a potential threat to be warded off or placated. For a long time, my only contact was with the head and her secretary. Although at times Mrs Ryman would mention a child, it was mainly to tell me that there had been a problem that had now been resolved. Once, her secretary telephoned the day before I was due to come and told me there really was nothing specific to discuss. It took a great deal of effort not to accept this invitation to enjoy a free afternoon instead of grappling with the problem. On another occasion, I was told, 'Please don't come today – we are having a problem,' making it crystal clear that my coming was seen as likely to compound the problem, rather than possibly being of help.

Towards the end of the first year, a member of staff would occasionally 'intrude', and we would discuss some problem they were having with a particular child. Very often, we would then attempt to arrange a meeting at which all staff concerned might meet in order to discuss the child in question. This often foundered on a difficulty of 'timing', particularly when it came to bringing staff from different professions together. The timetable was arranged in such a way that it was almost impossible for teaching and non-teaching staff to meet. Not surprisingly, relations between these two groups were very poor. What were consciously presented as timetabling problems actually represented interdisciplinary conflicts and rivalry; the timetable was an unconscious institutional defence to prevent these groups ever meeting to work together. None the less, it became increasingly apparent that there were a number of staff who would welcome meetings to discuss issues of common interest, and eventually one was arranged.

Development of the consultation

There is little doubt that the eventual institution of regular meetings for all staff was caused by the head's decision to retire early: in the ensuing vacuum, new opportunities for change were created. In the months leading up to her retirement, meetings with staff of several disciplines began to take place in the office more frequently. The notion that the children presented were not only there in their own right but as 'representatives of an institutional process' became more acceptable and understandable to the staff group. For example, a child presented for having stolen while the class went swimming was seen not only as an individual problem, but as a pointer to the issue of stealing in the school.

It was decided that regular staff meetings, to which I was invited, would be instituted at fortnightly intervals. It had taken three years for regular staff meetings to be instituted and for me to be invited to attend. Even then, the initial contract was for one term only, but this was subsequently re-negotiated to continue long term. Although I recognised the anxiety and expectation in the staff group concerning the coming meetings, I perhaps did not sufficiently acknowledge my own, but instead dealt with it by arranging with the school for a colleague to come with me.

My colleague and I wanted to adopt a model of being essentially non-participative but engaged in listening and attempting to understand the specific issues that were consciously and unconsciously preoccupying the staff. Our assumption was that an understanding of these processes would further their work. It was thus essentially a psychoanalytic model based on containing anxiety and searching for understanding which could then be used to inform decision-making. Not surprisingly, this model, though unspoken, proved too threatening and had to be modified. What was 'expected' of us was to participate specifically in our roles as child psychiatrists to the school. As such, we engaged in discussion as colleagues and fellow-workers, albeit in a different role and with different competence and experience. In addition, however, we would sometimes stand back and make 'consultative' observations on the interaction between ourselves and others. For example, 'Look at us, the way we're carrying on. I'm talking as a psychiatrist, you as a teacher, and neither of us seems to be able to listen to or understand each other.' This might then be further linked with professional preconceptions and the difficulty of interprofessional cooperation.

It is, however, not entirely accurate to say we were expected to behave in our original roles, because even that presented a threat. The least threatening position would have been for us to be 'one of them', and to behave like them. At the very first meeting, we were immediately asked what our topic was and what we were going to teach on that day – a model of teaching or being taught being what they were most at home with. It took some time for us to be accepted in our roles as being 'different' from them.

Over time, we attempted to capitalise on the fact that there were two of us. We did this by having one of us engage in the discussions from a professional stance, as child psychiatrist, while the other would adopt the role of institutional consultant and comment on the processes active in the staff meeting at the time. It took about a year from the establishment of the staff meetings for us to work as consultants to the institutional process as envisaged in our original model, and when my colleague left to have a baby, I was able to continue the work on my own.

The anxieties inherent in the task

Although some children at Goodman School had mild disabilities, the majority had a substantial physical disability. Many were in wheelchairs, and orthopaedic devices were common. Some children could not feed themselves, and were totally dependent on the staff for all caring functions. In some cases, the children suffered from progressive diseases, their condition deteriorating until they died.

Teachers generally understand their job to be helping pupils to acquire and use skills, developing their competence, and guiding them towards applying their learning so as to take up their roles in society later as independent adults. In this school, the teachers had to face the fact that much of what they taught would not be put to use, either on account of the deterioration, and sometimes death, of the child, or on account of the difficulty in integrating a person with disabilities into our present society. Similarly, the physiotherapists had to work with clients in whom there was seldom the sort of improvement or success that could be achieved in more acute conditions. In many cases, it was a matter of presiding over and slowing down as much as possible a process of deterioration. Even when there was a good and hopeful working relationship, the physiotherapists often had to witness the child leaving the school and their work being lost on account of the difficulties in continuing treatment outside, such as shortage of transport and treatment facilities, or lack of follow-up.

When there is so much pain inherent in the work, it is clear that some defences are necessary for the staff to remain in role and carry on with some hopefulness.

However, at times the extent and nature of the defensive processes is such that they not only interfere substantially with the primary task of the institution, but they are also ineffective in their intended purpose of protecting the staff from the pain of the job.

The institutional defence system

Defence mechanisms can be divided into two categories – personal and institutional. These are interrelated, partly because staff members with individual defences 'fitting' those of the institution are more likely to remain, while those whose individual defences are out of tune with the institution leave. It is worth commenting on the fact that several members of staff spoke about either having or having had a 'deformity' of a physical nature, or of having siblings or children who had physical disabilities. It is not clear whether this was because there was a higher incidence of physical disability in the histories of this group of teachers as compared with other teachers – and that teachers with this sort of history were more likely to be drawn into this work – or whether ongoing contact with children with physical disabilities made them more aware of their family histories. There is probably a link between choosing to work in this type of institution and personal history.

There is a further link between personal and institutional defences. Each individual member of the institution – and his or her defences – comes to represent aspects of the whole. The teacher whose personal defence is 'I treat them as normal' not only represents him- or herself, but also becomes the spokesperson for that part of everyone else in the institution that needs to regard the children as normal, and of that part of the institution itself that deals with abnormality by denial. When there is a 'good fit' between the personal and the institutional defence systems, neither will be challenged: reality-testing does not take place, and the defensive process continues.

The task of consultation at Goodman School was not only to name the defensive processes, but also to attempt to identify the underlying basic anxieties and their present manifestations. A model of school functioning based on a denial of the children's disabilities made it difficult to help the children towards an acceptance of these disabilities, and for this acceptance to become the foundation on which their transition from school to work and adulthood might be built. For example, Rodney, a 12-year-old boy with severe epilepsy, planned to be a bus driver. The acceptance of his epilepsy would have required his making a change of career choice; continued denial of his problem would make his transition from school to work a difficult one. School-leaving regularly created enormous problems for the leavers, but the pain of facing children's limits was avoided by the staff.

The need to deny the implications of physical disabilities was also supported by the way children entered the school. The entry procedure had traditionally been administered by outside agencies, separating the medical, social and educational aspects of the child's situation. Only at a late stage did the parents and child have contact with the school; they then usually met only with the head and focused essentially on academic matters. This process of induction, based on denial of the physical disabilities in word and deed, served the defensive needs of both staff and parents. Later, when the child's growing up or deterioration inexorably brought the impact of the physical disabilities to the fore, the relationship between staff and parents often deteriorated into mutual blame because the social and developmental implications of having a serious disability could no longer be ignored.

Meanwhile, parents in general were becoming more vociferous in their demands, more questioning of teachers and schools. As well, there was a growing movement away from hiving off children with special educational needs into specialised institutions, and towards integrating them into ordinary schools. These factors contributed to a situation where, if Goodman School were to survive, it had to provide the service it set out to – and it had to retain the cooperation of the parents. In the past, this had always been based on collusion between staff and parents, whose defensive needs were similar. Now there arose an increasing number of situations in which there would be protests from parents about the long-term costs of the traditional approach to working with children with disabilities, often followed by transfer of the child to another school.

Thus, the defensive processes not only did not serve to protect the staff very effectively from the pain of the work, but now also threatened them with the loss of jobs and the closure of the institution. As for the children, the damaging effect of abrupt changes of their environment can be readily imagined. It therefore gradually became clear to everyone that the defensive processes were anti-task, and that they urgently required review if the school were to survive at all. The role of the consultants became increasingly accepted, and staff meetings became a weekly event. Initially they alternated between 'administrative' and 'other', with the consultants continuing to attend on a fortnightly basis, but this fostered a split between action and understanding. To overcome this, the consultants then attended weekly, making links between issues arising in the two sorts of meeting.

Splitting and fragmentation

The weekly staff meetings were open to all members of staff: in practice they were attended by the head, deputy head, most of the teachers, most of the physiotherapists, the speech therapist and ourselves. The cleaning staff did not attend, being engaged in cleaning at that time; nor did the school helpers, who were taking the children home during the time of the meetings. The size of the group fluctuated between eight and 20.

Initially, the mere fact of the meetings being convened led to greater communication between individual members of staff and between different professional groups. Paradoxically, it became clear why staff meetings had hardly ever been held before – except to distribute administrative information – for they brought together various split-off aspects of a problem and initially resulted in increased distress. As put at an early meeting, 'It is good we are re-thinking issues and problems with children, discussing our problems with members of other disciplines, but when we are all in the same boat, we all feel helpless about the same child.' Staff meetings were clearly in the interests of the children, but were painful for the staff. The tendency was therefore for defensive splitting to take precedence over integration and its attendant pain. Splitting and denial (see Chapter 1) are among the most commonly used defence mechanisms in institutions. At Goodman School, they occurred between the school and the parents, the school and outside agencies, and within the school itself.

Splitting between school and parents

Splitting between school and parents was a common occurrence, and parental disturbance was often cited as a major source of difficulty, whether in communicating with a parent, or when a child was in trouble. If the parents were to blame, then by implication the teachers were not, and could therefore do nothing. An aura of helplessness would set in, everyone feeling stuck, and the child was not helped.

> A good example of this sort of splitting was the case of Mrs Langham, the mother of a child at the school, who wrote a newspaper article about the increasing educational and social deterioration of her daughter, suggesting that the school system was to blame. Although the article was fairly reasoned, there was little doubt that the mother herself was in desperate pain about her child. At the staff meeting following the publication of the article, there was uproar. There was a point-by-point dissection of the article and several inaccuracies were pointed out. Then there was a discussion of the child's family history, with particular emphasis on the parents' neurotic disturbances. Nowhere was there any acknowledgement of the fact that the article raised issues vital to the school, nor any awareness of the possible underlying dynamics of the situation. The entire initial exchange thus took place within the paranoid–schizoid position (see Chapter 1).
>
> With time, it became possible for us to interpret the denial that Mrs Langham's concerns and doubts were also held by many of the staff. It then became possible for the school to relate more sympathetically with the Langham family, but also for them to look at the issues raised, and to think constructively about families in the grip of similar dilemmas. At a subsequent meeting, a teacher spoke of another parent as a 'neutron bomb just about to go off'; the staff were able to consider ways of intervening before the situation got out of hand.

Splitting between staff and outside professionals

There were frequent complaints that the children often went to clinics or specialists of one sort or another but that no reports were ever sent to the school. There were endless discussions concerning the need for better communication with outside agencies, and plans to write letters to certain regularly used clinics and specialists requesting information, as if the staff believed, 'If only they told us what was going on there would be no difficulties'. They held tenaciously to this belief, despite their experience that when they *did* get reports, they generally found them of little value, adding minimally to what they already knew. They also expressed indignation when outside agencies involved with the children did not seek their opinion.

Here again the issue was one of splitting, in which the 'helpful information' was either held outside and not passed on, or else held by the staff but not requested. The depressive position (see Chapter 1) counterpart of the above view would include an acknowledgement of the difficulties involved in working with people with disabilities, and an acceptance of the fact that nobody knew the answers or had a simple solution. Recognising this led to greater sharing of difficulties and uncertainties, moving towards teamwork rather than competition and blame.

Splitting personal and professional parts of the self

Splitting up competencies among the disciplines was a common occurrence. For example, at one staff meeting there was a discussion about showing the children a film on epilepsy, which parents might also attend. When I asked who would lead the discussion, the answer, given as if to a stupid question, was 'The school doctor, of course.' Undoubtedly, the school doctor had a major contribution to make. However, the 'of course' answer also highlighted a splitting process in which staff insisted on regarding epilepsy as a medical problem. The result was that the many years of experience of other members of staff in how to deal with epilepsy were lost. The split safeguarded the non-medical staff from discussing a painful area in the lives of many of the children and their families. Yet it was precisely this nonmedical discussion that might best help the children and their parents with the process of accepting the disability and integrating it into everyday life. Here again, the splitting process protected some members of staff, but interfered with the overall work of the institution.

A similar split arose regarding helping children at puberty to develop their sexual identity. Our observation was that the physiotherapists had a central role in this. What could professionally be perceived as hydrotherapy to enable a child to have freer limb movement was, at another level, an opportunity for close bodily contact and discussion of the feelings aroused by puberty. However, the teachers stated categorically that the physiotherapists were not equipped for such discussions, and suggested that a lecturer be invited to bring a film on sexual development. Although this might well have been of interest, it was not a substitute for the discussion that might have taken place in the ongoing physiotherapeutic relationship, one that had often developed over several years. This splitting of professional and personal parts of the self led to the loss of a wealth of personal experience acquired by the physiotherapists (and other staff) in reaching their own bodily and sexual adjustment. Although personal privacy needed to be safeguarded, there was little doubt that if the professionals could draw on this personal experience and not split it off from their professional expertise, they could greatly facilitate the adolescents' coming to terms with the changes their bodies were undergoing.

Similarly, when the staff were able to stay in touch with their personal experience of being parents or siblings, they had no difficulty at all in sharing the dilemmas of the children's families and hence in being more understanding of their reactions, rather than complaining, 'How can they behave like that?' When staff spoke of their experiences in taking children on outings or on holiday, they often marvelled at the patience and fortitude of the parents, yet this experience would soon be 'forgotten' when they returned to school, and the old complaints would resume.

Integration and development

As a result of growing integration within the staff group, and diminishing the split between the personal and professional parts within individuals, new ways of working began to develop. One of the first was a physiotherapy group for new children, where they were allowed and encouraged to examine their own physical strengths and impairments, thus developing their own body image. However, the group had been going for some time before the physiotherapists told the rest of the staff about it. As one of them said, 'At training school, we were always taught never to mention the disabilities, and to instead develop exercises that would require the use of the handicapped limb.' This supported the institutional defence system, based on denial, while reducing the physiotherapist role to body manipulation. It took time and support to enable the physiotherapists to break free of this and develop a new and more effective approach, one incorporating mind and body for both child and worker.

Similar developments took place among teachers, so that, for example, one teacher who two years previously had spoken of his role as 'only a teacher and that's it', transformed some classroom sessions with his children into wide-ranging general discussions. This was not an avoidance of the task of teaching but rather an augmentation of it, in which a personal component was made available in furtherance of the school's work. Yet, here again it took some time for the teacher to make his new approach public. As with the physiotherapists, the change conflicted with his teacher training, and he therefore worried it might be considered unprofessional.

At the organizational level, too, support for questioning old assumptions led to change, for example, regarding admission procedures. The school clearly had the potential and the knowledge to develop its own system of intake, better geared to the real needs of children, parents and staff, but this process was constantly slowed down by their reluctance to question that the old practices were the 'right' way, and any deviation from these were 'wrong'. Only gradually, through the staff discovering again and again the defensive nature of many of their traditional ways of working, could these be questioned, reviewed and, when necessary, changed.

Although the shift from the paranoid-schizoid position to the depressive one has been described as if it were steadily progressive, it is by its very nature unstable. Whenever anxieties increase, defensive processes are fuelled and there is a tendency to return to splitting. This oscillation, with pressure to shift away from the depressive position, means there is repeated loss of the capacity to face painful reality, guilt and concern. There is thus a need for the ongoing containment of institutional anxieties to safeguard depressive functioning (for further illustration of the need for and usefulness of containment, see Chapter 8).

Conclusion

In this chapter, I have attempted to draw a parallel between the paranoid-schizoid/depressive position spectrum in individuals and in organizations. The chapter illustrates how the functioning state of an organization can be assessed by monitoring measures such as splitting and projective identification, and how – just as for individuals – a containing intervention can shift the functioning towards the depressive end of the spectrum.

None of the institutional processes mentioned in this chapter is unique to this school. They occur in other schools, in other 'people' institutions and in society at large. For staff to function to the best of their ability, they must have an external and internal framework that allows for a sense of security – a security that can be used as a base from which to explore personal and institutional issues. A regular timetable with clearly defined staff meetings is essential to bring together all the groups involved in providing care. It is my belief that an outside consultant to the staff meeting is invaluable in making sure that such meetings do not become infiltrated and bogged down by institutional defence processes. This consultation must be managed so that it is supportive of the institutional management structures, neither in collusion nor in collision with them.

It is only with the provision of a containing environment that the institution can settle down to working at its task. Members need time to get to know each other and their roles in a task-oriented setting; 'chats' during coffee break or lunch-time are not sufficient, as they invariably shirk the most difficult issues of the day. It is only with time and ongoing work that staff can reach the important stage – personally, professionally and institutionally – of having the freedom to think their own thoughts, as opposed to following the institutional defensive 'party line'. Only then will they be able to develop their own style of work, and contribute fully to the task in hand.

Note

1 The original title of this chapter was 'Fragmentation and integration in a school for physically handicapped children'. Terminology has been updated throughout except in direct quotes.

10

WHERE ANGELS FEAR TO TREAD[1]

Idealism, despondency and inhibition of thought in hospital nursing

Anna Dartington

The organization of rudimentary care systems around the processes of birth, death, injury and disease is as old as human interest in the survival of the tribe. Indeed, it is the inevitable social necessity of nursing, whether professional or unpaid, which produces emotive and ambivalent attitudes to this work both in society and in nurses themselves. Nurses remind us, as doctors also do, of our potential vulnerability and dependency in illness, and of our mortality.

Society's contradictory attitudes to nursing, often referred to in the psychosocial literature as 'idealisation' and 'denigration', are reflected in, for example, newspaper stories of selfless heroism among nurses, set against the reality of low pay and poor working conditions. The corresponding responses of the nurses themselves are flights of idealism, sometimes accompanied by illusions of omnipotence, and feelings of deep despondency.

Contemporary nursing is dogged by a negative expectation that nurses should not think. By thinking, I do not mean remembering whether Mr Jones is prescribed one sleeping tablet or two, but the processes of reflection about one's work, its efficacy and significance: registering what one observes of the patient's emotional state, the capacity to be informed by one's imagination and intuition, the opportunity to criticise constructively, and to influence the working environment. This is not to say that nurses do not think, but that it is an effort of will to make the space for reflection in a working life dominated by necessity, tradition and obedience. What is usually absent is the opportunity to ask the question 'Why?' of someone in authority, someone who is not surprised by the question, who is interested in the answer, and who can engage in a spirit of mutual enquiry.

Although the expectation not to think may have something to do with the denigration mentioned above, it is not simply a symptom of this. On the contrary, nurses are sometimes valued for a capacity to be passive at work, which itself is an example of the ideal of stoicism that pervades hospital culture. Nor can the expectation not to think be accounted for simply in terms of a doctor/nurse polarity of functions. It is true that many doctors are unreasonably expected to have a bright idea at a moment's notice, and are relentlessly pressurised to come up with an answer when they have no answer to give. But nurses may also collude in their own unthinkingness, in the same way that doctors may sometimes collude with a pseudo-know-all-ness.

Those of us who think about unconscious processes in organizations are bound to look at the total organization for the origins of these collusive defensive patterns which are so wasteful of human resources. We could examine the nurses' collusiveness with a non-thinking expectation in terms of the conventional role of women at work. Gender issues can hardly be irrelevant in the consideration of a largely female workforce. However, while general nurses working so consistently in a 'maternal' role is highly significant in many ways, it has been my experience that nurses feel themselves to be oppressed not by men *per se*, but by social systems. In the context of this book, what is of most interest are institutional and societal dynamics that can be observed that will explain the necessity for an unthinking workforce operating at the interface between the patient and the institution.

The impact of the hospital culture

Most people who have spent time in hospital either as patients or employees will remember the initial impact of the sights, sounds and smells that assailed them as they left the world behind. The memories linger because they are associated with fear. It is perfectly understandable to feel afraid when we put our bodies, and possibly our lives, in the hands of strangers. It is more difficult for staff to admit their own fear: that because strangers are prepared to trust them, the burden of responsibility and its attendant dependency might prove overwhelming.

I will now discuss the impact of entering a new institution from two different vantage points: one as a nurse student myself, the other, 25 years later, as a group-work consultant to nurse tutors. Both hospitals were large London teaching hospitals.

Some personal recollections

I joined the nurse training school soon after my 18th birthday. Most of the students were middle-class, and the majority had chosen nurse training as an alternative to university. Several were devout Christians and viewed nursing as a form of religious vocation. The culture was largely serious, committed and inhibited.

When talking to my friends who were at university, I realised that, by comparison, we were given little opportunity to question our teachers. Certainly we had not encountered seminars; although the nursing school seemed to pride itself on recruiting intelligent young women, it then seemed incurious about what was going on in their minds. Our teachers were pleasant but consistently distant; the expectation was that we would not be curious either. We asked questions about facts, of course, but we lacked both the innocence and the ruthlessness of any freethinking three-year-old. We remained silent, possibly experiencing the teachers as rather fragile.

We had yet to learn that we too were fragile, afraid of all the horrors the hospital might contain. The memory of my first visit to a surgical ward remains particularly vivid.

> I stood at the end of the bed of someone with tubes coming out of every orifice. He was gripping so tightly to the bedframe that his knuckles were white. I felt giddy and faint. In my imagination the man was being tortured, a thought so terrible I could not even voice it to my friend, who was asking sensible questions about the temperature chart. Later, as I sat recovering in the cool corridor, I felt foolish. It occurred to me that the new patients arriving on the ward might have similar waking nightmares, and like me feel ashamed of themselves.

From this experience I learned something of how hospitals are bursting with intense primitive anxieties about the potential sadistic abuse of the power staff have over patients, and that everybody has these dreadful thoughts but nobody ever speaks about them. Staff and patients alike are expected to exercise stoicism and repression. Once I started working on the wards, I found these fears lessened. I could chat to the man who had clung to his bed. He might ask me the results of a football match, or I might change his urine bag. In this way I was reassured, and, in the course of these ordinary and practical exchanges, so was he. It is often easier to be an active participant than to be an observer in hospitals.

My other abiding recollection is from my second week on my first ward, a male medical ward.

> Most of the patients were much older than the new nurses, except for a boy aged nineteen who was pleased to have other young people to talk to. For me, he represented a link with the more light-hearted world of my friends outside the hospital. In those days, the wards were well staffed, and there were opportunities to talk to patients. David had been admitted for tests. He looked healthy and handsome, and quite out of place among the elderly coronary patients.
>
> One afternoon, my friend Kate, a fellow student, erupted into the ward kitchen. She had overheard a conversation between the consultant and the ward sister – they had been discussing David's imminent death. I wanted to disbelieve her, but I knew from Kate's expression that it must be true. 'It's leukaemia,' she added. I continued with my duties, leaden with anger. I avoided David, but at one point he called me over. 'I was wondering,' he said, 'if you'd like this box of chocolates. I've got too many.' Without

thinking, I remonstrated, 'No, you keep them. You'll enjoy them when you're better.' David looked at me with exasperation and pity. 'I'd like you to have them,' was all he said. I accepted the chocolates, and he accepted the weight of my apology. David died three days later.

Three years earlier, Isabel Menzies had written in her now famous study of the nursing service of a teaching hospital:

> There is no individual supervision of student nurses, and no small-group teaching event concerned specifically to help student nurses work over the impact of their first essays in nursing practice and handle more effectively their relations with patients and their own emotional reactions.
>
> *(Menzies 1960 p. 61)*

I needed to understand why David had died. The ward sister made time to speak to me in broad terms about leukaemia. 'You'll get used to it,' she said. It was meant kindly, but what did it actually mean? Her invitation was to the world of experience, of greater objectivity; but without personal supervision or the opportunity for mental digestion, it could only become an invitation to avoidance and denial. In such well-intentioned and innocent ways the system perpetuates its defensive organization against anxiety.

The student nurse group project

Twenty-five years later, I was approached by a nurse tutor at a large teaching hospital, who had noticed her students were increasingly raising issues to do with their feelings about patients. She asked me to join her in a project in which weekly discussion groups would be offered to new nurses during the time of their early ward placements. Each group would be led by a tutor, and I would act as group consultant to the tutors themselves.

> The students seemed a confident group; the mixture of sexes, styles, races and accents gave the overall impression of a comprehensive school sixth form. The tutors were welcoming and informal. They appreciated their colleague's initiative because they thought it would support the students. The notion of support was always prominent, and the groups came to be known as support groups, although I preferred to think of them as exploratory meetings about work. The danger, as I saw it, was that support in the form of reassurance would replace exploration, but I was regarded as fussy and somewhat truculent for taking this stance.
>
> The initial student take-up of the groups was about 60 per cent. The older the students, the more interested they seemed to be. One hypothesis was that the younger students were still struggling with adolescent identity issues, and that this, together with the pressures of assuming a new role in a new

institution, would have represented a considerable onslaught on their psychic defence mechanisms. Any additional emotional exposure in a group could have been anticipated as intolerable.

The project started with four groups of six or seven members. The themes of the groups, as highlighted by the students, are broadly categorised below:

- Potential and actual abuse of power by hospital staff: for example, forcing unwanted treatments on a terminally ill patient.
- Dealing with patients who exercise independent thought; for example, the Roman Catholic patient who objected to being in a gynaecology ward where patients were being admitted for termination of pregnancy (the administration refused to move her).
- Coping with one's own response to tragedy while maintaining a professional role; for example, with regard to a teenager, brain-damaged in an accident, who will never regain consciousness.
- Shame associated with mistakes; for example, forgetting a patient had requested her son should be called before her death.

The tutors were quite shaken by some of the incidents and dilemmas described in the groups; the discussions forced them to think about something they had forgotten or repressed. They became preoccupied with the discrepancy between what was taught in the nursing school and the reality of busy ward practice. The tutors felt the sense of disillusion and helplessness that the nurses experienced. Sometimes they felt it necessary to give talks on topics such as how to care for the dying, to inject not only concern for standards but also some hope into the situation. Providing a forum for the students to think had, it seemed, pushed the pain of helplessness and of failed idealism upwards into another part of the nursing system. The tutor group became restless, and their attendance at the supervision group became erratic.

Some of the tutors were not particularly willing to acknowledge the degree of mental pain among the students, and at times I felt quite irritated by their unwillingness to try a more interpretative approach, which perhaps could help the students to feel contained and understood. For a while there was a wish to anaesthetise me. Did I represent an anarchic threat to the hospital? Although this seemed a mad and grandiose idea, I felt I was being experienced as pushing them into something dangerous. Gradually it became clearer. The consequence of an accurate and helpful interpretation is likely to be increased intimacy and dependency. It was as if, once the students were aware of the extent of their distress at work, they would lay their burdens at the door of the tutors: 'You have helped me to recognise this. Now what are you going to do about it?' The tutors imagined they would be held responsible. This seemed to mirror the students' fear of direct personal contact with patients and attachments that would involve impossible demands.

What I, the students and the tutors were all experiencing at first hand were the unconscious assumptions of the hospital system, which were that attachment should be avoided for fear of being overwhelmed by emotional demands that may threaten competence; and that dependency on colleagues and superiors should be avoided. One should manage stoically, not make demands of others, and be prepared to stifle one's individual response.

If, for a moment, we consider the institution as the patient, it is as if emotional dependency is experienced as the most dangerous and contagious of diseases. Everyone is under suspicion as a potential carrier, and an epidemic of possibly fatal proportions is likely to break out at any moment. The only known method of prevention is stoicism, which is administered by example and washed down with false reassurance. Since the patient/consumer is already seriously infected, by virtue of their institutionalised role, he or she must be kept at a courteous but safe distance.

We all know of small-scale health care institutions, such as hospices, where appropriate dependency in patients and staff is acknowledged with remarkably favourable consequences. Unfortunately, most nurses are trained in large hospitals, where institutional processes lead to a kind of madness in which dependency is simultaneously encouraged and punished.

Motivation, frustration and satisfaction

Despite the stress and distress of institutional life, nurses continue to find pleasure and satisfaction in nursing. Job satisfaction is notoriously difficult to define. The reasons why we choose the work we do and the elements that provide satisfaction are largely unconscious and related to complicated emotional needs (Main 1968; see also Chapter 13). However, it is possible to make the general observation that many people are drawn to the caring professions because they have a need to put something right. This need to make reparation may be only partially conscious. It arises from guilt or concern, and its aim is to heal emotional wounds: one's own, and those of the damaged figures of one's internal world. It can be expressed in a socially acceptable way by helping others. While reparative wishes are healthy (one might even say that to heal ourselves while promoting healing in others is a good psychic economy), problems can arise when there is a compulsive quality. We see this, for example, in the driven motivation of the do-gooder who appears self-satisfied, out of touch with his or her own vulnerability, seeing problems only in others, and determined to 'save' people with or without their consent.

Whatever it is that engenders the wish to nurse, job satisfaction will depend not simply on the presence of a patient, but also on the presence of a patient who needs a nurse.

I was asked by a trainee psychotherapist, Jane, to supervise her on a difficult piece of work. She had been asked to offer some support to a group of qualified nurses who worked on a liver unit. The nurses had been suffering from stress. Some had complained of it openly, others had taken long periods of sick leave for apparently minor illnesses, one had resigned, and still others had asked to be transferred to another unit. The hospital administrator had been alerted, and some money was made available to provide staff support. A series of whole-day meetings was organized at which Jane intended to offer the nurses an opportunity to relax and to talk about their stress. Out of a total of 12, only five wished to attend.

> Jane had planned to start with some brief relaxation exercises, but the nurses were unable to relax. One lay on the floor like an ironing board, another said surely it was all pointless, and two others said they were afraid of what might 'come out'. Jane then encouraged them to sit in a group and just talk.
>
> They talked, not surprisingly, about the number of deaths on the ward, the liver transplant patients whom they lost after days or weeks of painstaking intensive care, the distress of the relatives, their own exhaustion. The most difficult thing to talk about was the resentment and even hatred they sometimes felt towards the patients who seemed to thwart their every effort and care. These were the alcohol- and drug-dependent patients who returned again and again to be repaired, with the single intention, or so it seemed to these nurses, to continue to connive at their own death.

These nurses may or may not have been sophisticated in their knowledge of the complexity and intransigence of addiction. Our intellectual knowledge often makes very little difference when we are faced, day after day, with the hopelessness of persistent self-destructiveness in others. The nurses felt deprived of the opportunity to make reparation; they could not experience any gratification or significance in their work because they could not help the patients to get better. Jane could at least help these nurses to recognise the basis of their stress. Acknowledging and understanding their hatred of their patients for (as it seemed to them) refusing to get better could help them not to retaliate by ignoring the patients' distress.

In this sort of extreme frustration of work satisfaction, workers need opportunities to mobilise appropriate defences against pain and anger. For this to happen there has to be someone, most helpfully a senior colleague, available to share the burden. In a highly stressed and increasingly petrified system, it may be necessary for an outsider to be called in to ask the question 'Why?', and to be a catalyst and container for thinking.

If there are no such opportunities, and appropriate defences are consistently blocked over time, there are two types of response. One is the breakdown/breakout solution. This would include the development of psychosomatic symptoms, the avoidance of work, long periods of sick leave, depression and, ultimately, resignation. Such things get noticed, of course, as happened in the liver unit, when it led rather late in the day to an offer of support to the remaining staff.

A second solution is the evolution of pathological psychic defences in the worker. This does not get noticed in the same way because it develops gradually.

Sometimes people erect a shell around themselves which serves to deflect and anaesthetise emotion. This is largely an unconscious development. If such a shell becomes a permanent feature of the personality, it is at great cost to the individual, who can no longer be fully responsive to his or her emotional environment. The resulting detachment is dangerous to clients, patients or colleagues, who will sense the potential cruelty inherent in the indifference.

Appropriate defences are those which are mobilised in the recognition that a situation is painful or downright unbearable. They involve attempts to protect oneself from stress in order that the work-task may be preserved. Pathological defences are those which are mobilised in order to deny reality, to allow an unbearable situation to continue as if it were perfectly acceptable, when in fact it needs to be challenged in order to preserve both the workers and the work-task. The soft end of pathological defence is stoicism; the hard end is manic denial, a psychotic process that attempts to obliterate despair by manufacturing excitement. In manic states of mind people are oblivious to both pain and danger.

Maternal transference and countertransference

Dr D. Winnicott, who helped mothers to feel that being merely 'good enough' was all right, extended his ideas to those in the helping professions. He listed many reasons why an ordinary mother may at times hate her ordinary baby, among them that the baby 'is ruthless, treats her as scum, an unpaid servant, a slave' (Winnicott 1947 p. 201). In caring for disturbed, frightened, angry, dependent patients, nurses may experience similar feelings. The constant demands to be in attendance and available can give rise to much resentment and self-denigration, in the way that mothers at home with children complain they feel relegated to a low-status activity. They complain about this despite the fact that they love their children and want to be with them. Availability seems to be associated with denigration. We could say that the 'good enough' patient is one who provides enough job satisfaction to enable the nurse to continue with her work despite its unpleasant aspects. The 'good enough' patient senses that the nurse needs to be needed, as well as needing some protection against excessive emotional demands.

There are inevitably intimate moments between nurse and patient. The nurse knows she will be remembered. She knows, too, that very strong feelings will temporarily be transferred on to her. She knows that when patients wake up after major, life-risking surgery and see her face, they may experience her as an angel, not because they are hallucinating, but because she is associated at that moment with the beauty of being alive. At such a moment, each will experience the individuality of the other. Yet the hospital culture, as we have seen, does not encourage the nurses to be moved by their experiences; attachment is felt as a threat to the system. Nurses therefore often keep these moments of intense job satisfaction to themselves. This may also be because the patient unconsciously conveys embarrassment to the nurse, embarrassment about being an adult but feeling like an infant. The nurse 'holds' the embarrassment for the patient, and does not speak about it.

It is as if a pact is struck between them: the fulfilment of the nurse's reparative and maternal instincts, and the patient's appropriate dependency needs.

Conclusion

Many nurses have told me that when they step outside the training environment of the hospital to take up various nursing roles in the community, they experience an acute fear of their new professional autonomy, and also of the autonomy of their patients. Community nurses become retrospectively aware of their previous protected and even infantilised status as professionals who were not expected to think for themselves, nor to take initiatives while working in hospitals. If the institutionalisation has not become chronic, and if the new working environment is sufficiently tolerant of individuality, nurses will in time rediscover their curiosity and capacity for thought.

Most of us have an unthinking area of our work where we operate on assumptions. These are subjectively experienced as innocuous habits, but when challenged, despite the fact that no one is able to articulate the reason for them, the rules persist. These no-go areas of institutional life are usually those in which the most anxiety is generated. These areas of anxiety in society's humane institutions can be identified with ways of managing the containment of suffering, death and fear, in the clients and the workers. The intense emotions aroused are felt to threaten not only efficiency, but also the fabric of the institution itself. In a vast and perhaps literally unmanageable organization like a national health service, it seems to be the fate of those who work on the staff/client boundary to carry and attempt to contain this anxiety so that the rest of the organization can experience an emotion-free zone in which to operate. In order to maintain this, these frontline workers must be silenced, anaesthetised, infantilised or otherwise rendered powerless. Student nurses in particular often feel disempowered by infantilisation; because they feel afraid but must pretend to be strong for the patients, they experience themselves as merely playing nurses. They are frequently asked, 'Did you always want to be a nurse?', the implication being that this career choice did, or should, stem from some sweet and innocent notion.

Over the past 30 years, nursing has gone through an intense period of professionalisation, partly in response to the increasing sophistication of treatments, partly to raise the status of nursing and to do away with old stereotypes and hierarchies. With the implementation of Project 2000 in the 1990s, nurse training increasingly moved from hospitals into universities, with growing encouragement to take degrees and postgraduate diplomas.[2]

Much of 'nursing care' is now undertaken by unqualified workers called healthcare assistants. One danger is that the healthcare assistants are coming to bear the brunt of the emotional impact of care instead of the student nurses.

One can only hope that the changes in nursing education may have positive consequences in wider systems of social and physical care management, causing old assumptions to be questioned. If, on the other hand, we continue to behave as if emotionality in the workplace is best managed by denial, splitting and projection, then we will continue to inhibit the functioning of society's humane institutions, and continue to squander the potential thoughtfulness of those who work within them.

Notes

1 A fuller version of this chapter was first published in the journal *Winnicott Studies*, 7, spring 1993: 21–41, and later reprinted in Davenhill, R. (2007) (ed.) *Looking into Later Life: A Psychoanalytic Approach to Depression and Dementia in Old Age*, London: Karnac (pp. 160–183). Reprinted here by permission of Taylor & Francis, LLC.
2 All nurses have been required to have a degree since 2013.

11

TILL DEATH US DO PART

Caring and uncaring in work with older people

Vega Zagier Roberts

Caring for older people brings with it particular stresses, insofar as ageing is the fate of all who live long enough. It inevitably stirs up anxieties about our own future physical and mental decay, and loss of independence. It also stirs up memories and fears about our relationships with older generations, especially parents, but also grandparents, teachers and others, towards whom we have felt and shown a mixture of caring and uncaring. This chapter discusses how these anxieties were dealt with in one geriatric hospital. However, the processes described exist to some extent in all caring work.

A note on language

Readers who have struggled to promote the personalisation and dignity of clients and patients in institutions like the one described here may object to the use of words like 'incurables' and 'inmates'. However, these stark terms, used by Miller and Gwynne in 1972, have been retained here not only for historical reasons but also to underline the harshness of the experiences being discussed, which can be glossed over by using more modern and politically correct language.

The institution

Shady Glen was a specialised hospital for severely impaired older people who, without being particularly ill, required intensive, long-term nursing care. It had two wings: the smaller North Wing had three rehabilitation wards for those patients who were thought likely to be able to leave the hospital eventually; South Wing had four 'continuing care' wards for those who were not expected ever to be able to live outside the hospital again.

The four wards of South Wing were particularly bleak and depressing. The beds were arranged in a circle around the edge of each ward, pointing towards the centre, from where the nurse in charge could keep a watchful eye on everyone. Squeezed between each bed and the next one stood a small wardrobe and chest of drawers; there was little space for personal possessions, and virtually no privacy. A few patients could move about with walkers, but the others spent most of their time in bed or sitting immobile in chairs. Most were totally dependent on the nursing staff for all their physical needs, and were fed, toileted and bathed on a fixed schedule.

The nurses maintained a high standard of physical care. There were few bedsores or accidents, little illness, and the patients were clean and well-nourished. However, the managers of Shady Glen were concerned about the poor quality of life for the patients in South Wing, and asked the senior nurses of the South Wing wards to form a working party to explore what could be done to improve the situation. It quickly became apparent that patients' quality of life could be examined meaningfully only in conjunction with the quality of life for the staff working on the wards, and also that other significant hospital staff could not be left out of the project if real change were to take place. The working party was therefore expanded to include the heads of other departments providing patient treatment. Two external consultants were brought in to assist the working party in thinking about the stresses in the continuing care wards, and considering how these might be coped with better. They were then to present their findings and recommendations in a report to the senior managers of Shady Glen.

Stress and interprofessional conflict

Morale among the nurses was very low, and relations between them and the other professional groups involved in the treatment of patients were antagonistic and competitive rather than collaborative. The nurses felt, not without some justification, that they were left to bear the brunt of the strenuous but thankless routine of physical care, unsupported and unappreciated. This kind of work has low status within the nursing profession – just as the patients on these wards could be said to have low status in society – and many of the older nurses at Shady Glen lacked the training and technical expertise needed for jobs elsewhere. They felt their wards were used as a dumping-ground for people that everyone else – doctors, families, society – had given up on and wanted kept out of the way, but well enough looked after that no one would have to feel too guilty about having rejected them. Not only did the nurses get little positive feedback from colleagues, patients or patients' families, but they got little inner satisfaction from the sense of a job well done. None of them felt these wards were a place where they would wish themselves or their loved ones to spend their last years.

The division of the hospital into two parts, one for patients who would improve, and another for those who would not, exacerbated the problem for both patients and staff. Many patients died soon after being transferred from North Wing to South Wing, as if they had received a death sentence. Staff on the continuing care wards were deprived both of hope and of the satisfaction of seeing at least some of their patients improve and move back into the community. The alleged rationale for this division was that the two kinds of patients required different treatment approaches, and that the presence of 'incurables' would retard the progress of the less impaired patients, as if their condition were contagious, though there was little evidence for this.

At the same time, the nurses were not in the business of helping patients to die, as in a hospice, since most deteriorated only very slowly and remained on the wards for many years. It was as if the patients were 'on hold', the nurses just struggling against the gradual encroachment of decay. In the face of all this, any idealism or enthusiasm in newly arrived nurses was rapidly extinguished. New ideas they offered were rejected as impractical, or even sabotaged. As a result, those with ideas and choices rarely stayed long, and the staff from departments other than nursing tended to focus most of their efforts on the rehabilitation wards, adding to the continuing care nurses' sense of being abandoned.

In the absence of the usual nursing goal of assisting patients to get well, the nurses did the best they could to keep patients as well as possible, which translated into keeping them safe: preventing accidents by keeping mobility to a minimum, discouraging the keeping of personal possessions which might get lost or stolen, keeping patients out of the kitchen in case they burned themselves. This policy, while depriving the patients of individuality and dignity, added to the quantity of work to be done by the nurses, so there were rigid schedules for meals, drinks, toileting and dressing in order to get it all done. Furthermore, since other professionals, like occupational therapists and physiotherapists, were mainly oriented towards increasing patients' mobility and independence, and since the services they offered tended to clash with ward routine, friction between the various disciplines was inevitable.

The consultation

The antagonism between the nurses and staff from other departments was so great that the two consultants initially worked separately, one consulting to the senior nurses on South Wing and the other to the heads of the departments providing specialist inputs to the wards: speech, occupational therapy and physiotherapy. The plan was that the two groups would each first explore their own concerns and develop their own ideas for improving the quality of life on South Wing, and later come together to work on joint recommendations to make to management.

The nurses were at first apathetic and resistant to the whole project. They had worked on the continuing care wards for a long time, were cynical about managers implementing any of their suggestions, and were in any case sure that very little could be done, given the extent of the patients' disabilities.

Everyone found their attitude very frustrating; even the senior nursing officer, who usually defended 'her' nurses from criticism from outsiders, chided them for undermining the project.

In contrast, the members of the other group were young, enthusiastic and full of ideas. As heads of their own departments, they were accustomed to making decisions fairly autonomously, and for many weeks they worked eagerly at coming up with new programmes and plans for improving the quality of life on the wards. But the initial excitement gradually gave way to discouragement, as they anticipated – or actually encountered – the nurses' resistance to their ideas. Finally, the group became listless and work ground to a halt, everyone complaining, 'What's the point when they just won't cooperate?' The project had reached an impasse.

A chance occurrence some months into the consultancy changed this. Someone interrupted a meeting to ask for a patient's record, and it was revealed that many speech, occupational and physiotherapy records were months behind. This was the first time that any deficiency in the work of these departments was recognised. The group now began to work at reviewing their own services and improving them, rather than blaming everything on the nurses and focusing on how to make *them* change. They worked without the earlier excitement, but with more effect. At the same time, without there having been any formal contact between the two groups, the nurses became livelier in their meetings with their consultant, coming up with ideas of their own to contribute to the project. Within a few weeks, the two groups started joint work on what could now be experienced genuinely as a shared task, rather than a vehicle for apportioning blame. They drafted proposals for a new approach to continuing care, and these became the core of the consultants' report to management of their findings and recommendations (Millar and Zagier Roberts 1986).

The report

The central recommendation was to redefine the primary task (see Chapter 4) of the wards. Up to this point this seemed to have been to prolong physical life, keeping the patients in as good physical condition as possible for as long as possible. The proposal was that it should be 'to enable patients to live out the remainder of their lives in as full, dignified and satisfying a way as possible', which might or might not include their moving out of the hospital. This definition would mean that all the various professionals involved in patient care could see their particular work as contributing to a common purpose, rather than having conflicting and competing aims.

This change in task definition had major implications. It invited re-examination of practices previously taken for granted, such as the nurses' emphasis on safety as a priority, with its consequent depersonalisation and loss of dignity for patients. Instead, the new aim required considering how to encourage such independence and autonomy as were possible, identifying differences between patients, so that some could make their own tea or leave the ward unescorted, even if others could not, and even if some moderate risk were involved (provided the patient wished to do so). This not only gave patients more self-respect and choices, but lightened the workload for staff and restored some meaning to their work. The greater dignity and sense of personal identity for patients if they wore their own clothes, no longer had wristband identification and had their personal possessions around them came to be regarded as outweighing the risks involved.

The new primary task definition also had implications for how the hospital was structured, that is, where boundaries needed to be redrawn. Boundaries delimit task-systems (see Chapter 4). Whereas before each discipline or department had had its own discrete task, and was therefore managed as a separate system, the new definition of a shared task required a new boundary around all those involved in patient care (this is described in more detail in Chapter 17). Furthermore, the separation of rehabilitation from continuing care wards no longer had any rationale, since their previously different aims were now subsumed under a single task definition. By doing away with this, some hopefulness could be restored to the work.

Finally, the report recommended developing improved support systems for staff, particularly during the period of transition from the old way of working to the new. This is discussed further near the end of this chapter.

Anxieties and defences in institutions for incurables

The situation of people who are neither dying nor likely ever to improve enough to leave an institution produces particular anxieties both in the residents and in those caring for them. Miller and Gwynne (1972) made a study of institutions caring for people with incurable, mostly deteriorating, physically disabling illnesses, but much of what they described is very similar to what was happening on South Wing. For the residents, entering this kind of institution is inevitably accompanied by a sense of having been rejected – by family, employers and society generally. Those inside such institutions are not necessarily more dependent than those outside, but they have actually been rejected, if only by having no family to look after them, or no money to pay for care at home. Crossing the boundary into such institutions means joining the category of non-contributing non-participants in society: they lose any productive role they may have had, and with this, often, all opportunity to continue making decisions for themselves. Being treated differently from self-caring and able-bodied people, they experience great loss: 'I am no longer what (who) I was'. It is as if they are already socially dead, although they may be years away from physical death. The staff of such institutions can also have feelings of having been rejected and abandoned. Projective identification processes (see Chapter 2) can contribute to their over-protectiveness of the patients and their anger at patients' relatives and their own colleagues.

These were not the only difficult feelings which emerged during the consultation to Shady Glen. Others included staff members' anger at uncooperative patients and hatred of their failure to improve; discomfort with being still relatively young and healthy; anxieties about their relationships with the ageing members of their own families, and about their own ageing; and guilt for preferring some of their charges and treating them differently, while wishing they could be rid of some of the others, which could happen only through death.

Defences by the staff against becoming too aware of these disturbing feelings included depersonalising relations with patients by treating them as objects, and by sticking to rigid routines; avoiding seeing common elements between themselves and the patients; illness, absenteeism and exhausting themselves to avoid feeling guilty. There was also an enormous anxiety throughout the care staff about being blamed. This probably arose largely from their internal and unconscious conflicts, but was attributed to their being held responsible for keeping patients safe and well. It produced a preoccupation with patients' safety, rigid routines designed to minimise the chance of making mistakes, and a hostile defensiveness towards colleagues and patients' relatives. The widely felt, but largely denied, doubts about the adequacy of the service contributed to the pervasive tendency towards blaming others.

Two models of care

The anxieties inherent in any work give rise to institutional defences in the form of structures and practices which serve primarily to defend staff from anxiety, rather than to promote task performance. Miller and Gwynne (1972) identified two models of care in institutions for incurables, each involving a different central defence. The first, the *medical* or *humanitarian defence*, was based on the principle that prolongation of life is a good thing. This tends to be accompanied by denial of the inmates' unhappiness, lack of fulfilment and sense of futility. Inmates' ingratitude is an affront to these values. This defence produced what the researchers called the *warehousing model* of care, that is, encouraging dependence, and depersonalising inmate–staff relations and care. A 'good' inmate is one who passively and gratefully accepts being looked after.

The second, the *anti-medical* or *liberal defence*, was based on the view that inmates were really normal, 'just like everyone else', and could have as full a life as before, if only they could develop all their potential. This defence produced what Miller and Gwynne called the *horticultural model* of care, defining the aim of the institution in terms of providing opportunities for the growth of abilities, while denying disabilities. There tends to be excessive praise for minor achievements, like the praise adults give for a small child's first drawings, and denial of inmates' failure to achieve social status. A 'good' inmate here is one who is happy and fulfilled, active and independent. Eventually, of course, nearly all of them fail.

It is easier to see the inadequacies of the warehousing model, but the other is also inadequate: the demand for independence may be distressing to some people whose physical and mental strength is declining. In many cases, they have been struggling for years against increasing infirmity, and some may give up this struggle with relief upon entering a nursing institution. Others want to continue to fight. These two types need different kinds of care and different attitudes in their carers. When models of treatment are based on defensive needs in the staff, however, these kinds of distinctions among different clients' needs may not be made, since they require thought and facing reality. Instead, one model is likely to be applied indiscriminately to all, on the basis of being the 'right' way to work, rather than as appropriate for the needs of a given individual at a particular time.

Both models represent unconscious psychological defences against unbearable anxieties aroused by the work, and by the very meaning of the inmates' having entered the institution. There is guilt about the social death sentence that has been passed, and ambivalence about whether at least some of the patients might not be better off dead than alive. Similar splits occur in other institutions, for example, between cure and care in work with people who are mentally ill (see Chapter 14) or dying (see Chapter 12). In all these cases, care tends to be unjustly devalued, while cure is pursued against all odds.

Moving towards integration

Both the medical and the liberal defences were operating at Shady Glen, the first among the nurses, the second among the specialist therapists. Each group was unquestioningly committed to its own model. The therapists blamed the poor quality of life for patients at Shady Glen on the nurses being uncooperative and too set in their ways to entertain new ideas. The nurses agreed they were resistant to the quality-of-life project, but insisted this was for good reason: no one else was placed as they were to realise the full extent of the patients' disabilities. They also felt hostile towards the more privileged staff who could leave work at 5 p.m. and did not have to dirty their hands with the 'real' work: easy for them to have these airy-fairy ideas! Only *they* behaved realistically and responsibly; it was thanks only to their disciplined care and unswerving routines that the patients had any quality of life, free of the bedsores, illnesses and injuries so prevalent in other geriatric care settings.

Each group had split off and disowned unacceptable parts of themselves, projecting these into the other group, who were identified with the projections (see Chapter 3). The therapists unconsciously counted on the nurses to attend to details, and so did not take responsibility for these, which led to the nurses being all the more weighed down and having to stick to routine all the more rigidly. Similarly, liveliness and hopefulness were split off in the nurses and projected, defending them against guilt and disappointment, while the therapists became virtually manic in their planning. As a result of these intergroup projections, the nurses actually *were* rigid, and the therapists *were* inclined to be careless.

In the first phase of the consultation, members of the specialist group were excited and hyperactive in producing ideas and plans, the impracticality of which they blamed on the nurses – and the nurses accepted this blame. Over time, the euphoria associated with this kind of manic defence – that everything was possible, if only others would not stand in the way – gave way to angry helplessness and a listless feeling of being stuck. The recognition by the therapists of a shortcoming in themselves – small enough not to have to be immediately denied, but significant enough to provoke self-examination – led to their beginning to re-introject split-off parts of themselves, including responsibility for routine, and recognition of their own and also their patients' limitations. Taking back these projections not only increased their capacity for realistic work, but permitted them to value more the actual and potential contribution by nurses to patient care. Freed of the projections, the nurses were enabled to re-own hopeful parts of themselves, previously split off to defend against disappointment and depressive concerns, and to begin to relinquish some of their own obsessive preoccupation with routine. As each group became more able to value the other, less anxious about being blamed and therefore less prone to blaming the other, it became possible for them to think together about how to bring about improvements in the patients' quality of life, and thus also in their own.

The need for support

The recommendations to the management, to redefine the primary task and redraw the defensive boundaries between professional departments (see Chapter 17) and between rehabilitation and continuing care wards, were designed to reduce the institutional splits which were impairing rather than supporting the quality of life at Shady Glen. However, since institutional defences arise in response to the anxieties inherent in the work, dismantling defensive structures requires providing alternative structures to contain these anxieties. The final part of the report, therefore, focused on ways of developing new kinds of support systems. These were of three kinds.

In the first instance, because of the stressfulness and strenuousness of their work, the staff needed their efforts to be recognised and valued, with explicit acknowledgement of work well done. They also needed more face-to-face contact with the hospital management to counteract their sense of being marginalised, rejected and of low status. This might be achieved through regular visits to the wards by senior managers to review staff needs and the development of their new practices.

Second, staff needed a time and place where it would be possible – and actively encouraged – to reflect together on their work and how it was carried out. In small groups with continuity of membership, and with positive support from management, staff might then begin to acknowledge some of the unacceptable feelings aroused by their work: the fear, dislike and even hatred they sometimes felt towards their work and the patients, and the anxieties stirred up by the constant proximity to human decay. Otherwise, they could only defend themselves in the kinds of counterproductive ways we have seen. Often, just being able to face these feelings with colleagues can reduce the need for such defences. This, in turn, can lead to more effective task performance, which produces more work satisfaction, which further reduces anxiety: a benign cycle (for further examples of this process, see Chapters 8 and 12).

Finally, there needed to be mechanisms for inviting, considering and implementing ideas for change from everyone in the system, whatever their status (including patients and their relatives), so that everyone could participate in joint problem-solving and feel a sense of contributing towards a shared purpose. Such a forum could serve to support thoughtful institutional self-review and development, as described towards the end of the next chapter, in place of the rigid, stagnant working practices and entrenched intergroup conflicts which had previously characterised Shady Glen.

Conclusion

Dictionary definitions of care range from affection and solicitude, to caution, responsibility, oppression of the mind, anxiety and grief. Care staff can experience their work in all of these ways. Containing such a spectrum of emotions is psychologically stressful. Since ageing is the inevitable fate of all who live long enough, personal anxieties and primitive fantasies about death and decay add to the strains of looking after older people. The pressures to split positive from negative feelings are likely to be particularly acute. We have seen how at Shady Glen this splitting was exacerbated by the way the hospital was organized, with its divisions among the disciplines and between rehabilitation and continuing care.

In all caring work there are elements of uncaring. To be 'weighed down by responsibility' invites flight from the caring task, which can at times be hateful. Obsessional routines of care can serve to protect patients from carers' unconscious hate, from what staff fear they might do to those in their charge if not controlled by rigid discipline. At the same time, these routines can provide organizationally sanctioned ways of expressing hate of patients who exhaust, disgust or disappoint staff. Alternatively, all hate is projected, and the patients' hatefulness denied by seeing them as totally curable.

In his short but seminal paper, 'Hate in the countertransference', Winnicott (1947) discussed the hate inevitably felt by psychoanalysts for their patients, and by mothers for their babies. He stressed that the capacity to tolerate hating 'without doing anything about it' depends on one's being thoroughly aware of one's hate. Otherwise, he warned, one is at risk of falling back on masochism. Alternatively, hate – or, in less dramatic terms, uncaring – will be split off and projected, with impoverishment of the capacity to offer good enough care.

Winnicott's paper has given 'permission' to generations of psychotherapists to face previously unacceptable – and therefore denied and projected – negative feelings towards their patients. Indeed, to become conscious of such feelings has become a fundamental part of their training. Such permission – from within ourselves and from the environment – to acknowledge and own the uncaring elements in ourselves and our 'caring' institutions is crucial, both for individual well-being, and for the provision of effective services.

12

WORKING WITH DYING PEOPLE

On being good enough

Peter Speck

For most people, death only enters their lives a few times. When it does, it can precipitate a significant crisis as the individual seeks to adjust to the impact of the event. But what of the professional who in some settings faces death almost every week, if not every day? How does he or she cope with this abnormal exposure and still manage to maintain a professional role? Death is universal and will come to us all and to those we care about at some time. We know this intellectually, but we may well try to defend ourselves from the emotional impact of personal death or the death of someone close to us.

Stresses of working with dying people

Working intimately with people who are dying can put one in touch with personal loss; unresolved feelings and anxieties may be evoked by the death of someone we are caring for professionally. Attempting to suppress or deny the personal impact can be stressful, leading to fatigue, sickness, compensatory over-activity, loss of effectiveness at work and at home, together with other symptoms often referred to as 'burn-out'. Attitudes expressed by others may add to this excessive stress. People may make comments such as, 'Oh, those poor people! All that suffering! You must have to be quite hard, or very dedicated'. Or, 'I don't know how you do it, day after day. Isn't it all terribly depressing? I mean . . . they die'. Comments such as these make explicit an expectation people have that the carer must be an extraordinary person offering perfect care. If the carer knows that the reality can often be somewhat different, then the expectation can be a source of stress. If the carer shares the expectation, then this gives rise to stress, too. One often shared expectation is that good care will make for a 'good' death. But death is not just sad or beautiful; it can be ugly, painful and frightening.

One of the unconscious attractions to working with dying people is that the work-role can serve to maintain the fantasy that death happens only to other people. When this defence breaks down because the work situation is too close to one's own, there is a real risk that one may be disabled from working – or staying in role – at all, as the following vignette illustrates:

> In my role as chaplain, I was called one morning to the hospital intensive care unit (ICU) to see the parents of a dying boy. John, aged thirteen, had been knocked down by a lorry on his way to school. His mother, Mrs Brown, explained how he had been late for school and she had shouted up the stairs, 'You're late! Get out of bed or else . . . !' John eventually ran downstairs, dressing as he made for the front door. He said that he was too late for breakfast, ran off down the road, and at the corner ran out into the path of the lorry. He had been diagnosed as probably brainstem-dead, and the final definitive tests were awaited.
>
> As Mrs Brown talked, I became more and more upset and unable to listen to her. I just wanted to shut her up and to get away. It was increasingly difficult for me to stay in the room, let alone in my role. I realised I needed to leave and sort myself out; eventually I apologized and left the waiting room. Outside, a senior nurse, René, asked me what was wrong. I said I was very distressed about David. 'David who?' she asked. I said, the David who was in ICU and brainstem-dead. 'But we haven't got a David,' she said, 'Only a John. Come and see.' She took me into the side room where John lay. I realised it was not David, my son.
>
> Then I remembered how that morning, as I was leaving for work, I had heard my wife shouting up to our son 'You're late! Get out of bed, now!' When Mrs Brown had used almost exactly these words in telling me her story, she momentarily became my own wife, telling me that our son was dying. In the ICU waiting room, I had been so identified with the situation that I became a stricken father, not a chaplain. Once I realised what was happening, I returned to the waiting-room. As I apologised again for leaving, Mrs Brown threw her arms around me and said, 'It's all right, vicar. I could see you were upset.' We were then able to work together on how she and her husband might face the impending death of their son.

Through over-identification, my sense of reality and my professional identity had both broken down for a while. After an experience such as this, it is tempting to try to defend against its ever happening again, and to make sure we are no longer touched by such events. But in the field of terminal care, identification will always be a possibility: there will always be patients who resemble us or someone who is significant to us in ways which stir up anxiety. We are repeatedly put in touch with past losses and reminded of the certainty of future ones. Each time, we are confronted with the reality that our work does not confer any special protection against death.

Defences against the fear of death

Identification, the consequent loss of boundaries and the difficulty of managing oneself in role in the face of death can lead the professional to develop strategies to minimise the possibility of this happening – conscious and unconscious defences against the emotional impact of the work.

Avoidance

Some people, for example, may avoid the difficulty of talking about death in a personal way by rationalisation (the patient doesn't really want to know . . .); or by intellectualisation (talking in terms of statistics); or by hit and run tactics (telling the patient bluntly and then leaving, avoiding all further contact). Others may try to avoid direct contact with death altogether.

> A senior ward sister on a busy male surgical ward became quite hysterical one morning after a patient died while she was standing at the bedside. It was only the second time she had been present at a patient's death since qualifying over twenty years earlier. As a student nurse, she had witnessed a very traumatic death. When she had become distressed, the then ward sister told her, 'Pull yourself together and go and lay him out, then get the rest of the beds made.' She had vowed that she would never put herself in that situation again. Once she qualified, she always ensured that any dying patient had another nurse assigned so that she could avoid getting involved. She had managed that quite successfully until now.

Task-centredness and aggressive treatment approaches

The tendency to defend oneself by adopting a task-centred approach is not new. The priest can hide behind the ritual of prayers and sacraments, avoiding inter-personal contact; the doctor can use a stethoscope to silence the questioning of a patient. Such defences are often a way of protecting oneself from death, and of reassuring oneself that 'It won't happen to me'.

For clinicians, another way is to move into aggressive treatment approaches with techniques which may prove beneficial in some cases, such as radical recon-structive surgery, heavy doses of radiotherapy or highly potent cocktails of che-motherapy. The focus in such approaches is on potential cure, the 'breakthrough', which can confer a great feeling of omnipotence on the clinician. Such a disease-focused approach may be accompanied by a distancing from the patient as a person, and any patient who dies represents failure. Meanwhile, the human caring aspect is vested in the nurse or other paramedic who remains close to the patient and is identified with all that is good, loving and nice. When the patient dies, the nurse may become the recipient of the doctor's negative feelings because of the unad-dressed rivalry that has developed between them. The rivalry may relate to a covert competitiveness for the gratitude of the patient, who may seem to have shrugged off dependency and asserted his or her autonomy in the only way left – by dying.

An attempt to address this split is seen in the developing speciality of *palliative care*. Here a partnership is sought between the doctor, patient and nurse, with both doctor and nurse involved in a personal way with the patient for whom they are caring. Surgery, radiotherapy and chemotherapy may still be employed, but the focus is shifted from cure to symptom control and pain relief.

Chronic niceness

Staff who work in hospices, which specialise in care for the terminally ill, usually appear to be cheerful people who work extremely hard to provide the highest standard of care for their patients and patients' families so that the dying can achieve a 'good' or 'nice' death. While there is little doubt that hospice staff are caring and dedicated people, one of the dangers which face them, and others who work long term with dying people, is that of 'chronic niceness', whereby the individual and the organization collude to split off and deny the negative aspects of caring daily for the dying. There is a collective fantasy that the staff are nice people, who are caring for nice dying people, who are going to have a nice death in a nice place. This protects everyone from facing the fact that the relationship between the carers and the dying can often arouse very primitive and powerful feelings which are disturbingly not-nice.

Having relinquished some of the traditional defences described above, carers can fall victim to this chronic niceness, as if acknowledging any negative feelings and thoughts about patients or colleagues might threaten the unity they have established. In order that everyone can continue to be nice to each other, the not-so-nice feelings get split off and displaced outside the staff group. For example, there may be much complaining about managers who 'don't understand the pressures . . . are always demanding more and more of us . . . don't seem to value what we do'. This can, of course, be true, but it can also indicate that the group has moved towards a paranoid-schizoid position in order to retain staff cohesiveness (see Chapter 1). In this case, whatever management may intend will probably be misperceived by the work group. Similarly, the split-off negative feelings may be projected on to the patients' relatives, who are then perceived as hypercritical of the standard of care and of the way in which the staff are looking after the patient. The staff's image of themselves as competent, caring and nice people may seem to be under attack, and it may feel like it is only the patient – who is already in a dependent relationship – who really appreciates what they are doing.

Survivor guilt and the need for gratitude

In my encounter with Mrs Brown described earlier in this chapter, I experienced a large measure of relief in finding it was not *my* son who was dying in the ICU.

This feeling, which psychoanalysts refer to as 'manic triumph', often arises in the course of caring for dying people and brings with it a sense of guilt (Freud 1917). It can be difficult to acknowledge to oneself, let alone to others, that one feels pleasure in knowing that it is not one's own death or the death of someone important to oneself that is about to happen. In the face of the obvious distress of those who *are* experiencing death, one may then also experience guilt for having survived. There may be a strong desire to split off and deny such painful feelings. However, if one can contain simultaneously contradictory feelings of concern and relief, it is possible to tolerate the pain without resorting to excessive splitting, projection and denial (Klein 1959; see also Chapter 1).

Patients' gratitude can do much to alleviate survivor guilt. But patients are not always nice and appreciative, and carers will then have to find ways to deal with the negative feelings this arouses if they are to continue to manage themselves in role, as the following example illustrates:

Robert was a 35-year-old married man with two very young children. The day he received his diagnosis of cancer of the pancreas he was initially very distressed, and then withdrew and became uncommunicative. In the course of my routine visit to the ward, the staff told me they were worried about Robert and I agreed to visit him. At this first meeting, Robert made it clear he was not religious, and that the events of the past few days had done nothing to change this. I explained that I was not in the business of 'arm-twisting' religion, but was available to listen to his feelings about the events of the past few days.

Robert remained silent for a while, and then became tearful. Eventually, he said, 'It's not being able to see the kids grow up . . . but I can't talk about it now.' I said I recognised that he might not feel ready to talk at present, but asked for permission to visit again, explaining that staff could contact me at any time. Over the ensuing weeks of treatment and care, I visited Robert regularly. There was no formal religious ministry during these meetings, but we talked about what it meant to him to have an inoperable tumour, and about the impact of the treatment on Robert and his family. Some of this he was able to share with other staff as well. Robert expressed his grief over the loss of a future, his concern for his wife and young children, and his anger at what was happening. Once he discovered that I was concerned to relate to him *where he was* in his understanding of life, Robert was able to use me as a support and resource.

Then the time approached when I would be away on annual leave. I tried to prepare Robert for my absence, and introduced a colleague who would be available in my place over the holiday period. At this point, Robert developed a blocked duct, and had to have some palliative reconstructive surgery. Although he made a good recovery from the operation, it was clear his condition was deteriorating. His anxieties concerning his children became more acute. Although there had been several family sessions when the children had all been able to talk about the impact of their father's disease and probable death, there was much that Robert still wanted but felt unable to say to them. Following a suggestion from me, he decided he would write letters to each of his children and to his wife. The letters took a long time to write, but eventually he finished them and gave them to me for safe-keeping, telling his wife what he had done. He then asked me to promise to visit him the night before going on holiday.

When I made that visit, Robert was reasonably comfortable and wanting to talk. He reviewed much of the ground we had covered over the previous weeks, and also highlighted the areas which he still needed to explore. I felt Robert was trying to face the ending, but at the same time indicating there was much to be done and not much time. He expressed gratitude to me for the work we had achieved, but the overriding feeling was regret for all that had not been done. At this point I began to experience feelings of guilt, of having let Robert down by not being available for this new work, and a sense of failure for not having helped Robert achieve what he wanted in the time available. While I was trying to make sense of these mixed feelings, Robert suddenly asked me if I were going on holiday tomorrow. Then he asked if I were taking my wife and children. Again I said yes. There was a silence, and then, loudly and angrily, Robert said, 'Well, it's bloody well all right for you isn't it? I'll be dead when you get back. Have a bloody good holiday!' He then turned over in bed, away from me, and pulled the sheet over his head.

I felt very angry at this 'unfair' outburst, and for being made to feel guilty for going on leave. I felt unsure whether to tackle the issue with Robert or to leave and risk that Robert might later feel bad about his final farewell. At that moment, too, a part of me wanted him to feel bad for 'spoiling' our good relationship in this way. It was proving difficult for me to retain any capacity to think through what was happening. After a moment I said, 'I'm sorry we are parting in this way, Robert. I appreciate you're very angry with me for going, but that's the way it is. I must now say goodbye,' and I touched his arm as I said this. There was no response, so I left the bedside and went to find the ward sister. I told her I needed to talk through what had happened because I felt very angry. We went to the office, had a cup of coffee, and I tried to understand what had happened between Robert and me.

The need for support and containment

It is understandable that dying people should expect their carers not to desert them. The chaplain, especially, is expected to be available and nice at all times, remaining calm, pleasant, able to receive and contain anything 'dumped' on to him or her. This expectation is often shared by the other care staff of the institution which employs the chaplain. When staff feel stressed and fragile, it can be very useful to have a chaplain on board to be the recipient of negative projections.

In this case, having managed my difficult feelings as best I could, I needed support myself, which I got from the ward sister.

As we talked things over, I realised that some of my anger was at Robert's illness and the inability of any of us to 'put it right' and restore him to health. I also recognised that I felt guilty not only for leaving, but also for not having worked more on Robert's anger earlier. I had thought we had addressed it, but now I experienced a strong desire to 'turn the clock back' and do it better, which is a characteristic aspect of endings. My feelings mirrored Robert's: a mixture of gratitude for what had been good, sadness and anger, and also guilt and anxiety about not having done all that might have been possible. By being able to ventilate some of my feelings with the ward sister, I came to see that for some time I had not properly acknowledged the anger that Robert had been feeling inside while on the surface he had been saying appreciative and nice things. I could also recognise how my need for Robert's gratitude had led to our colluding in niceness. Robert *was* appreciative, but he was also very envious of the fact I was fit and well, and going away on holiday, while he faced death.

In this case, I was able to get the help I needed from the ward sister. However, often colleagues are experiencing such similar feelings that they cannot contain them for each other. Such situations cry out for consultation to the staff group and/or management so that these feelings can be contained rather than acted out or projected. Just as I, in my role as chaplain, needed some space in order to regain my ability to think, so as not to go on holiday feeling excessively guilty or angry, so staff groups need space to understand what they are carrying psychologically as a result of the work they do. The hospice or other care institution may then be able to re-engage with its primary task. It is the ability to tolerate ambivalence that can restore integration and the capacity to think, or, in Kleinian terms, move a group from the paranoid-schizoid to the depressive position (see Chapter 1).

Conclusion

The tendency towards 'chronic niceness' is an aspect of the desire to be the perfect carer (see 'Guilt and reparation', pp. 136–138 in Chapter 13). This desire can create great stress for the individual carer, the group of carers and the patients. The recognition that one can perhaps be a *good enough* carer for dying people or their families, without being perfect, can be very liberating.

> Out of the working through of the depressive position, there is further strengthening of the capacity to accept and tolerate conflict and ambivalence. One's work need no longer be experienced as perfect . . . because inevitable imperfection is no longer felt as bitter persecuting failure. Out of this mature resignation comes . . . true serenity, serenity which transcends imperfection by accepting it.

> *(Jaques 1965 p. 246)*

Dying people frequently create in their carers a desire to do everything possible to ensure that this part of the person's life is quality time. Striving for perfection may, however, cause considerable stress for all concerned. It may be more realistic to aim at being a 'nice enough' carer for that particular dying person. In this way, it may be possible to discover a strength which allows each to let go of the other in an appropriate and healthy way.

Part IIb   Challenges, crises and change

13

THE SELF-ASSIGNED IMPOSSIBLE TASK

Vega Zagier Roberts

The preceding chapters in this part of the book have described how the nature of the work in various settings across the helping services affects the workers, giving rise to collective or institutional defences, which in turn determine organizational structures and practices. This chapter looks at what the workers bring to the work, their needs and inner conflicts, and how these make them particularly vulnerable to getting caught up in the institutional defences arising from shared anxieties.

Choosing a helping profession

The choices we make regarding which profession to train for, which client group we will work with, and in what kind of setting, are all profoundly influenced by our need to come to terms with unresolved issues from our past, as the following example shows:

> Marian was the eldest of six children who were abandoned by their alcoholic father when she was 13. Their mother, who had to go out to work, looked to Marian to care for the younger children, often repeating, 'I don't know what I would do without her.' This left Marian little time for her studies, and she was the only one of the six who did not go to university. She stayed at home until the youngest child passed his 'O' levels. At the age of 30, Marian found her first paid job, as an assistant in an inner-city nursery school for children with disabilities. Here she maintained a familiar source of self-esteem, dedicating herself to helping young children get the best possible start in life. Like her mother, the teachers at the school often wondered how they would manage without Marian. At a less conscious level, Marian was working through issues related to a view of herself as handicapped by her lack of education, and by the social isolation of her adolescent years.

Violet, one of Marian's younger sisters, who had been only four when her father left, became a family therapist. While she was consciously motivated by a powerful desire to keep families together, it was a constant battle for her to control her rage at parents when they behaved in ways she considered harmful to their children. This made it difficult for Violet to work effectively, until personal therapy enabled her to disentangle her own experiences from those of her clients.

A brother, Harry, had been an unruly child, and was often told he was making life even more difficult for his mother. Harry became a teacher, and later headmaster of a boys' boarding school. He was a stern disciplinarian, and his internal image of his school was of a place where unruly boys were sent to be kept under control, and to relieve parents of a burden they could not cope with.

Ideals and defences

Many of the conscious choices made by helping professionals are based on idealism. However, ideals also have unconscious determinants, and these can contribute to defensive institutional processes.

Fairlea Manor was a private psychiatric hospital, famous since the 1940s for its pioneering work in applying psychoanalytic methods to the treatment of severely disturbed and previously untreatable patients. It retained a reputation as a place of hope for people who no longer responded to more conventional psychiatric intervention. At a case conference, Veronica, a fairly new psychotherapist, presented Dan, a young man with whom she had been working for 15 months. As was usual at Fairlea Manor, all his medication had been stopped when he arrived, and for many months he had been very agitated and often assaultive. Now, although he was still too disturbed to leave the ward unescorted, his symptoms were subsiding. Veronica thought that together they were coming to understand his illness, and was hopeful that Dan would be one of the rare and highly prized patients who recovered without medication. However, the ward staff were pressing for a decision to re-institute medication to hasten Dan's improvement. This was agreed at the case conference, over Veronica's strenuous objections. She was angry and bitterly disappointed, experiencing the decision and the nursing staff's focus on promoting 'normal' behaviour as an attack on her work. In supervision, she described feeling drugged and sleepy during sessions with Dan, as if she too were being medicated. For their part, the staff regarded Veronica as dangerously out of touch with the reality of Dan's time-limited health insurance and his lack of real progress towards being able to live outside the hospital.

This was not uncommon. Acrimonious arguments between therapists and the nursing staff were a regular feature of case conferences, and there was little dialogue between the two groups. Many of the therapists had come to Fairlea Manor because they believed passionately in the value of psychoanalysis and this was one of the few hospitals where it was still a core treatment. They disregarded the external reality that the environment had changed dramatically since the 1940s, when the absence of alternative treatments meant that patients could remain at Fairlea Manor indefinitely if necessary. Now the insurance companies paying for treatment demanded that hospitals demonstrate they were keeping patients' length of stay to a minimum.

This disregard, even hatred, of external reality is typical of the basic assumption mode of group functioning, where the task pursued by a group is more the meeting of members' internal needs than the work-task for which it was called into being (see Chapter 3). It is associated with an absence of scientific curiosity about the group's effectiveness, an inability to think, learn from experience, or adapt to change, and is most likely to dominate when there is anxiety about survival (Bion 1961). The therapists were under threat in a number of ways, not least from the nature of their work with such deeply disturbed people, its assaults on their safety and sanity, its unrelenting demands and its often disappointing results. In addition, their survival as specialised professionals was threatened by the decline of psycho-analytic psychotherapy as a psychiatric intervention. Finally, many were still in analytic treatment themselves as part of their training, and deeply needed to believe in its efficacy.

In response, they set themselves an impossible task: to prove they could cure any mental illness, however serious, with psychotherapy. No one defined their task to them in this way; it was self-imposed, unarticulated, powerful and very persecutory, since, thus defined, it was unachievable. They had to find most of their satisfaction in their endurance, and in their shared disdain for those seeking merely external, superficial improvement in the patients. They split off any doubts they had and projected them into the ward staff. They also split off their rage at patients who refused to get better, and blamed the hospital for not providing the resources – especially unlimited time – which would enable them to achieve their self-assigned impossible task.

Meanwhile, they unconsciously entrusted to the ward staff the task of 'exporting' sufficient numbers of patients who had recovered enough to return to the community, the task on which the hospital's economic survival depended. To the outside world, Fairlea Manor presented a united front, defending its costly and time-consuming approach to treatment from all criticism. In this way, it provided the therapists with a place where they could continue to do the work they needed to do in order to meet their unconscious needs.

Task performance and unconscious needs

To the extent that people are drawn to work in a particular setting because it offers opportunities to work through their own unresolved issues, these settings may well attract staff with similar internal needs and a similar propensity to fit with certain kinds of defences. Bion (1961) refers to this phenomenon as *valency*, and its part in determining one's choice of profession has been discussed in Chapter 3. This gives rise to collective defences against the anxieties stirred up by the work which can seriously impede the task performance.

> Swallow House was a social services residential unit for children who had been removed from their families for their own safety. Its task was to prepare for the children's return to family life, either with their original parents or with adoptive parents. Although discharge planning was ostensibly central from the first day, in practice the staff focused their efforts on providing as secure and home-like a place as possible. This in itself was positive, but difficulties arose when it was time for a child to move on; the staff could never see any parents as being good enough or ready enough to take the child on. It was as if only Swallow House staff could meet the children's needs, and almost every departure was traumatic.
>
> When the manager tried to help the staff with this in supervision, his efforts were violently resisted. Staff were very suspicious and distrustful of the manager, casting him in the role of a 'bad parent' who was too preoccupied with his own concerns to have the children's best interests at heart.

The self-assigned impossible task in this case seemed to be to provide the children with the (ideal) parenting they had never had: impossible in any case, but actually anti-task in an institution intended for children in transition. This very young staff's unresolved issues – several had themselves been in care, or came from broken homes – both about themselves as children, and also as potential parents, led on the one hand to unrealistic expectations of the parents to whose care the children were discharged, and on the other to attacks on their manager for failing to be an ideal parent to them. This made it difficult to make use of the 'parenting' he did offer; supervision sessions were often cancelled, and his authority constantly challenged.

The staff over-identified with the children, partly as a result of the key-working system, which meant that children were assigned to particular staff members who took primary responsibility for them. This system, originally designed to reduce the psychological trauma of institutional care, put a dysfunctionally strong boundary around the child/key worker pair, a boundary which supported the as-if task at the expense of the task which needed to be done (see Chapter 4, p. 45). The special and exclusive intimacy of 'key working', consciously intended to meet the needs of the children, was also a product of the need for intimacy in the staff.

Professional idealism and group identity

At both Fairlea Manor and Swallow House there were difficulties in the export process – discharging the patients or children. This had to do with a collective sense of everything good and helpful being inside the organization, and of the outside world as harmful and dangerous. In both institutions, group identity was based on being a superior alternative to another form of care. At Fairlea Manor, this was explicit: it set out to be an alternative to 'revolving-door' hospitals offering short-term treatments aimed at symptom control. At Swallow House, it was less conscious: key workers strove to be better parents to the children than those in whose care they had previously been, whom the staff blamed for the children's situation.

A group's identity is linked to its definition of its primary task – its reason for existing (Rice 1963; see also Chapter 4). To some extent this always includes a dimension of being an alternative to some other group. 'We make shoes' is a start, but we identify ourselves with a particular group making particular shoes, more stylish, cheaper or more comfortable than others. In organizations caring for people, identity and task are often linked with ideals and ideology. For example, Chapter 11 described models of care based on a 'warehousing' ideology, where patients are treated as creatures with purely physical needs, and an 'horticultural' ideology, where patients are treated as individuals with unfulfilled potential which needs to be developed (Miller and Gwynne 1972). Workers using this second approach tended to be so persuaded of its superiority that it was difficult for them to recognise how it, too, failed some of their clients.

Since the personal meaning of the work tends to be vested in the ideals underlying the choice of working methods, it can be very anxiety-provoking to question them. Instead of space to reflect on what is most appropriate for whom, there is often polarisation around 'right or wrong', as illustrated in the following example:

> At the Tappenly Drug Dependency Unit (previously described in Chapter 4), the growing waiting list became such a pressing problem that the service managers asked the staff to revise their methods, so as to reduce the list as quickly as possible. The team saw this as devaluing their good work, and united to defend long-term counselling, without showing any interest in comparing outcomes for clients receiving different amounts or types of counselling. The argument, which was bitter, remained anecdotal and highly personalised.
>
> As reforms in the health service threatened to make evaluation a requirement, staff predicted that this would be based purely on numbers, without any regard for clients' welfare; yet they were unable to suggest any alternative criteria when they were invited to draft their own. The introduction of a computer to collect data was perceived as a way for managers to spy on and control the unit, rather than as an opportunity to gather the information they needed for service planning. When a researcher offered to train them how to use the computerised data to answer their own questions about how clients were using their service, they were so suspicious that he was an auditor that they were unable to formulate questions that might have enabled them to use their limited resources more judiciously.

Many teams and organizations are set up as alternatives to other, more tradi-tional ones, often by someone disaffected by personal or professional experience of other settings. However, identity based on being an alternative, superior by some ethical or humanitarian criterion, tends to stifle internal debate. Doubts and dis-agreement are projected, fuelling intergroup conflict, but within the group every-one must support the ideology. Any questioning from within the group is treated as a betrayal of the shared vision. In the Tappenly team, for example, some doctors and nurses ventured to express alarm about the risks to health and life for people on the waiting list, and suggested diffidently that it might be better to take some staff time away from counselling to assess the physical state of the waiting clients. The panic and anger which greeted this 'selling out' to the opposition quickly led to the proposal being dropped. Similarly, some Fairlea Manor therapists would from time to time question whether the use of medication or more emphasis on symptomatic improvement necessarily undermined the psychoanalytic work, but the prevailing anxiety about 'becoming just like anywhere else' made this feel too dangerous to talk about. Thus, internal differences were constantly stifled (see Chapter 16).

The self-assigned impossible task becomes the 'glue' which holds these alterna-tive organizations together. It serves as a defence against the difficulty and stress of working at the possible. Problems inevitably arise when the alternative approach proves limited. Working with chronic schizophrenics or abused children or heroin addicts is intrinsically difficult, and success is never as great as one hopes. The alternative approach is based on a hypothesis that by changing certain conditions far more success will be achieved. When outcomes fail to support this belief, disap-pointment and anxiety set in. Failure is experienced as a punishment or envious attack for having dared to set themselves up as a superior alternative. This serves to reduce guilt and anxiety about the institution's shortcomings, but at the cost of leaving staff feeling under attack, helpless, abused and unable to learn from their experience.

Guilt and reparation

From a psychoanalytic point of view, it is the drive to effect reparation, partly conscious, but largely unconscious, that is the fundamental impetus to all creative, productive and caring activities. This drive has its roots in our own experiences with our earliest caretakers – let us say with mother. In the earliest months of life, the infant splits his perception of mother into good and bad: the good, nurtur-ing mother he loves, and the bad, depriving mother he hates and attacks. With maturation comes the awareness that mother is a single person for whom the baby feels both love and hate. With this realisation come remorse, concern and guilt for the damage his greed and aggression have caused and will cause her. From this stems the drive to reparation: to atone, to protect, and also to express gratitude for the good care received. Normally, the child's reparative activities will keep his anxieties at bay. When guilt is too strong, however, reparative activity will be inhibited. Instead, the infant – and the adult in whom these early conflicts are revived – retreats to the earlier, more primitive mental activity of splitting objects into good and bad, which can be unambivalently and separately loved and hated.

Usually, by repeatedly discovering that mother and, later, others survive his attacks, the infant comes to trust that his love predominates over his hate, and that his reparative activities are successful. This lessens his fears of persecution and retaliation by the bad mother he has attacked. But when external reality fails to disprove the child's anxieties, for example, if the mother dies, or withdraws, or retaliates, then depressive anxieties may become too great to bear. The individual then gives up his unsuccessful reparative activities, resorting instead to more primitive paranoid, manic and obsessional defences.

Paranoid defences involve denial and projection of aggression so that it is experienced as coming from outside oneself in the form of persecutors. Manic defences are directed at denying that damage has occurred, and involve omnipotent fantasies about magical repair. Unlike genuine reparation, which requires the ability to face that damage has been done and cannot be undone, manic reparation must be total, so that no anxiety, grief or guilt need be experienced. Manic reparation tends to be impractical and ineffective; when it fails, individuals may use obsessional defences, the ritualistic repetition of certain acts, as a further effort to control and master anxiety, especially about their aggressive impulses (Klein 1959; Segal 1986). Those in the helping professions inevitably and repeatedly encounter failure in their work with damaged and deprived clients. If this arouses intolerable guilt and anxiety, they, like the infant, may retreat to these primitive defences in order to maintain precarious self-esteem, and to defend themselves against the retaliation anticipated for failing to heal.

Two features distinguish caring work from most other work. The first is that the reparative activities are carried out in direct relation to other human beings. This means the job situation often very closely resembles early-life situations that the worker may still unconsciously be dealing with, and which drew him or her to this particular line of work. The second feature is that the worker's self is felt to be the major tool for producing benefit for the client. The helping professions are often regarded both by their members and by their clients as vocations requiring special qualities. Skills and 'technology' – the syllabus, the treatment programme – may be used defensively to ward off anxiety about personal adequacy for the task. Often, however, they are put in second place, with primacy being given to personal attributes as the instrument of change. By offering themselves as such instruments, workers unconsciously hope to confirm that they have sufficient internal goodness to repair damage in others. This is a source both of individual and organizational ideals, but also of much anxiety.

> Haply Lodge was founded as an alternative to statutory provision for homeless mentally ill people. The staff strove to abolish all distinctions between themselves and those they served, living with them in a community where the tasks of daily living, such as cooking and cleaning, were shared by all. There were no rotas or shifts: everyone lived full-time at Haply Lodge, with

minimal personal privacy and no demarcations between on-duty and off-duty periods. The vision, to which staff felt deeply committed, was that by doing away with any barriers between themselves and their clients, such as they believed had contributed to the reluctance of many homeless people to use statutory services, they would bring about healing through love and mutual respect. That the absence of limits on what they offered generally led to their own physical and emotional breakdown within a year or two was built into the culture of the organization. Despite the fact that this burn-out was expected, it was usually accompanied by disappointment, anger and guilt in both management and workers.

When the consultant explored with staff how they had come to work at Haply Lodge, it turned out that nearly all of them had painful personal experiences of homelessness – actual or psychological – and had no meaningful home to go to, were they to work more conventional hours. They found the intimacy and sense of belonging at Haply Lodge deeply rewarding, at least at first, and were shocked when their clients drifted back to 'life under the bridges' as they always had.

Although the impossible task here was explicit rather than self-assigned, this example highlights unconscious processes which operate across the caring services. Staff at Haply Lodge were stressed both by the similarities and by the differences between themselves and their clients, and both played a part in their choosing this particular work. They felt guilt for being better off than their clients, having more education, skills and material resources, and therefore more choices about where and how to live; guilt, too, for being glad this was the case. By obliterating these differences, the staff unconsciously sought both to reduce their guilt and to find the loving home missing in their own lives.

The aim of helping or healing through one's love and goodness is two-pronged. Success is deeply validating, strengthening the capacity to act constructively. But failure, or even limited success, is felt to demonstrate inner deficiency, and is intolerable. At Haply Lodge, the burn-out served to assuage guilt about lacking sufficient goodness to bring about the intended result. It was also the only way staff members could get away, since their investment in the organization's ideals precluded their actively choosing to leave at an earlier stage.

Conclusion: managing anxiety in the helping services

To understand, and therefore to be able to help, another person requires a capacity for empathy: to stand momentarily in the other's shoes and experience their pain, using what one has learned as a guide as to how best to respond. However, the close resemblance between workers' own most painful and conflicted past experiences and their experiences at work constantly threatens this capacity. In some institutions, the dominant defence is to accentuate differences: 'they' (the clients) are the sick or mad or needy ones; 'we' (the staff) are the well, sane, strong, helping ones. The work in this case will be structured to support the distance between staff and clients, using rigid timetables, programmes and hierarchies. In other institutions, particularly those dominated by a self-assigned impossible task, the dominant defence is more likely to be to deny differences, to stand so much in the others' shoes – identifying with the clients as victims – as to be overwhelmed by their pain and despair. In both cases, there is a failure to manage the client–worker boundary in ways that support task performance (see Chapter 4).

It is therefore of the greatest importance for helping professionals to have some insight into their reasons for choosing the particular kind of work or setting in which they find themselves, and awareness of their specific blind spots: their valency for certain kinds of defences, and their vulnerability to particular kinds of projective identification. It can be helpful to explore this with colleagues, in the process gathering clues as to the source of some collective defences. Personal therapy can also be of assistance, as in the case of Violet (described at the beginning of this chapter), to disentangle one's past from the present, and to find alternative ways of resolving unconscious conflicts, rather than needing to do this entirely through one's work.

By recognising consciously the internal task definition they are working to, staff groups can become more aware of the associated anxieties and defences. A more realistic task definition can then be formulated, one that is meaningful but also possible, and which relates to the overall task of the wider institution. Realistic task definition, by making some success possible, increases the capacity to tolerate depressive anxieties. Managers can take a lead in this, provided they maintain their position at the boundary of the system and are not too caught up in the defensive processes themselves (see Chapter 4).

Coherent thought and the capacity for problem-solving are possible only when depressive anxieties – and hence reality – can be tolerated. When paranoid anxieties prevail, thought and memory, which link reality to consciousness, have to be attacked and eliminated, and there is no curiosity about causation. In this case, problems cannot even be stated, let alone solved (Bion 1967). In the depressive position, omnipotent fantasy, obsessional ritual and paranoid blaming can give way to thinking: one can seek to know, to learn from experience and to solve problems. Reparative activities can then become more realistic and practical, allowing workers more solid satisfaction from their very difficult work.

14

INSTITUTIONAL CHAOS AND PERSONAL STRESS

Jon Stokes

In this chapter I wish to make some links between the increasingly uncertain and sometimes chaotic nature of life in present-day organizations and the personal experiences of stress felt by those working in them. Essentially my argument is that in order to understand many apparently personal experiences of stress, it is important to place these in their organizational context of uncertainty about the future, and a related confusion about the organization's primary purpose or mission.

The organization-in-the-mind

The conceptual framework I wish to use is based on the idea of an organization or institution 'in the mind'. This term was first introduced by Pierre Turquet in the 1960s when he was working at the Tavistock on group relations with applications to organizations (see also Armstrong 1991). It refers to the idea of the institution that each individual member carries in his or her mind. Members from different parts of the same organization may have different pictures and these may be in contradiction to one another. Although often partly unconscious, these pictures nevertheless inform and influence the behaviour and feelings of the members. An organization is coherent to the extent that there is also a collective organization-in-the mind shared by all the members. In what follows, the terms 'organization' and 'institution' are used somewhat interchangeably. However, a distinction can be made between the relatively stable aims of something called an 'institution' with an emphasis on continuity and solidity, and the relatively more flexible and change-able connotations of an 'organization'.

Gordon Lawrence (1977) has shown that whilst an organization may have one publicly stated idea of its primary purpose or mission, there are often also hidden conceptions at work. Put simply, there is the level of 'what we say we do' but there are also the levels of 'what we really believe we are doing' and also 'what is actually going on'; the members of an organization may be quite unconscious of this third level (see Chapter 4). In Chapter 18, Anton Obholzer suggests that at this third level the health service is unconsciously seen as a 'keep-death-at-bay service'; whilst the stated task is the treatment of illness, there is also an unconscious task of providing each member of society with the fantasy that death can be prevented. Many of the extreme feelings about the provision of health services can be understood more accurately as having their roots in anxiety about death; death as one of the inevitable outcomes of hospital work is denied. In one case this actually took the form of a hospital in London being built without a mortuary. It turned out that the architect had forgotten to plan for this, and no one had noticed. The drive to preserve life as an organizational imperative then becomes dominant, often irrespective of the quality of life that the patient will have.

When the medical model of cure is transferred to the field of psychiatry, the result can be a denigration of ordinary care, often the only hope that people with a serious mental illness have. What is idealised are the latest fashions in cure, which succeed one another with manic rapidity. The result is very self-destructive both to the organization's conscious primary task, which is disrupted by this more unconscious emphasis on the task of cure as above that of care; and also to the morale of the staff, whose abilities to care and to act realistically rather than omnipotently are consequently undermined. Since care is a slow process and does not provide the dramatic result desired, it is denigrated as being ineffective, whereas 'cure', which is exciting and offers a defence of omnipotent denial of the chronic nature of the problems, is idealised. This is also an expression of professionals' use of 'treatment' as a defence against the inevitable experiences of helplessness and failure inevitable in this kind of work.

A second form of denial sometimes found in psychiatric institutions is a political analysis of mental illness which denies its reality and claims it is only a consequence of social inequalities. Rather than having to care for and treat ill patients, an often difficult and sometimes unsuccessful process, the staff are drawn into seemingly endless power struggles over irreconcilable ideologies. A frequent dynamic of staff meetings in such institutions is centred on who has the 'power' and who is 'powerless' within the team. This is a defensive shift away from the real powerlessness that the whole team shares in its relative inability to 'cure' the patient. For example, in a psychiatric unit to which I consulted there was, in the course of the staff meeting, a heated debate about a patient who had requested her social security cheque. The doctor's view was the patient was currently ill with a manic-depressive illness and would simply spend all her money on some useless article. The social worker disagreed; in his opinion it was a contravention of the patient's rights to withhold the cheque. There was a furious argument with the majority of the nurses and other staff supporting the social worker's view. The patient subsequently spent her entire cheque on alcohol and chocolates. I don't think it is possible to say that either the doctor's or the social worker's view was right or wrong, instead there was a painful choice – to restrict the patient's 'freedom' or to 'collude' with madness. One of the feelings that the whole team found difficulty in facing was their shared sense of helplessness in relation to this particular patient. A focus on action and quick decision was used as a defence against this painful feeling.

As we have seen again and again, moving the mentally ill out of mental institutions (which were, it is true, sometimes very cruel) often results in their being abandoned to live on the streets. In my view, this in part involves an unconscious attempt to solve the problem of currently incurable forms of mental illness through denial by allowing the sufferers to die from exposure in a hostile environment.

I am not arguing for a return to the large mental hospitals of the past, but it is necessary to acknowledge the complex emotions and often ambivalence surrounding the activities of cure and care. Unless this ambivalence is acknowledged and managed, and worked with rather than denied, there is a danger of a considerable amount of cruelty in any care system. Here, the underlying and unconscious institution-in-the-mind is one of a powerful cure for all mental illness, and hence each failure to do so is a threat to the identity and sense of effectiveness of each individual member of staff. This idea can become a persecuting presence and drive the staff to acts of rejection and cruelty towards those in care, which would not be the case in an institution with a less idealised picture of its primary purpose.

As a final example of the complexity caused by diverse pictures of the organization-in-the-mind of the members of an institution, I turn to the prison service. Here, there are at least three competing views of its primary purpose: to contain dangerous and violent criminals, to punish those who have broken the laws of society, and finally to provide rehabilitation. Different prison officers will emphasise one or other of these in their everyday work; likewise individual members of society will have different expectations of the prison service. This gives rise to conflict and confusion both inside and outside the prison service about the role of the prison officers. Are they to be controllers, punishers or rehabilitators? Any decision about action in relation to a particular person needs to take account of these conflicting and competing roles. Failure to acknowledge this will result in muddled and unreflective decision-making in the staff team, as well as stress for individual officers.

These different, and to some extent conflicting, pictures of the prison institution-in-the-mind and of the role of a prison officer need to be distinguished. Prison staff are of course aware of this, but nevertheless feelings about the priority of one purpose over another do often impede day-to-day decision-making, and also policy-making both at institutional and societal levels. Here, as for the other examples above, shifts from one to another view of the primary task can contribute to the felt need to 're-structure' organizations, as if re-structuring will solve the difficulties inherent in the work.

Institutions as containers

I want now to return to how the individual member of an organization may be affected. Although often felt to restrict, constrain and limit the individual, institutions can also provide a sense of psychological and emotional containment. Much of the sense of constraint in organizations is produced because each individual member projects parts of the self that he or she does not want to be aware of into other, more distant parts of the organization. These not only provide a focus for blame for the frustrations and conflicts inherent in working in the organization, but also 'lock' individuals and groups into unconscious roles.

In all of us, there is the impulse to work and there is the impulse not to work (see Chapter 3). Where can this impulse against work be located? Very conveniently, in the department or office down the hall, or in the other building; *they* are the lazy ones, or the reason we are not doing well at the moment. This is one unconscious reason why we form and join organizations: to provide us, through splitting and projection, opportunities to locate difficult and hated aspects of ourselves in some 'other'. Internal personal conflicts can be projected on to the interpersonal or even inter-institutional stage. This also happens at the international and the inter-ethnic levels, but it is most immediately evident inside our own organizations. However, this process of splitting and projecting requires a reasonably coherent, clearly structured and relatively unchanging organization. If 'they' keep changing, how do we know who 'they' are? Stability is not a prominent feature of most organizations today; continual change and re-organization are in progress almost everywhere. Who is 'them' and who is 'us' has become less and less simple.

The current trend towards fundamentalist religions is perhaps related to this, reflecting a wish to find an exceedingly stable framework where one's actions are prescribed by a religious text, whether it is feeding, sexual behaviour or a ready-made and socially sanctioned enemy. In this way, anxieties about choices are reduced, which brings a reassuring feeling of stability, predictability and familiarity. The problem, of course, is that it requires an out-group to fight against, and in doing so one can provoke counter-attack from them. Whilst this may have been a tenable method of managing things in the past, particularly where the 'enemy' was always at some distance and less likely to be provoked, the increasing interdependency between nations and the rapidity of communications means that it is now a much less viable form of psychological defence. Additionally, national economies are now so interdependent that this psychological myth also becomes economically counterproductive.

One of the things that a good 'old fashioned' institution provides is something that we can really love or something that we can really hate. And it will be there tomorrow, no matter how hard we love or hate it. Nowadays, one is hard-pressed to find such a thing. In the past, the institution could be blamed for being too conservative, too rigid, too bureaucratic or whatever, and very convenient that was too, since it provided the individual members with places to locate these conservative and rigid aspects of themselves. Nowadays, you will be lucky if the other department or the other unit is still there next year. Certainly the people may not be, and certainly the task is continuously changing. As a result, institutions are not so available for the working out and working through of the ambivalent feelings surrounding work that each individual has. It is often hard to be sure what one's organization will be doing in a year's time, and what its structure will be, and this causes anxiety.

The changeability of organizations means they do not provide such easy targets for projections. This results, I believe, in the widely shared experience of an increase in interpersonal tension and personal stress within sub-groups inside organizations, instead of the more familiar and simpler tension between workers and management. This is perhaps even more obviously true in public sector organizations, such as the health, education, social, civil and police services, than in commercial ones, though even the largest and most successful companies are changing out of all recognition. Whereas our public institutions used to provide a reliable and stable container for the nation, helping to manage issues concerning inequality, sickness and disorder, they no longer provide a dependable environment for its citizens.

One result is an obscuring of the psychological task of public sector organizations by an over-emphasis on cost-effectiveness. In the case of the police, the public are now called 'customers'. While no doubt an important change in the sense that the police are trying to view us in a different way and asking us to do likewise, this can bring with it a different problem. We need the police to be available, psychologically speaking, for the projection of certain of our attitudes towards authority. Indeed, accepting these projections, working them through, and handing them back to society at large is part of the task of the police. If the police see themselves only as providing a service, and do not realise that psychological containment of tensions within society is also a central function, there is likely to be an increase in disorder rather than a reduction. If the police are no longer available in this way to society, they will not provide the necessary sense of authoritative containment.

The shifting focus of organizational conflict

With the increasing recognition of the plurality of our society, which contains many sub-groups each demanding representation and influence, the primary task of many established public sector institutions requires re-negotiation. Furthermore, existing authority structures are continuously being challenged, creating considerable additional stress and confusion for the members of these institutions as they attempt to adopt and modify their working practices to take account of these changes. The conventional model of hierarchical top-down organizations is being replaced by negotiations between sub-systems of organizations with fewer levels of hierarchy. Where previously authority was ultimately patriarchal and matriarchal in character, we are now seeing conflicts not so much with 'the authorities' but between sub-groups within society and within organizations. To extend the family analogy, many organizational conflicts today are more akin to sibling rivalry between brothers or sisters competing for resources and power.

One result of these changes is that difficulties that were previously managed by projection up and down hierarchical levels, or between established departments and units, may be forced down to the interpersonal level between members within an organization. For instance, there is a notable increase in 'bullying' in organiza tions (Adams and Crawford 1992), and other forms of scapegoating of certain individuals within organizations who are then subjected to intolerable pressures and are often driven out in one way or another. The individuals who experience this sort of treatment are very often at the boundary of two parts of the organi- zation, like heads of departments, or at its boundary with the outside world, for example, receptionists or secretaries; these positions are particularly vulnerable to institutional pressures. No doubt the individuals involved unconsciously choose these jobs, which in some way suit their personality, but their personal character- istics are also fed by institutional demands and unconscious needs, as discussed in the next chapter. Sometimes there can be a happy match between the unconscious needs of the individual and those of the organization. An effective receptionist, for example, should perhaps have what Bion (1961) refers to as valency for fight–flight (see Chapter 3), which can be used appropriately in role in the work. But when the match is unhappy, or a job changes so that an earlier match is lost, the individual is at risk of breaking down. The question of responsibility for this is complex.

> Janice, the head of an adult education centre, came for a consultation regard- ing her role as manager. She was under considerable personal stress, and felt that her personal problems were causing her to fail as a manager. Although she was nominally the head of the organization, it turned out that she was really not allowed to use the authority appropriate to this role. She was undermined at every stage by the executive committee; when problems arose, they would not ask her in role as manager how she saw the problem or what the solution might be, but instead would set up innumerable working parties, task groups and so on. Ostensibly this was in order to 'involve' mem- bers of the committee in the work of the organization, but the effect was to undermine her authority. In addition, because the centre was in a multi- ethnic area and Janice was white, the committee expressed great worry about being accused of being racist, although there was no evidence of this. Indeed, Janice seemed to be a very competent manager. In the interests of 'enquiry' and 'democracy', the management structure had been undermined, leading to poor morale throughout the organization, and great difficulty making decisions.

It seemed to me that a good deal of the problem had to do with the internal power struggles and feelings of envy between members of the executive commit- tee. These were dealt with by giving each member an 'equal' share of the respon- sibility. This disabled Janice from operating effectively, since she had a very limited range of choices. It usually fell to her to carry out only the more unpleasant tasks, such as sacking staff, the actual decisions having been taken by the committee, often without her involvement. The committee were also expressing their envy of her role by undermining her. The result was incoherence and confusion in both policy and organization. Through our work together, she was able to understand these dynamics better and to devise ways of tackling them through gaining the proper support of the committee chairperson, and ways of negotiating more appropriate delegation of authority to her by the management committee. Her symptoms of personal stress, ill health and anxiety disappeared. As a by-product, the chair of the executive committee also became better able to manage her own task, partly through advice from Janice.

Tolstoy wrote that he felt his freedom consisted in his *not* having made the laws. Perhaps what he had in mind was that, precisely because he was not responsible for creating the laws, he had a choice about what role he could take up in relation to them. The laws provided him with a framework, but not one that he was himself directly responsible for making, and thereby he had a certain degree of freedom even though constrained by these rules. But what are the rules in today's organizations? Often the only rule seems to be that nothing will stay the same.

Freedom comes not necessarily from changing the organization, which is too often seen as the only solution to almost any problem. It can also come from finding, making and taking a role in relation to the task and the structures available to support this (Grubb Institute 1991). Often, greater actual change is achieved in this way. Where adaptation is required, then changes should of course be made; but nowadays it seems that a new manager is not seen as having really taken up his or her post unless everything is re-organized. Re-organizing may have as much to do with the need to establish identity and mark out territory – the organizational equivalent of a dog urinating on a lamp-post – as it has to do with improving organizational functioning.

The result is that people, such as nurses in psychiatric institutions, who have been doing things in a certain way for many years are made to feel not only that this way is now outmoded, but that it was never of any use anyway. This inevitably corrodes morale. Change can be driven by a manic and contemptuous attempt to triumph over difficulty and conflicts. Feelings of compassion are cut off and the capacity for concern is projected on to others who are then seen as weak. The organization may well need someone who can represent or 'carry' weakness, such as a part-time worker or a member of a minority group. This individual is scapegoated and may even be driven out. Again, personal stress is caused by unconscious organizational conflicts, but because the conflict has been forced down to the individual and interpersonal levels, it becomes impossible to address.

Conclusion

In the face of constant change and chaos, we cannot either full-heartedly love or hate our institutions any longer, but we continue to be dependent on them, often far more so than we care to realise. Witness, for example, the sudden decline of individuals who retire or who are made redundant. An externally containing and coherent organization supports us, yet we also hate, envy and fear institutions for their apparent power over us, and they can easily become personifications of persecuting figures from our internal worlds (see Chapter 1). However, when organizations seem fragile and unpredictable, they become more like a rather inadequate foster parent than a second home. Then the inevitable feelings of hostility and envy towards parental objects, previously projected into management, have either to be denied or directed elsewhere, usually into intergroup and interpersonal conflicts, contributing to personal stress in organizations. This process can be compared to the somatisation of internal conflict in the individual; when we are unable to deal with conflict at a mental level, it is pressed down into the body and finds expression in physical complaints.

Unless the management of organizations is sufficiently stable to be able to provide a clear definition of purpose and a reliable container for the inevitably ambivalent feelings of those they employ towards those in authority, then the organization will express its disorder through individual and interpersonal disorder in its members. This comes to replace a more appropriate and creative struggle with the task of the organization, a struggle supported by the structure of the organization. Interpersonal and intergroup conflicts can easily provide scapegoats, and the real problems remain unaddressed.

Alongside this continual clarification and working at the primary task of the organization, its purpose and aims, there is also the need for a parallel working at the roles best designed to carry out the primary task. As has been discussed, roles have both an overt and conscious aspect (for example, a job description) and a covert or unconscious element (for example, the flight–fight basic assumption underlying the 'unconscious job description' of a receptionist in an organization). Also, as in the prison service, there may be a series of conflicting and competing roles implicit in the organization. Unless management includes the management of opportunities for staff to understand these pressures, there will inevitably be an increase in stress at the personal level. Role consultation for managers is one way for staff to understand and work in these normal pressures and tensions of organizational life.

15

THE TROUBLESOME INDIVIDUAL AND THE TROUBLED INSTITUTION

Anton Obholzer and Vega Zagier Roberts

We would all like to believe that the world is fundamentally a logical, well-managed place. Since the evidence against this is overwhelming it is inevitable that we seek a defence against finding it so frighteningly unsafe. A popular explanation, going back at least to the Old Testament story of Jonah, is that all would be well if only the evil ones, the trouble-makers, could be got rid of. Similarly, in institutions there is a great deal of blaming – between departments, between staff and management, or between the organization and the outside world, the politicians and policy-makers, whose wrong-thinking is the cause of all our troubles.

As discussed in the previous chapter, institutional difficulties are often attributed to the personalities of particular individuals, identified as 'troublesome'. Here, we will look at how such individuals are unconsciously 'selected' by the institution, and how both the individual and the institution can deal more effectively with what is troubling them.

Trouble-making as unconscious communication

Sheldon Road was a residential unit for sexually abused children. One summer the staff were feeling particularly pressed because several old-timers had recently left, and had been replaced by relatively inexperienced workers. They asked their manager, Nick, not to accept any more referrals until later in the year. Rather abruptly, there was an emergency admission of a nine-year-old boy, Terence. Nick explained to the staff that he had done all he could to avoid this, but that no other place could be found for the child, an explanation which the staff appeared to accept.

Around this time, Tony, the only part-time worker on the staff, told his colleagues he had seen the manager leave the room of one of the girls late at night, looking dishevelled. A week later he placed a formal complaint about this against Nick, adding that Nick had been coming to work intoxicated. There was an inquiry, the allegations were judged to be without foundation, and Tony was warned about the consequences of making unwarranted accusations.

His colleagues had been aware for some time that Tony was in difficulties. He had recently left his wife, had been coming late to work, calling in sick, and getting very behind in his paperwork. They were worried about him, and suggested he seek professional help, wondering among themselves if he might not be heading for a breakdown. After the inquiry, Tony became more and more agitated, and made even wilder accusations against Nick. Finally, he saw a psychiatrist, who prescribed medication and recommended extended sick leave. The staff were angry and upset about what had happened, blaming Nick for reprimanding Tony too severely, but were also relieved that Tony, who had been unable to carry his share of the workload for some time, had left.

Just as things were beginning to settle down, the behaviour of the new boy, Terence, became a serious problem. He was quite abusive to staff, and on two occasions got involved in fights with other children which resulted in injuries. The staff protested to Nick that they were not trained to deal with this level of physical violence; they could no longer contain Terence, particularly now that they were more short-staffed than ever. Nick gave every support he could: extra meetings were held with the staff, additional supervision was given to Terence's key worker, and money was provided for extra locum staff. However, Terence's behaviour continued to worsen. On the day that he threw another child off the swing so hard that she had to be admitted to hospital with concussion, Terence was removed from Sheldon Road and transferred to a psychiatric ward. The staff again breathed a sigh of relief; with their most difficult charge gone, they could 'get back to normal' at last.

Many groups and organizations have a 'difficult', 'disturbed' or 'impossible' member whose behaviour is regarded as getting in the way of the others' good work. There may be a widely shared belief that if only that person would leave, then everything would be fine. This view is very attractive, hard to resist and tempting to act upon. At Sheldon Road, the staff had lost confidence in their manager when he proved helpless to protect them from taking on another child at a time when they felt very vulnerable. Tony's breakdown expressed the vulnerability they all felt, and could be regarded as a strong unconscious message to management to attend to their difficulties. At the same time, staff needed to locate their vulnerability in one member: 'It is he, not we, who is breaking down'.

It is significant that the precipitating event, Tony's allegations against Nick, while unfounded, served to express the desire of all the staff to accuse management of misconduct, the real misconduct being Nick's untrustworthiness in failing to prevent Terence's admission. Tony was the best candidate to express this, given his family difficulties and argumentative style, and could be regarded as having unconsciously 'volunteered' for the task. And, as happens very often, no sooner had one troublesome person left, than another one appeared. When management failed to take sufficient heed of the first spokesperson, Terence was 'selected'. The child who was hurt by Terence represented all of the staff: 'Look what is happening to us as a result of your decision'. Terence's behaviour expressed not only his own rage, but also the rage all the staff were feeling at parental figures who abuse and fail those whom they should protect. At the same time, first Tony and then Terence were used to voice the group's unacknowledged anxieties about the quality of the service they were offering, anxieties which were split off, projected and finally got rid of by the removal of the 'whistle-blowers'.

Selecting a trouble-maker

This unconscious suction of individuals into performing a function on behalf of others as well as themselves happens in all institutions. For instance, the individual who gives the chairperson a hard time, holding up a whole committee by question-ing and arguing every move, needs to be viewed not as a difficult or 'troublesome' individual – though he may well be that – but as an institutional mouthpiece, into whom all the staff have projected their disquiet. Sitting embarrassedly in the same room, signalling with their eyes that they wish to dissociate themselves from the trouble-maker, they are disowning that part of themselves which, by a process of projective identification (see Chapters 1 and 2), is located in the trouble-maker. So, too, with the chronically tardy staff member, or the reactionary, or the person given to violent emotional outbursts. Rather than seeing them merely as among the inevitable hazards of working with other people, we can more usefully regard their behaviour as a response to the unconscious needs of the institution.

> The manager of Links, an organization providing community support for the elderly, had been plagued for some time by the lack of competence in the staff he had inherited from his predecessor. This had been ascribed to their having been recruited in haste from among a very small number of not very suitable candidates. When vacancies arose and posts were advertised, there were dozens of applicants. Selection was a long, careful process, at the end of which the manager was asked by a colleague whether he was relieved to have the highly trained staff he had been longing for. 'Well, I'm not too sure about one of them,' he replied. 'She doesn't seem as clear as I would have liked about the kind of approach that is needed in community work.' Indeed, this new staff member – despite her excellent qualifications on paper – soon took up a group role of the confused, argumentative staff member who neither understood nor agreed with fundamental policies and procedures in the organization, the very same role her less well-trained pre-decessor had held before her.

At an unconscious level, the new staff member had responded to a job advertise-ment that read between the lines something like this: 'Wanted: volunteer required to voice the difficult, disowned, anti-task elements of the staff. Both internal and external candidates are welcome, but only candidates with suitably difficult per sonalities should apply'.

The difficult person unconsciously acts on behalf of all the staff, and the problem, rather than being attributed to personality, needs to be tackled on a group and institutional level. Instead of 'Isn't it terrible how X is behaving?', there needs to be a psychological and institutional move to 'We all have ambivalent feelings which we need to own, and those that relate to our work in the institution need to be taken up at work'. It is only from this position that some headway can be made in improving the functioning of the organization. At the same time, this helps the 'difficult' person shift out of the role into which he or she has been locked, as other members of staff become able to withdraw their projections. However, as it is often the most vulnerable or least competent group member who is selected to voice the dilemma, it can be all too easy for others to dissociate themselves from the spokesperson and to treat his or her behaviour as a personal problem. Identical processes occur between groups and departments, as described in Chapter 11, where the nursing and non-nursing staff were locked into antagonistic roles until the intergroup projections and underlying anxieties were addressed.

Dealing with institutional dilemmas

Very often, the particular nature of the work of the institution determines the type and style of the problem that the 'difficult' person is asked to act out.

> Thorne House was regarded as a particularly progressive therapeutic community for the treatment of disturbed adolescents. It deliberately recruited staff with varied backgrounds and experience, on the basis that this would offer the adolescents a wide range of potential role models. Week after week, a great deal of time was taken up in staff meetings by rows between two of the men. Rodney was young, trendy and 'laid back'; he thought the staff should overlook what he considered minor infractions of the rules. Richard, who was older and had previously worked in a psychiatric hospital, on the other hand, insisted on taking these very seriously: 'If our boys don't know where they stand, things will get out of hand'. He was perceived by his colleagues as rigid and authoritarian, while Rodney was referred to as a 'bit of a flake'. The arguments between Richard and Rodney about how to manage the adolescents were endlessly repetitive. Other staff sat back and watched, some amused, some bored, and many irritated at the waste of time and the lack of change in either party.

The risk in situations like this is of seeing the process in terms of individual personality – or, in a therapeutic institution, in terms of individual psychopathology. This leads to a blind alley. It was not within anyone's authority at Thorne House to insist that staff have personal therapy. Even if it had been, it is likely that

Rodney and Richard would have resisted, at least until they were freed from the institutional projections having to do with unresolved unconscious dilemmas, in both staff and residents, about issues of authority, managing themselves and being managed by others.

An intervention focusing on the institutional process could serve to draw all members of staff back into role, and enable them to resume work on the primary task of the institution. By contrast, an intervention focusing solely on the difficulties of the two individuals could produce only an unsuccessful therapy group, or a road show for a vicarious audience. Personal psychopathology is relevant in this kind of situation only inasmuch as it determines who will be used for what institutional purpose: their personal *valency* for particular unconscious roles (see Chapter 3). Seeing the individuals concerned as expressing a wider conflict directly related to anti-task processes puts the problem into a different framework.

Thus, what needed to be recognised at Thorne House was the two sides of an unexpressed institutional debate on permissiveness versus control, so that the fight could become the public, ongoing debate within the staff group as a whole that it needed to become. Indeed, this debate taps into the very essence of the adolescent process, with its unconscious struggle between authoritarian and anti-authoritarian parts of the maturing self. Similarly, at Sheldon Road, fundamental tensions in working with abused children – for example, between avoidance and intimacy, between the wish to expose and get rid of an abusing parent and the wish to keep the family intact, between trust and mistrust of both children and parents – were avoided. Instead, anxieties were projected into vulnerable group members with a valency for expressing one or other aspect of these dilemmas. As a result, Tony and Terence both behaved in such extreme ways that they were expelled from the institution, leaving the underlying issues unresolved and likely to re-erupt as a new crisis at any time.

From this group-as-a-whole perspective, troublesome individual behaviour must be perceived and treated as an important indication of a problem in the group. Thus, the adolescent who is caught smoking marijuana needs to be thought about and managed as representing drug-taking 'on behalf of the entire group'. Whether they are kept on or expelled, the meaning of the drug-taking behaviour needs to be taken up as an institutional issue, resulting from a complex network of protective processes. It is the most-vulnerable-to-drug-taking adolescent who is unconsciously selected to take the drugs; but merely to treat the individual is to guarantee that the problem will crop up again, in the same or in a different form. The difference in the two approaches to the situation is of major consequence. Treated as a group process, the underlying problem, as well as the individual's, is addressed. To treat it as one person's misbehaviour allows everyone else to continue disowning and projecting aspects of themselves into the targeted individual, and the process will continue unabated, to the cost of both the individual and the institution.

Institutional dilemmas, like personal ones, are anxiety-provoking, and regularly give rise to the kinds of defensive projective processes described above. These processes can then lead to individual stress and scapegoating, as happened at Sheldon Road, and as described in the previous chapter. Alternatively, the unconscious roles particular individuals are pulled into may be fairly comfortable for them, as seemed to be the case for Richard and Rodney at Thorne House. In this case, the collusive lattice (Wells 1985), in which each member of a group accepts a tacitly agreed unconscious role, may continue indefinitely, to the serious detriment of the organization's primary task.

Implications for management

At a minimum, each of us must manage ourselves in our various roles. This requires an ongoing awareness of the issues of tasks and boundaries (see Chapter 4) and of authority (see Chapter 5). It also requires awareness of institutional process, and our own particular susceptibility or *valency* to being drawn into certain unconscious roles on behalf of the institution-as-a-whole. Even just recognising that one is being used – has been 'enrolled', so to speak – to perform some unconscious task on behalf of others can be immensely liberating. This understanding also makes one somewhat less vulnerable to institutional processes.

Developing awareness of unconscious process

Transference and countertransference are both useful concepts in helping to make sense of how one is perceived and treated, and also how one feels oneself (see Chapter 1). Paying attention to our feelings, particularly when they are more intense than usual, may tell us when we are reacting to others in ways more determined by our past than by the present.

> Crystal, a charge nurse on Langham Ward, noticed she reacted defensively whenever Claire, the ward sister, criticised her in any way. She would feel anxious, hurt and angry, and would try to justify her actions in great detail, exasperating Claire with lengthy, argumentative explanations of trivial incidents. Crystal knew that Claire liked her and thought well of her work. Indeed, Claire had gone to great lengths to arrange for Crystal, who had worked on Langham Ward as a student, to work there after she qualified, and had supported her rapid promotion. So why, Crystal wondered, was she so defensive and anxious now?
>
> In therapy, Crystal talked a lot about her feelings towards Claire, how special their relationship felt when she was a student, and how upsetting she now found Claire's constant fault-finding. She came to recognise that she was re-experiencing aspects of her relationship with her mother, whose favourite child she had been. Her mother had been a pianist before her marriage, and had been very enthusiastic in supporting her daughter's musical talent. But when Crystal won a major prize and decided to study music professionally, her mother became very critical of her playing, and sceptical about her ability

to make a successful career in music. Her interest and affection seemed to shift to Crystal's younger sister, and Crystal became quite depressed for a period. Finally, she abandoned her musical studies to take up nursing.

Crystal realised that every time Claire criticised her, she reacted just as she had with her mother, feeling the old anxiety about losing her special place in the other's affections. The student role had been an easy, comfortable one, repeating the easy, close relationship she had had with her mother during her early years. However, the more proficient Crystal became, the more frightened she felt of arousing dangerous rivalrous feelings in Claire, and the harder she felt compelled to try to regain Claire's approval. Once she could stand back from her intense and irrational responses to Claire, seeing how they had more to do with the past than with the present, Crystal was able to respond more appropriately to criticisms, learning from some, accepting others as prompted by tension, and asserting herself calmly when the criticism seemed unfair.

Personal therapy can be very helpful in providing access to parts of one's past. As Santayana put it, 'Those who cannot remember the past are condemned to repeat it' (1905). Even without therapy, however, one can work at developing a self-observing stance towards one's reactions, noticing when these seem more intense than the current situation warrants, or when one's emotional state is similar to ways one has felt in earlier significant relationships.

This can help, not only to understand and manage one's own behaviour, but also to understand and manage others more effectively. In the above example, even if Crystal had not changed, Claire might have recognised that Crystal was reacting to her in an overly emotional way, and suspected this was based on transference. She might then have handled Crystal's mistakes differently, or at least not have felt so hurt and exasperated by the changes in her protégée's attitude towards her.

Managing oneself in role

The risk in this way of thinking is that one may use knowledge about transference and countertransference defensively, disregarding every complaint made of one's behaviour on the basis that 'it is their problem, not mine', rather than examining one's own part in the difficulty. To guard against this requires constant monitoring of our own state of mind, and how this is determining our actions. Since we are in a much better position to change our own behaviour than that of others, insight into unconscious processes needs to be used primarily to manage ourselves.

The process is further complicated when projective identification comes into play, and one gets pulled into behaving like the person the other perceives us to be.

Students on a psychodynamically oriented management course complained that the tutors treated them in a harsh, uncaring and disrespectful way. The tutors found this frustrating and hurtful. They continually tried different ways of teaching, but it seemed to them that whatever they did was misinterpreted and distorted. It was puzzling, too, since in their other work contexts, even as tutors on other courses, they were regarded as supportive and helpful. They suspected that the students' perceptions of them were based on their experiences of their managers at work, whom they regularly described in identical terms. Since this was a psychodynamic course, the tutors shared this hypothesis with the students. This proved quite unhelpful; indeed, the students claimed this was but further evidence of the tutors' refusal to attend to their point of view, and of using their knowledge 'to put us down' rather than to be helpful.

Over time, the tutors began to notice they were discussing the students with each other in increasingly disparaging and judgemental tones. Whereas before they had been clear that something 'not me' was being projected, they now found themselves behaving and feeling in the very ways the students described. It was as if they had become the harsh, punitive managers they had been accused of being. At first the tutors rationalised this as a natural reaction to the students' seeming resistance to learning, but as they recognised the intensity of their punitive feelings towards the students, they realised they had become caught up in a process of projective identification. Only after they acknowledged their own part in this process, how they actually *were* being unreasonable in their expectations of the students, did the climate of the course begin to shift in a way that allowed the students to begin learning again.

Here, the tutors were helped to extricate themselves from the roles they had been sucked into by there being two of them, so that they had the benefit of each other's observations. Furthermore, their knowledge of unconscious group processes enabled them to recognise the 'numbing sense of reality', as Bion (1961) puts it, that accompanies taking up a particular role based on others' projections and becoming identified with the projected role. The impetus to reflect on what was happening came not only from the discomfort the role suction (Wells 1985) was causing them, but also from their holding in mind the primary task of the course, the students' learning, which was so obviously being impeded.

Re-framing the presenting problem

Besides personal insight, whether acquired through therapy or otherwise, it is immensely useful for managers and other professionals to have training in understanding group and institutional processes. Ideally, in addition to theoretical input, this should have an experiential component (see Chapter 5) so that they can become attuned to the interplay between their own personal valency for particular unconscious roles, and the institutional process. This can enable them to stand back from demands to sort out problems as expeditiously as possible, in order to identify the underlying issues requiring attention.

However, as institutions typically develop ways of functioning that serve defensive ends, and since institutions of a particular type tend to bring together staff with similar personal valencies, it may be necessary from time to time to get help from someone outside the organization. This may be an institutional consultant, or it may be someone whose role is sufficiently outside the immediate problem situation that they can help restore the capacity to think, which those inside have temporarily lost because they are caught up in the process.

> Roxanne, an educational psychologist, kept getting referrals from Stepside Comprehensive School of boys who were accused of bullying. Each referral appeared sound enough in itself, and each invited her to give an opinion on what to do about the pupil involved. She noticed, however, what a steady stream of bullies were being referred, far more than from any other school in the area, and how few other kinds of referrals Stepside made. This raised for Roxanne the possibility that the referrals might be saying something not only about the children, but also about the school. It might be that the message was, 'We have this problem of bullying, therefore of authority and power, in this school'. The referred boys might be those with the greatest difficulty with these issues, who were being 'used' to deliver this message.
>
> Instead of continuing to assess each boy who was referred, Roxanne suggested meeting with the staff at Stepside to look at what the bullying might be about. What emerged was a serious management problem. The headmaster was perceived as a bully, and in fact was using bullying tactics to manage the staff. Once this came out into the open, and with the help of individual role-consultation to the headmaster as well as consultation to the staff group as a whole to discuss these issues, there was a dramatic reduction in the number of referrals for bullying.

Because Roxanne was an 'outsider', she was able to notice a pattern in the referrals, rather than – as was happening within the school – seeing each incident of bullying as a crisis requiring immediate action. Her awareness of unconscious group processes helped her to intervene in a useful way, by tackling the problem as one belonging to the whole institution rather than to a number of individual trouble-makers. Work with the whole institution to take back its projections and deal with the institutional problem proved beneficial to the staff, the headmaster, the boys referred – and also to Roxanne herself, who was no longer inundated with more referrals than she could deal with.

Conclusion

The management role requires maintaining a position at the boundary between inside and outside (see Chapter 4). This applies both to managing oneself and to managing others. If one is too much inside – caught up in the internal group process or one's own inner world – one is likely to enact what is projected, rather than managing it, as was initially the case with Crystal. If one stands too far back, one is likely to lose touch with the important information the emotional experience can convey, or to use knowledge of group processes defensively. We have described some of the ways institutions use individual members to express fundamental institutional dilemmas, and how awareness of these processes can assist both individuals – who can begin to move out of the unconscious roles they have been locked into – and the institution as a whole to move forward.

16

FINDING A VOICE

Differentiation, representation and empowerment in organizations under threat

James Mosse and Vega Zagier Roberts

In these days of widespread cuts, closures of services, and restructuring of jobs and management systems, many organizations feel under great threat. Often, they request consultation because they want help with managing the disturbances produced by these threats. In other cases, the request is for help with organizational development, such as training or team-building. Yet here, too, exploration often reveals a threat to survival, albeit an internal and unacknowledged one. We shall describe here a particular kind of institutional defence we have encountered repeatedly, which severely impairs an organization's capacity to deal with the threats to its survival.

An external threat

As part of massive financial cuts across the whole education authority, the South Trenton Resource Development and Training Department, an advisory service for South Trenton schools, was about to be disbanded and its staff redeployed. We were asked to design a training day on managing transitions, which might help the staff to cope with their anxiety about the impending changes. To help us prepare for the day, we were sent a mountain of documents; buried in these was a small diagram which showed that the proposed changes were going to affect some of the staff far more than others. No mention had been made of this when we were briefed, and when we asked about it, everyone professed surprise. Meanwhile, the trade unions had been mobilised, and on the day we met with the group, there was an excited fighting mood around. When one person said she did not feel like fighting, she was told they all had to stand united or 'they will pick us off one by one.'

The first exercise of the day consisted of a role-play. Participants were randomly divided into three groups: one to speak as the managers of the education authority, the second as the staff of the training department, and the third as the users of their service. Each group was to prepare a statement to present to the other two groups.[1]

The 'users' group was very energetic in criticising the service, saying they had never been clear what it was for, and that they foresaw no great loss to the schools if it were to close. Up to this point, the value of the service had been treated as a given, the identified problem being that 'they' were not caring enough to appreciate its importance to the schools. That the 'users' could express their scepticism so quickly suggested to us that anxiety about whether the department really achieved anything had been near the surface, but not acknowledged openly and hence not dealt with.

The second part of the day was designed to start a process which might enable them to respond more effectively to their situation. We asked each of the four teams within the department to prepare a proposal for alternative ways of cutting the budget of the service, and to select a representative to meet with the representatives of the other groups to prepare a joint proposal to the external management. This exercise became chaotic when whole groups insisted on attending the representatives' meeting, either because they had failed to select a representative, or could not trust one to work on their behalf at a distance. This made negotiation impossible, both internally and with the external management.

Here we see the interplay of internal and external threat. The depressive anxieties (see Chapter 1) about the usefulness of their work pre-dated the crisis for which consultation was requested, but had been suppressed: the cuts proposed by management may well have felt unconsciously like 'just deserts'. In defence, any blame of themselves or each other had been projected into the managers. This kind of shift, from feeling guilty to feeling persecuted, that is, from depressive to paranoid anxieties, makes it very hard for a group to think and act effectively. The pressure to band together and to blame problems on outside enemies was exacerbated in this case by the covert awareness that the proposed re-deployment would affect some of the staff far more than others. Indeed, all internal differences within the group had to be denied. This made it impossible to empower anyone to act or speak on behalf of the group.

The objectives of the consultation were two-fold. First, the group needed to begin to 'own' both the doubts about the usefulness of the service, and the need for financial cuts, rather than experiencing these as attacks from outside. In other words, they needed to face reality, to shift from basic assumption mentality (see Chapter 3), with its focus on personal and group survival, to work-group mentality, with its focus on the primary task, self-evaluation and survival of the organization in the outside world. The second objective was to help them begin to differentiate internally, so they could empower some of their members to negotiate on their behalf: to find a voice which stood some chance of being heard.

Away-days in times of crisis

Away-days have gained much currency over recent years, and have characteristics affecting both design and outcome. At the conscious, rational level, the 'away' component is about removing participants from their everyday work setting with all its impingements, creating a space for reflection, debate and new thinking. However, the return to the office the next day is also a movement away – this time from the setting where the newness or learning took place, making it possible to leave these behind. If external consultants are invited to facilitate the away-day, the bounded timeframe of the contract means they will play no part in the process of implementing the away-experiences in the natural setting. They, and their ideas, can be used or forgotten according to the unconscious needs of the group.

In our experience, such away-days are often planned at times of crisis, whether acknowledged or not, with the participants having become locked into a particular stance in relation to the crisis. Some groups manifest a strong us-and-them polarization, 'fighting from the trenches' where they have dug themselves into defensive positions. Others are more obviously immobilised, waiting passively for the axe to fall. Typically, a fog of supposition and speculation replaces facts, which are neither sought nor recognised when available. The group seems to be paralysed by fear that any differences among the members will lead to fragmentation, or to sapping energy needed to resist the 'real' enemy.

In order to enable participants to shift out of the defensive positions into which they have become locked, we often use designs which contain an element of play, replacing the pressure to find immediate solutions with an invitation to 'play with ideas'. However, we set a real-enough task: not so real as to evoke the same degree of anxiety as the actual back-home situation, but resembling it closely enough for participants to have real investment in the outcome, rather than dismissing it as just a game of make-believe. The design usually includes an element of taking up roles different from members' everyday roles, both to encourage a shift in perspective, and because this requires participants to differentiate. Furthermore, the design includes some negotiation between sub-groups; this offers an immediate here-and-now experience of how difficult this is, and also a dramatic demonstration of how high the cost is of failure to differentiate roles sufficiently. Similarly, the disastrous consequences of excessive investment in consensus management and of inadequate delegation of power and authority are highlighted.

The whole design is intended to support a process of easy transition back and forth between playful as-if-ness and participants' back-home working reality. At its most successful, the day not only enables participants to begin to plan how to negotiate more effectively with other parts of their institutional system, and thus to better manage the external threat facing them, but also decreases the previous regressive pull towards differentiation, so that individuals can engage in internal debate.

An internal threat

The Felham Internal Counselling and Support Programme (FICS) had been established by the Felham Health Authority to provide practical and psychological help to any of its employees who might need it. Initially, FICS had a team of six counsellors, offering individual counselling sessions at the FICS offices. Later, a new project, staffed by a team of five experienced group workers, was set up to offer consultation to staff groups complaining of stress. FICS staff had always had an annual away-day for development and training. For one such day, we were asked to design some team-building exercises to help integrate the two parts of the service.

We began by asking each team to list issues which were affecting the development of FICS. In the course of this discussion, we discovered that the group-work team had been set up as a one-year pilot project, which was unlikely to be renewed in six months' time because of cuts in funding. Having completed their lists, each group was asked to prepare a proposal for a training event to address the issues they had just identified. They were then to meet with the other group to negotiate a joint proposal for their next away-day.

The group workers worked hard on the task we had set, while the counsellors spent most of their time arguing among themselves about whether or not they were obliged to do it. When the time came to negotiate a joint proposal, they brought only some vague, last-minute ideas. The other group's carefully worked-out plan caused them some surprise and embarrassment, but it was not debated. At the end of the day, it remained posted on the wall, unamended, neither accepted nor rejected.

By proposing nothing, the counsellors avoided the task of negotiation, since there was nothing to negotiate. The group workers had put great effort into their proposal, despite the fact that they would almost certainly no longer be working at FICS by the time the next away-day took place. Having complied with the task, they had no further interest in their proposal, and left it on the wall to be removed by the cleaners. Thus, they too avoided negotiating with the other group. Our hypothesis was that acknowledging differences within the total staff group was intolerable, because of anxieties about guilt and envy in relation to the imminent demise of the pilot project. This significant event had not even been mentioned to us when we were briefed, and its importance continued to be played down throughout the day.

In our closing meeting with them, we pointed out that the issues they had listed in the morning were different for the two teams, and that some of them might be tackled more effectively if the teams worked separately, rather than hoping that their difficulties would disappear if only they all worked together. The evidence had been that when they tried to work together, the need to avoid acknowledging even the most obvious differences within the group made negotiation and debate impossible. Instead, anything either team came up with had to be forgotten or ignored to preserve unity.

The problem of differentiation

FICS was facing a similar situation to the one at South Trenton, namely, that it was about to be broken up and many of its staff re-deployed. Why had nothing been said to us about this when we were briefed? Why had we been invited to do team-building with a team that would soon no longer exist? Underlying the apparent differences in the situations of FICS and South Trenton, there were fundamental similarities. In both organizations, there was an external threat affecting some staff more than others. It was this, particularly, that could not be faced: both groups denied their internal differences. Both had invited consultants to help them bond even more closely together; in effect, to collude with their defensive dedifferentiation. In both cases, the denial of differences and avoidance of expressing clear views – which might conflict – prevented their negotiating ways to affect their future.

Threats to survival produce extreme anxiety. One of the commonest defences in groups under threat is to try to strengthen the emotional ties which bind them together. This includes denying any differences which could contribute to the dismemberment of the group. It is at such times that one is most likely to find groups under the sway of basic assumptions (see Chapter 3). South Trenton used basic assumption fight, demanding that its members join together to fight the enemy. FICS used basic assumption dependency, one team in a compliant way, the other by debating whether or not to depose us. Both looked to the consultants to provide basic assumption leadership by supporting their defensive dedifferentiation, and were very hostile to our efforts to identify differences, or even to name external realities that everyone was aware of but had 'agreed' not to voice. However, the inability to acknowledge and debate internal differences makes it impossible for a group to do effective work. The next example further illustrates this:

Argyll House, a day centre for people with physical disabilities, had been working for some time with a small number of very dependent clients, who were grateful for any help offered them. The premises had just been enlarged in preparation for the centre taking on much larger numbers of people with less severe disabilities. The staff anticipated these new clients would be far more articulate, demanding and aggressive. Their request for consultation was framed in terms of shared anxieties, resistance to change, and difficulties in planning how to set up the new programme.

At our first meeting, it became clear that this was misleading. Some of them had found the old work tedious and were very much looking forward to more active and varied work in which they could mobilise skills for which there had been no scope before. Others were anxious both about the loss of the intimacy and predictability of the old work, and about lacking the skills that the new work was likely to require. In the meantime, they had been unable to plan their services for the new clients, who were due to arrive shortly. Ideas would be put forward tentatively, and quickly dropped when alternative suggestions were made.

One of the first interventions I made was to ask the staff to work in pairs to prepare lists of the aims of Argyll House and of the activities they thought they should be engaged in with the different kinds of client, and then to order each list in terms of priority, or the amount of time to be allocated to each item.[2] There was almost total match across the lists in terms of what was included, but extreme disagreement about the relative importance given to each item. I then asked them to produce a joint list before our next meeting: these would form the basis for their new operational policy.

Unacknowledged disagreements about priorities and about how the work was to be carried out had paralysed the team from making any decisions about the new shape of the service. Since neither consensus nor debate had been possible while the team felt so anxious about the potentially fragmenting impact of the new work, they had been unable to move forward. Now they were able to begin re-writing their operational policy. However, when they reviewed it six months later, they recognised it had troublesome shortcomings because many items had been worded too vaguely to be of guidance. This ambiguity resulted from their unconscious need to blur differences in the group. Instead of overt conflict, there was muffled antagonism in the team, which occasionally erupted in the form of personal criticism rather than as debate about the work itself. When the contentious items were more clearly defined, two team members who disagreed with what had been decided began to look for jobs elsewhere. This was initially perceived as evidence of catastrophic failure, as if it should have been possible to find a way to satisfy everyone. However, having clearly stated aims, values and policies made it possible to recruit staff who had a fairly accurate picture of what sort of organization they were joining, and of what would be expected of them. Instead of covertly sabotaging the work to move the group in one direction or another, team members were freed to manage their own work in relation to the agreed boundaries.

In groups under threat, the unconscious pressures on members to blur differences can be enormous – as if safety lies only in oneness. New members are required to make a tacit pledge to defend the group from any disagreement, lest this make the group vulnerable to attack from the dangerous world outside. Even the capacity to notice when something is wrong has to be suppressed. The price of belonging is the submerging of individuality, and is often experienced by members as oppressive, although they cannot locate the source of oppression.

One newly arrived member pointed out how much time was lost in meetings due to people arriving late. Two weeks later, although she still arrived on time herself, she no longer seemed to feel any of her earlier annoyance. When I remarked on this, she looked blank, leaving me feeling I was either mistaken or extremely tasteless to have recalled the matter. Similar blankness greeted my commenting that the black workers never participated in group discussions, or that team members received different pay and had different statutory obligations and different levels of expertise. When I persisted in these observations, the group would become quite hostile towards me; as soon as I stopped, the atmosphere would immediately become amicable again.

Gustafson (1976) has called this kind of group 'pseudo-mutual': roles are blurred, vague terms like 'helping' are popular, everyone must be 'equal' and 'equal' means identical. Everyone tends to behave in a friendly and helpful way. If anyone questions anything, this is likely to be met first by concern and offers of help, and later by hurt surprise at the unnecessary unpleasantness. The misguided member usually quickly relapses into anonymity. If they do not, they are likely to be extruded from the group with considerable, albeit masked, aggression. Under the guise of friendliness, there is actually a great deal of oppression.

Effective work requires differentiation: defining a clear task (see Chapter 4) and allocating work according to skills and resources. The pseudo-mutual group, instead of being held together by the work-based bond of a shared aim, is held together by a kind of 'glue' of identification. The group cannot bear separateness, ambivalence, imperfection and other sources of depressive anxieties, nor risk the emergence of envy and rivalry. Hence, there is no room for healthy competitiveness or genuine mutuality, only for friends and foes.

The problem of representation

A corollary of being unable to differentiate internally is that it becomes impossible to empower anyone to speak or act on behalf of the group, since this implies their taking up a differentiated role. Consequently, negotiation with outsiders is impossible. It may be possible to have a spokesperson, but only to transmit a prepared message, since the group cannot delegate sufficient authority to anyone to engage in dialogue with others on their behalf.

In addition, there may be an unconscious need to make sure that negotiations do not succeed, since the more dangerous the outside world is demonstrated to be, the more likely the group is to maintain the solidarity it regards as indispensable to survival.

An employees' committee was set up at Shane Hospital as a vehicle for staff to express their grievances to the management. Each department was asked to send a representative of their own choosing. In almost all cases, since no one volunteered, the most junior member of the department became its representative. The committee was derided as window-dressing, and attending meetings was regarded as a pointless chore. Exploration of why the departments chose those least likely to be listened to suggested that there was unconscious investment across the hospital in proving that the invitation from management to set up the committee was not based on a genuine intention to take grievances seriously. When the nature of the relationship between the employees' committee and the management was debated and formalised, departments began to select more senior representatives, and the committee became an effective system for intergroup negotiation.

Effective representation requires thought about who is best able to take up the role of representative, based on explicit criteria such as being articulate, diplomatic or senior enough to be taken seriously by the other people involved in the negotiation. It also requires that groups delegate sufficient authority to representatives to enable them to pursue the task entrusted to them (see Chapter 17). This means being able to trust the representing member to act responsibly on their behalf. Yet often representatives are selected in an apparently random way. This serves to avoid both rivalrous feelings towards the person chosen and anxieties about differentiating a role, ensuring that nothing significant will happen. We have already seen how pseudo-mutuality at Argyll House led to suppressing individuation. Not surprisingly, this team also was unable to let anyone do work on its behalf.

> Whenever someone introduced a new idea at Argyll House, a working party would be set up to go away and think about it. Ostensibly, its task was to come up with a concrete proposal for implementing the idea, which the team as a whole would then consider. However, the invariable experience of these working parties was that when they brought back their plan, no one showed any interest in it, and the project died. With it, each time, died a bit more of the enthusiasm and commitment to the team of the individuals who had been involved in the working party, especially of the person who had first had the idea. Over time there were fewer and fewer individual initiatives, since their fate was so predictable.

In this case there was an apparent delegation of authority, a mandate to gather information and make a proposal. The outcome suggested that the creation of the working party was a way of getting rid of ideas, rather than of exploring them. A contributing factor was the membership of the working parties; since this was determined by who volunteered, only those committed to the idea were involved. Those opposing it could then kill it off by disregarding the proposal, without ever having to voice their objections explicitly, just as happened at the away-day with FICS (see p. 161). The whole process served not to develop the service, but to remove contentious topics which might otherwise have threatened group unity.

Conclusion: who needs to say what to whom?

Threats to survival stir up primitive anxieties about annihilation and fragmentation. Very often, the response is to withdraw from reality, which seriously compromises the capacity for problem-solving. Some threats come from outside, as when an organization is at risk of closure or of being taken over. Others come from within, in the form of threats to self-esteem or to group cohesiveness. Very often there is an interplay of these different kinds of threats.

The question 'Who needs to say what to whom?' is often a useful prelude to planning how to manage the threat facing a group or organization. The 'what' part of the question needs to be tackled first, since in any danger situation it is essential first of all to recognise what the danger is. The question 'Who needs to say what to whom?' is often a useful prelude to planning how to manage the threat facing a group or organization. The 'what' part of the question needs to be tackled first, since in any danger situation it is essential first of all to recognise what the danger is. Sometimes the stated challenge may be used to defend against facing a more fundamental threat that at some level everyone knows but no one dares to name. For example, the presenting issue in the work with the South Trenton service obscured a fear lurking just under the surface that their work was not relevant to their clients, while at Felham the presenting challenge of integration 'hid' the reality that one of the teams was about to be cut. Only when a state of mind has been reached where people can name the danger can they begin to think about what might be done about it.

The nature of the threat helps to answer the 'to whom' part of the question. For example, the external threat of funding cuts at South Trenton required negotiating with people outside the department, perhaps about alternative ways to achieve the necessary financial savings. Internal threats, such as the staff's anxieties about the usefulness of their work, on the other hand, needed to be discussed within the group. In many cases, this means bringing unspoken disagreements out into the open, and the group may well learn things which they would prefer not to know. Furthermore, internal debate involves relinquishing the fantasy that everyone will be pleased with the outcome. Usually there *are* winners and losers, but unless the group can bear this, everyone will lose (which may be psychologically less unbearable). It is crucial to have the right fight with the right people, so to speak; otherwise the fight will be displaced in ways that undermine the task.

Finally, having determined what needs to be said to whom, there remains the question of who will say it. Unless individuals can be empowered to speak, whether on their own behalf or on behalf of the group, the threatening conditions are unlikely to change. Denying the reality of internal differences is disempowering: neither internal nor external negotiation is then possible. In many cases, even the capacity to think will be lost. Yet now, more than ever, it is imperative to retain the capacity to think and act effectively under threat. If anxiety can be contained, then what needs to be talked about can be named, and some effectiveness recovered. Sometimes the threat itself can be overcome. Even when this does not happen, it is possible to regain some inner sense of having the power to affect one's own experience, rather than being a silenced victim.

Notes

1 We would like to thank Eric Milter for the design of this exercise.
2 Where vignettes describe situations involving only one of the authors, we have used 'I' to avoid cumbersome alternatives.

17

CONFLICT AND COLLABORATION

Managing intergroup relations

Vega Zagier Roberts

Throughout the human services, complex tasks require that members of different groups – whether departments within a single organization, or different agencies dealing with the same clients – work together. There is much talk about the need for better coordination, for collaboration, for teamwork. Yet services continue to be fragmented, intergroup rivalry and conflict are rife, and attempts to address these difficulties are met more often with frustration and failure than with success.

Interagency relations

As services for people with severe and long-term physical, mental or emotional difficulties and other high-need clients have increasingly moved out of the large institutions and into the community, the various activities needed for their care have been taken up by different agencies. Thus, an individual may be involved with his or her doctor, the local community psychiatric nurse team, a social services day centre, the housing department, a voluntary sector social club and a host of other helping professionals. Each agency deals with its own 'bit' of the client, and new problems are likely to lead to further referrals to yet other agencies.

Without coordination, gaps and/or overlap in services are likely to occur. As the client passes from one agency to another, each can blame the others for any difficulties.

> New Start was a voluntary sector organization set up as an alternative way of meeting the multiple needs of people leaving long-stay psychiatric hospitals to live in the community. Its aim was to provide the whole range of support services from within one team. Its members were surprised to get very few referrals directly from the local psychiatric hospital; instead, most of the referrals came from the housing department, which wanted help in reducing the

high rate of breakdown and emergency re-admission to hospital among the people they placed in bed-and-breakfast accommodation. However, the New Start team were turning down nearly two-thirds of the referrals from housing as not meeting their carefully thought-out criteria for which kinds of clients they felt able to take on. Each time they turned one down, they re-stated these criteria, complaining among themselves that, yet again, statutory agencies were disorganized and trying to use New Start as a dumping ground.

The housing department placement team suggested the two agencies do joint assessments of patients about to leave hospital, in order to determine who was most suitable for available accommodation. The New Start team refused, saying this was not their job. Meanwhile, patients referred to and placed by the housing department continued to break down and return to hospital in large numbers; referrals from housing to New Start were being turned down; and there were hardly any referrals from the hospital to New Start.

I had been asked to consult to the New Start team to assist them in developing their service. As we began discussing their aims, team members talked about their shared view of statutory agencies as being paternalistic and condescending towards clients, abusing their power and fostering helplessness. They were deeply committed to empowering their clients and to fighting abusive practices on their behalf. As a new and small organization, they felt vulnerable to being exploited by the larger and more powerful agencies, as did their clients, with whom they identified consciously and unconsciously.

They were also anxious to prove they were capable of supporting their clients effectively. To this end, they had evolved their criteria and defined their role as picking up where the others left off. They were very worried about those people who were 'getting lost' – the potential clients who were not being referred to them by the hospital and other community agencies – but were ambivalent about pursuing these lest they be overwhelmed by demands they could not meet.

Their refusal to participate in joint assessments could now be understood as having several sources. The most conscious was a fear of being exploited, which led to their holding firmly to the boundaries they had set on their task. Less conscious was anxiety about having power over clients if they got involved in making decisions for them, when they saw their role as protecting clients from others' abuse of power. Finally, there was anxiety about feeling more responsibility for clients' breakdown. Although they felt uncomfortable about the referrals they were turning down, as well as about the ones they were not getting, they could argue the blame did not lie with them. By disavowing power and locating it elsewhere, they reduced their guilt and sense of responsibility, but at the cost of feeling more helpless and vulnerable than was necessary.

Over time, the New Start team came to see that the problem of clients' successful transition from the psychiatric hospital into the community was one shared by all three agencies, and took the initiative in setting up what proved to be a very successful joint assessment scheme to replace the former sequential model of interagency referral.

Interdepartmental relations

The example on the previous page illustrates some of the problems which arise when different agencies are working with the same clients. Similar processes occur within a single organization where different departments are contributing to the overall task. For example, in a hospital, a number of departments – medical, nursing, housekeeping, volunteer services and others – are likely to be contributing to the well-being of the patients, but often with little coordination.

> The rivalry, conflict and mutual disparagement between nursing and the other departments at Shady Glen have already been described with regard to the need to define a task which was both meaningful and feasible, and to which staff from all departments could feel committed (see Chapter 11). The consultation, initially offered separately to nurses and non-nurses, eventually brought the two groups together into a joint working party, to prepare a proposal for improving patients' quality of life. This proposal contained many ideas for changes in working practices, but a central recommendation was to alter the boundaries of the task-systems.
>
> Originally, nurses of all grades, including students, were based full-time on a particular ward; everyone else was firmly based in their respective departments, visiting the wards or removing patients from them to provide their particular input. For instance, occupational therapists (OTs) ran cooking and art groups in the occupational therapy department, and waited there for patients to be brought from the ward. When the ward was short-staffed, there was often no one available to escort the patients to their groups, and patients would therefore not arrive that day. The OTs also ran current events and reality-orientation groups on the wards. Very often, they would arrive to find none of the patients ready, as they were still being bathed and toileted. After waiting for a while, the therapist would leave, angry at her efforts being sabotaged by the nurses. Physiotherapists and speech therapists encountered similar problems. The nurses, meanwhile, felt resentful that they were left to do all the heavy physical work of lifting and moving patients to clean and dress them while the OTs could 'swan in and out'.
>
> Our recommendation was to enlarge the boundary of the ward team to include everyone contributing directly to the re-defined primary task. This had the effect of reducing rivalry, conflict and unconscious sabotage of each other's work across departments. It also made possible some creative rethinking about how various activities related to the overall task. For instance, when an OT arrived to lead her current events discussion group but found that what was most urgently needed was another pair of hands to

help with toileting bed-bound patients, she could help out with this 'nursing' task. This might then free some nurses to join the group activity, rather than cancelling it because they were 'too busy'. Finally, patients' failure to improve was now a shared problem, rather than something to be blamed on someone else.

Intergroup relations in multidisciplinary teams

At Shady Glen, the glaring drawbacks of splitting up patient care among different departments led to our proposing a new task-system which would bring staff from all disciplines together. However, in many wards, day centres and community healthcare settings, such a system already exists: the multidisciplinary team. The hope is that these teams will plan and provide an effective coordinated service, since they have all the specialist skills needed under one roof. Instead, they often duplicate the same interdisciplinary fights and rivalry, or fail to coordinate their various activities, as described previously. Other teams, determined not to repeat these mistakes, encounter a new set of problems.

> Bradley Lane, a community mental health centre staffed by a multidisciplinary team, had been plagued for years by bitter splits and fights between the various professional groups. The psychologists, psychiatrists and social workers spent most of their time offering individual counselling and therapy to the centre's least-disabled patients. Nurses and occupational therapists ran group activities for the more chronic patients, and often resented being allocated this 'low-status' work.
>
> This changed when the newly created post of team manager was filled by an enthusiastic young psychiatric nurse, Anna. Anna had been working in a therapeutic community and brought with her an inspiring conviction of the value of team cohesiveness. Over the next few months, the team spent a great deal of time reviewing their working practices, including two days of team-building with an external consultant. On the basis of this, they decided to work genetically: all of the centre's activities would be shared across all the disciplines. Clients would be assessed by the whole team and then assigned to whomever had a vacancy, regardless of their particular profession. The groups offered to patients gradually shifted towards an emphasis on insight and change, rather than on training in social skills.
>
> At an annual review, the team psychologist noted there was a gap in their service, in that clients with full-time jobs found it difficult to attend any of the available treatment programmes, and suggested that an evening therapy group might be useful. As she could not run such a group herself because of family commitments, one of the nurses, Sharon, offered to do it. She spent many weeks planning and publicising the group, with help from colleagues. When Sharon went to her line manager in the nursing department to ask

for time off during the day in lieu of working one evening each week, he refused, saying the nurses' priority should be to expand the day programme for the most chronic patients; therapy should be offered either by psychologists or by social workers.

The whole team was shocked and outraged at having their plan overturned. After a burst of protest, including a letter to a more senior manager which had no effect, there was a steep decline in morale and three people left the team soon after. Even a full year later, they were still refusing to initiate any new projects on the basis that 'they won't let us do anything anyway'.

Intergroup collaboration

The word 'collaboration' is often used interchangeably with 'cooperation', to denote harmonious working together. In this chapter, however, it refers to the particular situation where a group of people come to work together *because of* their membership in other groups or institutions whose tasks overlap. For example, staff from New Start, the local psychiatric hospital and the housing department had been assessing many of the same clients separately and sequentially. Through forming a joint assessment team, they were able to carry out this task more effectively. At Shady Glen, members of previously competing departments came together in an enlarged ward team in order to provide a better service to their patients. At Bradley Lane, an intergroup system was already in place: the multidisciplinary team.

In Figure 17.1, the outer boxes represent the original or 'home' groups – the different agencies, departments or disciplines – and the inner box represents the intergroup system or 'collaborative' group.[1] The overlapping boundaries indicate that members of the collaborative group continue to be members of their home groups, which are task-systems in their own right for activities which do not require intergroup collaboration.

The problem of dual membership

Every member of a group is likely to be also a member of other groups. These may be outside groups – trade union, church, family – or sub-groups within a team, such as the old-timers and newcomers, or men and women. To this extent, every group is actually an intergroup, with intergroup relations which need to be managed. Each group membership carries a greater or lesser degree of *sentience* or emotional significance (Miller and Rice 1967). From this stem loyalty and commitment to the group's aims. Inevitably, individuals with membership in more than one group will sometimes have trouble with conflicting demands from the various groups they belong to, and their dominant group sentience may shift over time.

Most such multiple memberships are incidental as far as the work group is concerned. The teacher who is a member of the Labour Party, the nurse who is

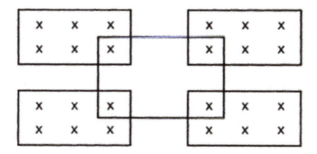

FIGURE 17.1   An intergroup system

a Catholic, the social worker who is a mother, all bring with them these other memberships, which affect how they do their jobs; but when they leave their jobs, they will be replaced by others with different affiliations. In other situations, one's membership in another group is part of the reason for being selected for a post: a team may wish to have a certain number of staff from ethnic minorities, or of women, or of residential social workers, in order to carry out its task better. Finally, there are situations where the home group membership is the main reason for being included in the collaborative group. For example, in the joint assessment team set up by New Start, each member was there as a representative of his or her home agency. Many committees, such as joint planning committees, are representatives' groups, made up of people sent to protect the home agency's interests, as well as to contribute to the joint project. In this case, it becomes crucial, both for the individual and for the group, to manage this dual membership.

When a new collaborative group first comes together, its members are likely to identify themselves predominantly in terms of their home agencies. This may well make it very difficult for the collaborative group to work effectively. Members with loyalty to different home groups are likely to be competitive, and the collaborative group may fragment into fighting factions. Often, however, members gradually invest more and more in the collaborative group over a period of time, as its task takes on meaning and importance. The group builds up a shared value-system, as well as personal relationships among members. As their sentience shifts, they may become more committed to the aims of the collaborative group than to those of their home groups, even to the extent of 'forgetting' their original membership. This is particularly likely to happen when the collaborative work is done outside or away from the home group, or when workers spend much more time in the collaborative group than in the home group (see Figure 17.2). Here, the collaborative group has become quasi-autonomous, a closed system whose members have lost touch with their dual membership and its linking function, on which their effectiveness depends.

For instance, in the case of Bradley Lane, if Sharon had held in mind that she was part of the nursing department, as well as of the multidisciplinary team at the centre, she might have kept her manager more in touch with her plans for an

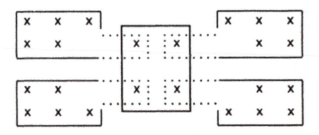

FIGURE 17.2 Changing sentience in an intergroup system

evening group, and even have gained his support. Alternatively, she might have been more aware of the nursing department's priorities and view of the nurse's role, and therefore not have put herself forward to run the group. The idea might then have been taken on successfully by another team member, whose department regarded it as an appropriate use of their time.

It was, of course, not only Sharon who failed to hold her dual membership in mind. The whole team was anxious to maintain their hard-won cohesiveness, hence the decision to work genetically. In the process, they had obliterated differences in skills, training and experience among members, as well as 'forgetting' their home group membership. One obvious cost was the damage caused by the 'veto' – damage to team morale, and the loss to the clients who might have benefited from an evening group. There was also a chronic 'running cost' in that the denial of differences disabled individual members from using their special skills – even the very ones for which they were hired – lest they arouse envy and re-kindle the old competitiveness and fights. Anything which could not be done equally well by everyone could not be done by anyone. The team – and their clients – were deprived of the richness of specialised contributions to the overall task, and individual staff members lost a major source of job satisfaction.

The effectiveness of collaborative groups depends largely on their members' ability to manage their dual memberships. Excessive commitment to either membership at the expense of the other will inevitably compromise task performance, and lead to problematic intergroup relations.

The problem of dual management

Often, collaborative groups have no formal management. The members are managed from their home-groups and come together as 'equals', that is, with no one within the group having authority over anyone else. Thus, when Bradley Lane opened, there was no manager of the centre, only a 'co-ordinator' to order supplies and plan rotas; staff were managed from their respective departments. This contributed to the difficulty resolving disagreements in the team, since it was up to individuals (and their department managers) whether or not they abided by any decisions the team made. Concurrently with the team-building work, the health

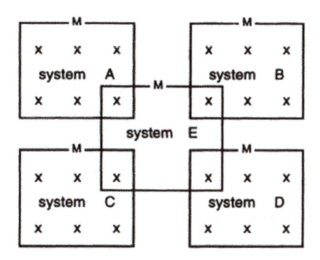

FIGURE 17.3   Dual management in intergroup systems

authority was restructured, and as part of this a team manager post was created at the centre. Each member then had two line managers. This is often the case in collaborative groups (see system E in Figure 17.3).

Where task-systems have overlapping boundaries, and their members are part of two management systems, the question of who is managing what – where authority is located – can become critical. Many collaborative enterprises founder because this question is not adequately addressed. For example, at Bradley Lane, the team assumed they had sufficient authority to decide to run an evening group and to decide among themselves who would do it. This proved not to be the case. But the nurse manager's refusing permission to a nurse was taken as a veto of the whole plan, which was abandoned without any consideration of the possibility that someone from another discipline might take on the project. Everyone felt equally injured by the decision, which might otherwise have been a blow only to Sharon. The situation was further complicated by the ambiguity about the nurse manager's authority. Was his refusal based only on priorities within the nursing department, or was it a message from senior management levels about what the team's priorities should be? This was never clarified, and contributed to the shared fantasy in the team that 'they won't let us do anything anyway'. With this, they projected all their authority, and lapsed into resentful apathy.

Similar difficulties arose at Shady Glen. The proposed new ward team boundary, which included staff from other disciplines, needed to be managed by someone with sufficient authority to make decisions about patient care. The most obvious person to take on this management role was the ward sister. Previously, all non-nurses had been managed from their own department; for the enlarged ward team to be managed as a system, some of the authority previously located in these departments would have to be relinquished to the most senior nurse on the ward.

This did not happen. While our report was still being discussed among senior managers, the specialist therapists became more involved on the ward, as described previously, and attended ward meetings, where some innovative ideas about changing working practices and personalising the patients' living space were developed. In the end, however, the necessary authority was not delegated to the ward sister, and as a result, fundamental change to the continuing-care system as a whole – and to the patients' and staff's quality of life – did not take place. The failure to implement the report came as a devastating disappointment to the therapists. The nurses' response was more along the lines of, 'Well, what do you expect?' – the beginning of a move back to the old splits along the fault-lines between the different disciplines.

Successful collaboration

Of the three collaborative groups described in this chapter, the most successful was the joint assessment team convened by New Start. Its task was the most circumscribed of the three, and could readily be seen to be in the interests of each of the home agencies, as well as of the clients. Furthermore, its work represented a relatively small proportion of the total work of its members, so that managing dual membership was not as difficult as in the other two examples. Furthermore, delegating sufficient authority to the collaborative system did not pose a threat to the home groups. All three agencies were needed for the task, and each had a specific contribution to make. Management of the intergroup system also proved fairly straightforward. Since the joint assessment team met to discuss how to plan for clients *before* they were discharged from hospital, the clients were at that point still the responsibility of the hospital. The meetings therefore took place there, so that the staff from New Start and the housing department could meet with patients before discussing them. The meetings were chaired by whichever nurse knew most about the patient's current situation and past history. In summary:

- The task of the collaborative group was clear and feasible.
- It did not conflict with the aims and priorities of the home groups.
- It was important enough to its members for them to invest sufficient commitment to do the work.
- It was important enough to the home groups involved for them to allocate sufficient resources (mainly staff time) and delegate sufficient authority to the collaborative group for the task in hand.
- Membership of the collaborative group related to its task, so that each person felt that he or she had and was seen to have a specific and needed contribution to make.
- The group created a management system based on what was needed to achieve the joint task.

To put it another way, the group and intergroup relations could be managed because there was sufficient sanctioning of authority, both from within the group ('below') and from outside ('above') (see Chapter 4). These are essential conditions for successful collaboration, and one or more was missing in the other cases described.

Conclusion

Working well together – whether between individuals or across groups and organiations – is generally considered a good thing and, as such, to be pursued without question. Yet before effective systems for working together can be set up or adequately managed, there are basic questions which need to be asked. The first is whether there is a task which requires collaboration. If so, who needs to work with whom in order to carry out this task? And finally, what authority will they need to have, and how (and by whom) are they to be managed? Without adequate attention to these questions, there is every likelihood either of too much togetherness or too little. Too much can give rise to numerous large meetings which feel pointless but take up a lot of time; or to the pursuit of 'cohesiveness' at the expense of individual initiative and the on-task exercise of specific competencies. Too little can result in insufficient co-ordination of related activities, and chronic strife. On the other hand, well-managed intergroup relations, including relations among sub-groups within a single team, can do much to improve both morale and effectiveness in the human services.

Note

1 The figures in this chapter are adapted from Miller and Rice (1967).

18

MANAGING SOCIAL ANXIETIES IN PUBLIC SECTOR ORGANIZATIONS

Anton Obholzer

When this chapter was first published, the dominant explanation for what ailed our public services (or public sector organizations) had to do with management: that financial criteria were not been adhered to, that workers had too much power, that working practices were outmoded, that we were not as successful a country as we might be. The implication was that we were too soft, that we needed firmer management based on sound economic principles, and that we needed less consultation and more action.

The response was a drive towards greater efficiency and tighter governance through targets and monitoring, cuts, restructuring and privatisation. While some of this has doubtless been useful, 'firmer management' has not been as successful as was anticipated. Public sector workers reel under the demands for paperwork to demonstrate they are doing what they are required to do, but without necessarily feeling this is resulting in better services, and the media highlights the failures of our public institutions on a daily basis.

Clearly, the growing gap between what citizens expect and workers want to provide on the one hand, and what is actually delivered on the other, has multiple and complex causes, including huge economic, political, demographic and social changes. But some things have not changed, notably, the core anxieties we face as human beings and how we unconsciously look to our public sector institutions to manage these on our behalf.

As a psychoanalyst, manager, and consultant to institutions, I am often struck by the parallel between human psychic processes and institutional processes. In individuals, it is a recipe for disaster to ignore the underlying difficulties, be they personal, marital or familial. Managing them by denying and repressing them invariably leads to further difficulties and disturbances. To avoid the underlying difficulties in institutions and to try to 'manage' them away has similar consequences. Awareness of underlying anxieties and fantasies enables us to manage ourselves and our systems in such a way as to make improved use of resources, both psychological and physical. It follows that neglecting to do so results in disproportionately heavy wear and tear of both human and physical resources.

Management, structure and organization are not unimportant – in fact, they are vital. Nor is the emphasis on money inappropriate: financial constraint is a reality. However, often little or no attention is paid to social, group and psychological phenomena. Consequently, by neglect, the factors that should be an integral part of good management become the very factors that undermine the venture.

As an example, it is common knowledge that any group numbering more than about 12 individuals is ineffective as a work group, incapable of useful debate and effective decision-making. Yet a great many committees are made up of many more than 12 people. One assumption might be that their purpose is not one of decision-making, but ornamental. An alternative postulate would be ignorance that it is not known that groups of a certain size have certain dynamics, and are only capable of certain tasks and not of others. If so, it confirms the lack of group-dynamics knowledge in management. A third possibility is that such groups are unconsciously set up this way to ensure work does not get done, an anti-task phenomenon (see Chapter 4).

Besides group size, other factors necessary for groups to be effective include clarity of task, time boundaries and authority structures. And yet it is quite common to receive the agenda for a so-called work group too late for it to be of any use in preparing oneself, for meetings not to start on time, and not to be clearly chaired. Not only are groups frequently too large for work, but it is also common for their membership to be so inconsistent as to make work impossible: if one representative cannot come, another is sent instead. Eventually it reaches a stage where individuals come and go and no one is sure who people are or what they represent. This makes for great difficulty in maintaining an ongoing strand of work. It is possible to see why representative groups have got a bad name: the conclusion can easily be that representation and consultation do not work. The problem, however, is with numbers and structure, not with the process of consultation; it is to do with how the group is constituted and how it is managed.

Often the response to these perceived inefficiencies is 'tighter' management and control, often involving restructuring. The previous systems of public sector management are understandably written off, but the new structures seem to be based on a lack of understanding of what went wrong in the earlier scheme. So we have repeated reorganization, each equally uninformed and unsuccessful. These changes, directed at improving organizational effectiveness, come from what Reed and Armstrong call 'purposive systems thinking', which focuses on input-transformation-output processes. However, effective management also requires 'containing systems thinking'. This focuses on how people's needs, beliefs and feelings give rise to patterns of relations, 'rules' and customs which often continue unaffected by structural changes (Grubb Institute 1991).

Institutions as containers of social anxieties

Here, I use the term 'institution' to refer to large social systems such as the health, education and social services. Each of these, besides providing for specific needs – healthcare, schooling and so forth – through its primary task, also deals constantly with fundamental human anxieties about life and death, or, in more psychoanalytic terms, about annihilation. As discussed in earlier chapters (see Chapters 1, 2 and 8), the individual who is prey to these primitive anxieties seeks relief by projecting these anxieties into another, the earliest experience of this being the mother–baby relationship. If all goes well, the mother processes or 'metabolises' the baby's anxieties in such a way that the feelings become bearable; we then say the anxieties have been 'contained' (Bion 1967). It is this process of containment that eventually makes possible the maturational shift from the paranoid-schizoid position, which involves fragmentation and denial of reality, to the depressive position, where integration, thought and appropriate responses to reality are possible. In an analogous way, the institutions referred to serve to contain these anxieties for society as a whole.

Healthcare systems

In the unconscious, there is no such concept as 'health'. There is, however, a concept of 'death', and, in our constant attempt to keep this anxiety repressed, we use various unconscious defensive mechanisms, including the creation of social systems to serve the defensive function. Indeed, our health service might more accurately be called a 'keep-death-at-bay' service.

All societies fear death, and a multitude of systems exist in every society in order to cope with this anxiety. Some may attempt to cope with death by viewing it as a form of continuation of life. In many religions, belief functions as a socially sanctioned form of denial: you will not die and be nothing; dying is merely a transition, a step on the path of life. However, it is not only religion that is called upon to protect us from our most primitive fears and fantasies of death: doctors have always belonged to a similar defence system.

Originally, priests and doctors were often one and the same profession. While in Ancient Greece the division took place early on, in other societies the two strands are still located in one person, for example, the African witch doctor. In many rural or isolated communities, priests are still assumed to have healing powers, and doctors need to have some 'magic' as part of their practice. Although the practice of magical rituals has waned in our so-called civilised world, we would seriously mislead ourselves if we believed they are no longer of significance. I believe that many of the organizational difficulties that occur in hospital settings arise from a neglect of the unconscious psychological impact of death or near-death on patients, their relatives and staff. Hospitals are as much an embodiment of a social system that exists to defend society and its citizens against anxieties about death as are churches; from a psychic point of view, doctors occupy a similar niche to priests.

In some countries, there is a national health service which is used as a receptacle for the nation's projections of death, and as a collective unconscious system to shield us from the anxieties arising from an awareness of illness and mortality. To lose sight of the 'anxiety-containing' function of the service means an increase in turmoil, and neither its conscious nor its unconscious functions are served adequately. Consider, for example, the outrage in developed countries when advanced medical technologies cannot be made available to all; or the unfounded hopes placed in experimental treatments; or the tendency to feel duped when interventions fail. In all these situations, both individuals and society at large are quick to blame, as if good enough medical care should prevent illness and death. Patients and doctors collude in this to protect the former from facing their fear of death and the latter from facing their fallibility.

Education systems

All societies have an 'education service', in the broadest sense, in order to teach their members to use the tools they need to survive. From an unconscious point of view, the education service is intended to shield us from the risk of going under. It is also, therefore, an institution that is supposed to cope with – whether by encouragement or denial – competition and rivalry. The debate about which nation has the best education system could be seen as a debate about who will survive and who will end up against the wall.

Institutions often serve as containers for the unwanted or difficult-to-cope-with aspects of ourselves. One source of anxiety in our society is our sense of responsibility for bringing up our children, and for their learning the skills needed to survive in society. Put this way, it is a fearsome responsibility, which, if put on to 'them' – teachers, schools and government education departments – lets us off the hook. For the office-bearers of the system, this is a double-edged sword. On the one hand, they welcome the power that comes with the job; on the other, the responsibility is terrifying, particularly as the expectations cannot be met.

At an unconscious level, what is hoped for from the education system is unreality: that all our children will be well-equipped – ideally, equally equipped – to meet all of life's challenges. For example, when I worked as a consultant to Goodman School, a school for children with severe physical disabilities, the head welcomed me with, 'In this school we treat all children as normal'. While at one level an admirable statement, this encapsulated the denial of the extent of the children's problems and hampered all attempts to deal with them. The teachers had been trained in and operated in the belief that if they did their best, and pupils and their parents more or less cooperated, then the end result would be most pupils making their way in society successfully. In fact, very few children managed the transition into the outside world; many went straight from school into sheltered work and accommodation, and those suffering from degenerative diseases often died (this is discussed in more detail in Chapter 9).

In how many ordinary schools are the hopes and ideals that staff had as train-ees met? How many children fulfil their own and our expectations? One way of reducing the pain arising from this disappointment is to alter the primary task, which is subtly modified to, for example, 'life skills', or to passing standard exami-nations which implicitly suggest the child is now equipped for life. A move to something more achievable is sometimes determined by the difficulty in reaching the original goals. And in subtly changing the goals, we lose the opportunity of assessing whether the goals are realistic or whether our approach to them needs to be altered. In other words, our falling into unconscious defensive manoeuvres interferes with our capacity to review the task and to adjust the system appropri-ately. From an insider's point of view, this process is often very difficult to detect.

Defensive structures in public sector organizations

For the container to have the best chance of containing and metabolising the anx-ieties projected into it, it needs to be in a depressive position mode (see Chapter 1), which means it has a capacity to face both external and psychic reality. For orga-nizations, this requires not only agreement about the primary task of the organiza-tion, but also remaining in touch with the nature of the anxieties projected into the container, rather than defensively blocking them out of awareness. In order for a system to work according to these principles, a structured system for dialogue between the various component parts is necessary. This depends on all concerned being in touch with the difficulties of the task, and their relative powerlessness in radically altering the pattern of life and of society.

The present position of many public sector organizations, however, is quite a different one. The new style of management is to give managers more power and to eliminate consultation as 'inefficient'. It has become a top–down model, with dialogue and cooperation between the different sectors seen as old-fashioned, and care staff increasingly excluded from policy- and decision-making. This style of management could be described as 'paranoid-schizoid by choice', fragmenting and splitting up systems instead of promoting collaboration. The splitting up of func-tions makes it more bearable for managers to make decisions.

For example, in healthcare systems, managers are kept at a distance from the clinicians and the patients. The structure thus enables managers psychologically to turn a blind eye to the consequences of their actions. In the short term, this gives an impression of effective change; in the long term, the consequences are disastrous. Meanwhile, the caring that has, so to speak, been 'leeched out' of the management system is precipitated into the carers, who in turn leave their admin-istrative/financial-reality side in the managers.

In Britain, the Griffiths Report (1988) on the re-organization of the health services anticipated that a fair proportion of new-style managers would be doctors. As it turned out, very few doctors put themselves forward, as if financial concerns and concerns about the quality of care could not be held within one role. As part of the ongoing effort to include doctors in management, all executive boards of

NHS Trusts must now include an executive medical director and an executive director of nursing, ostensibly to ensure that the executive board as a whole will attend to both clinical and financial requirements. At lower levels too, there are 'hybrid managers' with both clinical and managerial duties. However, there is some evidence that doctors in particular struggle to take up these role effectively: those who spend the majority of their time on clinical work tend to prioritise clinical and professional interests, while those who do little or no clinical work often lose credibility with the colleagues they are meant to lead (Clay-Williams et al. 2017).

As the necessity for rationing public sector resources has increased, the pull to splitting caring from management has intensified, with system failures attributed to uncaring managers and insufficient resources. The societal fantasy that a well-functioning healthcare system will 'keep death at bay' requires keeping this split in place. Any tampering with the unconscious social system creates a great deal of anxiety and resistance on all sides.

Facing psychic reality

In a management climate such as this, in which contact between the various component parts is fragile at best, it is easy for doctors to fall into a state of mind believing that much more would be possible in the fight against death if only more money were available. The shared fantasy between doctors, the public and the media seems to be that we could have eternal life, if only there were unlimited health funds.

Within the hospital, too, the staff need to protect themselves from the reality of illness, pain and death. Walk into one or another institution and you will probably be bowled over by the horror of the place. Mention it to a regular member, however, and they will not know what you are talking about. This is not because it does not exist, nor because they are used to it, which would imply a certain benevolent acceptance. What they are expressing is a denial, or a repression, of the substance of your observation. This flight from reality happens gradually and largely unconsciously. In the process of inducting new members, the group unconsciously gives the message, 'This is how we ignore what is going on – pretend along with us, and you will soon be one of us'. It can be called settling down, or it can be called institutionalisation. In fact, it is a collusive group denial of the work difficulties.

Another way of protecting oneself against what is unbearable is to organize the work in ways that serve more to ward off primitive anxieties, than to achieve the primary task. A great deal of what goes on is not about dramatic rescue but about having to accept one's relative powerlessness in the presence of pain, decrepitude and death. Staff are ill-prepared for this in their training, and in their work practice there is often no socially sanctioned outlet for their distress (see Chapter 10). This then expresses itself as staff stress and illness, absenteeism, high turnover, low morale, poor time-keeping and so on. In a study on nursing turnover (Menzies 1960), it was found that it was usually the most sensitive nurses, those with the capacity to make the strongest contribution to nursing, who were most likely to leave – perhaps those least willing to join in the institutional systems of denial.

At a seminar, top health service managers were asked to name their own worst personal anxieties. They mentioned death, debilitating illness, divorce, insanity, abandonment, loss of employment and so on. All of these are of course central to the work (and the workers) of our public sector services. They viewed their task as one of management, and stressed that the only requirement legally laid down was for them to live within their allocated budgets. It clearly was too painful for these managers to be in touch with the needs of the patients and the consequences of their actions, and psychologically more comfortable to focus on budgets – a classic example of splitting used to avoid depressive-position pain. A great deal of the disorganization, time-wasting on and off committees, bureaucracy and the like is a way of avoiding face-to-face contact with patients and their ailments.

Similar processes occur in our other public sector services: it is contact with pain – the clients' pain and our own – that regularly puts us in touch with our feelings, our impotence and the inadequacy of our training and of our professions. Many of our so-called administrative or managerial difficulties are in reality defence mechanisms arising from the difficulty of the work. Furthermore, a system of financial reward for 'effective' management further bolsters this defensive style of functioning. From a psychoanalytic point of view, we then have a system in which the caring depressive-position functioning of managers and management systems is penalised, and the defensive paranoid-schizoid component is rewarded.

Implications for management

Our public sector institutions can usefully be thought of as comprising three sub-sectors: the public and its consumer representatives (patients, pupils and their parents, etc.); the care sub-sector (the staff of the services); and the administrative system (representing government). So far, we have looked at the anxieties that are being defended against. There are, however, other factors at play of an intergroup nature. These take place within the sub-sectors, and have to do with a rivalry between various professional and administrative sub-groups. They have always been there, but in a climate of increased pressure and, therefore, of increased splitting and projective identification, they are exacerbated.

In the caring sector, the result is more strife between the various professional disciplines and heightened competition for resources. With greater rivalry and reduced communication, the situation is often not unlike the chaos found in group relations conferences (see Chapter 5). There it is for study purposes, to learn about the irrational unconscious processes in and between groups. Here, however, it is for real – and permanent. Within the administrative sector, it is also not uncommon to find massive divisions between the various departments. This of course hinders competent management and encourages a technique of playing one group off against the other. In order for any organization to function at its most effective, certain guidelines, based on group relations understanding and sound management principles, need to be laid down.

For *all* members of the organization, be they cleaner or managing director, there is the need for:

- clarity about the task of the organization;
- clarity about authority and accountability;
- the opportunity to participate and contribute.

In addition, for those in authority there is a need for:

- psychologically informed management;
- awareness of the risks to the workers;
- openness towards the consumers.

Clarity about the task of the organization

As an example, cleaning contracts in the health service now go out to tender. It is clear from the contracts that no account is taken of the fact that while cleaners are there to clean, they are cleaning in a hospital with patients bearing anxiety and pain. The human contact is important for both patients and cleaners. Cutting out the commitment to the overall task is to the detriment of all.

Clarity about authority and accountability

In public sector organizations, heads of schools, chief executives of healthcare organizations, directors of social service departments and others all contend with multiple and often competing requirements: from those using their services, from the public, and from government ministers. Neither authority nor accountability are straightforward, and heads of public sector organizations interpret their scope of discretion differently. Again and again we hear them say 'I have to dance to the tune of my political masters' or 'Going against government directives would be the end of my job'. At a leadership programme for over 100 CEOs of NHS Trusts, over 90 per cent of participants saw themselves as having little authority or power to set priorities. In a series of interviews with chief executives, similar comments were made by all but one who stated his priorities very clearly: 'Patient safety, quality of services, and coming in on budget, in that order'. It is hard – if not impossible – to serve two masters: for him, accountability for safety and care had to over-ride everything else. It is perhaps significant that he was the oldest of the group, on the verge of retiring, and thus more able to resist the pressures to put the bottom line first. Accountability to the public adds another strand of complexity, as discussed further on.

The opportunity to participate and contribute

Contract labour does not make for good staff morale or effective organization, first because contract labour does not have institutional allegiance, and, second, because of the ill-will created in the permanent staff. At one stage, more than half the secretaries in the health service were temps because they could get much better salaries that way than as permanent members of staff. An organization run on a *Gästarbeiter* ('guest-worker' – being a euphemism for disenfranchised staff) principle is not a good idea.

Psychologically informed management

This would include awareness of group and social factors that might interfere with the task of the organization. Such awareness can enable managers to take measures to combat anti-task phenomena. For example, most meetings not only do not start on time, but, more surprisingly, do not have a designated ending time. The logical-sounding rationale is that it depends on how much is on the agenda, and how long that will take. It is widely recognised that 90 minutes or so of committee meetings is as long as anyone can maintain useful attention. Yet this time-span is neither scheduled for nor taken account of. Decisions are therefore made on the basis of grinding down, rather than by working through. Decisions made on the basis of out-manoeuvring or wearing down the opposition do not lead to successful management; they are often Pyrrhic victories.

Awareness of the risks to the workers

For any organization to function effectively the managers must take into account the stresses on the staff as a result of the work they are doing. They need also to make adequate provision for dealing with staff distress, and to ask themselves whether seemingly unrelated anti-task phenomena might not be manifestations of this. It is crucial that a climate is created in which the stress of the entire system can be acknowledged openly, with an awareness of the particular risks to the workers from the nature of the particular task they are performing. These will be different for the helping professions – teachers, social workers, prison officers and so on. One can usefully think of pain, anxiety and distress as being as much a part of the atmosphere and as widespread as is coal dust in a mine. As in the coal mines, so also in the human services, attention needs to be paid to keeping the 'coal dust' to a minimum, and to detecting its ill-effects as early as possible, before a chronic or terminal illness develops in the worker.

Openness towards the consumers

Given the defensive tendency in the health service to push patients and what they so painfully stand for aside, it is not surprising that patients are, by and large, forgotten. It is much easier to deal with diseased organs than with a person who has a complaint (often a very genuine complaint), and staff often focus on organs to defend themselves against people contact. Similarly, senior health service managers may think and talk in terms of populations, again as a defence against the pain of thinking about individuals.

It is a moot point whether it is helpful for the public to know via the media that their local hospital has no beds available for emergencies. Administrators are loath to inform the media of relevant local or national issues. If the information does get out, much time and energy is spent trying to trace the source, and much anger is expended in the process. It seems that the authorities are accountable to those further up the line, and that public information and opinion count for very little. However, the authority for running public sector services derives ultimately from the public (the electorate), and accountability to the public needs to be held in mind and built into the system.

Conclusion

Looking at the various defensive patterns described – whether between institutions and their environment, or inter-institutional, or interpersonal – we can see how a style of work that is essentially and consistently defensive is bad not only for the work but also for individual workers. To be constantly out of touch with many aspects of psychic reality at work puts individuals at risk of being out of touch with themselves as a result of a combination of work defences and personal vulnerabilities. This can seep into one's personal life, affect marital and family mental health. The pattern can influence the behaviour of children and their reactions to stress, and therefore perpetuate itself. The chances of developing stress-related diseases are also increased. We therefore come to the end of the road – an unhealthy mind in an unhealthy body in an unhealthy organization.

Groups and institutions accept newcomers and mould them to the institutional ways of doing things, including joining in with their particular version of institutional defences. Eventually, the individual to a large extent loses his or her capacity to be detached and to 'see' things from an outside perspective. Yet, to maintain some outside perspective is essential if one is to retain a capacity for critical thought and questioning. Without these, our institutions are doomed to operate more and more on a basis of denial of reality – the reality that they exist to help people cope with pain, unfulfilled hopes, sickness and death. The more this is denied, the less effective the systems become, and the greater the toll on those involved in them.

PART III

The unconscious at work in business organizations

Kay Trainor (guest editor)

19

FAMILY PATTERNS AT WORK

How casting light on the shadows of the past can enhance leadership in the present

Francesca Cardona and Sheila Damon

There are times when, as managers and leaders, we may find ourselves gripped by surprisingly strong – sometimes seemingly irrational – emotions, or be disconcerted by puzzling patterns of behaviour, our own or others'. Relationships may become dysfunctional and resilience may be tested. The origins of such patterns and the feelings associated with them often lie in the 'shadows' cast by early life experiences, beneath the surface of what we are aware of. In this chapter, we will explore some of these shadows and how leadership can be enhanced if light is shone on them so that they can be understood and worked with.

Since the publication of Goleman's *Emotional Intelligence* (1995) and *Working with Emotional Intelligence* (1998), there has been increasing recognition of the importance of being in touch with feelings and using emotional information to guide thinking and behaviour at work. Goleman lists the key skills of emotional intelligence as self-awareness, self-regulation, motivation, empathy and social skill. Tools like 360 feedback are now widely used to raise awareness of how we are perceived by staff, colleagues and bosses, reducing 'blind spots'. However, this awareness may not in itself be enough to bring about change: insight into the links between past and present can enable deeper levels of emotional intelligence and thus have a transformative effect.

The shadows at work

As the psychoanalyst, Melanie Klein (1959) put it:

> The relation to early figures keeps reappearing and problems that remain unresolved in infancy or early childhood are revived though in modified forms (. . .) If we look at our adult world from the viewpoint of its roots in infancy we gain an insight into the way our mind, our habits, and our views

have been built up from the earliest infantile phantasies, and emotions to the most complex and sophisticated adult manifestations.

(Klein, 1959 pp. 14, 18)

It is, of course, widely accepted that relationships with parents and other key figures in early life can influence feelings and behaviours in adult life, for example in the choice of a life partner. Less explored is how impactful this can be in the workplace, particularly with regard to how individuals are or are not able to exercise authority effectively.

In Chapter 5, Obholzer explores three key sources of authority in organizations: from above (delegated), from below (sanctioned by those being managed), and from within (authorising oneself). With regard to the latter:

> This largely depends on the nature of their relationship with the figures in their inner world, in particular past authority figures. The attitude of such 'in-the-mind' authority figures is crucial in affecting how, to what extent and with what competence external institutional roles are taken up.
>
> *(p. 51)*

In practice, this may mean authority figures or other colleagues at work are experienced 'as if' they were significant figures from the past – the unconscious phenomenon known as transference. Where the relationships have been positive, these connections and echoes can be beneficial, enabling people to work effectively and resiliently with their feelings and those of others. However, the shadows of more negative early relationships can impair the ability to take up one's authority or trigger difficulties in work relationships that have more to do with the past than with the present.

Sometimes even our choice of profession, sector, or of a particular organization may have an unconscious meaning: we may unconsciously be seeking a place where we can repeat positive experiences or 'sort out' unresolved issues from the past. If our unconscious needs fit with the needs of the system in which we are working, things can go well. But this is not always the case, and even positive dynamics may become dysfunctional over time, as people, roles, tasks and demands shift.

Examples of family patterns, positive and negative, which can be triggered by the everyday experience of working together, include:

* *Sibling dynamics*: Colleagues feeling and acting towards each other as they did towards their siblings. These may manifest as collaborative or protective behaviour, or as rivalry, competitiveness, preoccupation with fairness or a pervasive sense of inferiority.
* *Parental dynamics*: Staff reacting to their managers as they did towards their mothers, fathers, teachers or other significant adult figures from their childhood. Experiences of being judged harshly or humiliated at home or at school may

affect work situations where performance is being judged or judgement is anticipated. Where parents were harsh or neglectful, the staff member may be hypersensitive to criticism or to being overlooked.

- *Caretaking dynamics*: Employees who, for one reason or another, took up a parental role in families with a psychologically or physically absent parent may find themselves taking up an inappropriate version of a managerial role, either trying too hard to meet others' needs, or alternatively warding off even reasonable demands.
- *Bullying dynamics*: Bullying, being bullied or feeling bullied at work may be connected with early experiences at home or at school.
- *Family businesses*: Family relationships from both the past and the present, within and between the generations, may become entangled with work roles and responsibilities.

Four examples follow to illustrate some of these phenomena. The first describes a shadow which had been inhibiting the realisation of potential. In the second, the shadow was causing intolerable stress. The third is an example of how shadows which had previously worked well became a hindrance towards the end of a successful working life. The fourth explores the dynamics of a family business.

Don't trust the boss!

> David, a well-respected middle manager in a multinational organization, found his relationship with his boss challenging. He did not feel understood or appreciated, despite his good performance and outcomes. He kept contact with his boss to a minimum and avoided developing a relationship with him. His superiors respected his abilities, but they could never get to know him well enough to feel confident in his potential to develop the skills needed for a more strategic and influential role.
>
> Why?
>
> David was very good operationally. He was focused, disciplined and self-contained. He had learnt this behaviour 'the hard way'. His workaholic father mostly ignored him and his mother was distant and extremely religious. He had gone through school and university without parental support or guidance. David's efficiency and self-reliance were his way of coping but had become like armour protecting him from the unconscious risks of a more engaged and dependent relationship with people in positions of authority. He felt he must never show any neediness or vulnerability.

Working with a coach, he began to realise that the emotional neglect he had experienced growing up had produced a 'shadow' in his relationship with his boss; he struggled to believe that anyone in a 'parental' role could have a genuine interest in him and his development, even when there was evidence to the contrary. David gradually changed his perception of his boss and started to develop a closer relationship with him. Colleagues and senior managers experienced David as more open and engaged. As a result, he gained more credibility and trust across the whole organization, and became more effective in building and motivating teams. He has been talent-spotted for development as a potential member of senior management.

David's insights into the impact of the shadows of his early emotional deprivation on his experience of people in authority created new possibilities for him at work. He may or may not choose to do further work on unresolved issues from his early years (through personal therapy for example), but at work he has learned how to be vigilant for early signs of unfounded mistrust towards authority figures and his tendency to seek distance from them, which he now understands to belong more to the past than to the present.

Who am I trying to impress?

Ella, an economist by background, was the leader of a successful social marketing organization, in the forefront of its niche field, with an emphasis on human rights, equality and diversity. She was good with people, created trusting relationships with clients, and was very skilled at problem solving. Yet despite her confidence, drive and success, she felt somehow unhappy and unfulfilled. Work dominated her life and she felt constantly guilty about neglecting her young family.

Colleagues respected her, but they were very demanding of her time and energy. She described herself as a 'milking cow' – feeling as if she had to supply all the sustenance for the whole organization. Throughout her career, she had felt driven constantly to compete, wanting a big job, influential and well paid. She also wanted to be a great mother to her children and be fully part of their lives, rather than being often distracted and irritable at home. But she was now the boss at work: why couldn't she choose to do things differently? Instead she seemed driven by a conviction that whatever she did, it was never enough, and so she constantly strove to do more.

Ella's family were immigrants. Her father was a high-achieving, very successful engineer. Her mother was a full-time housewife. As the only girl of her family she was not expected to have a proper career, unlike her brothers; despite her talents, she was not encouraged to go to university. She decided to go ahead regardless and supported herself throughout, going on to achieve a successful career.

The emerging shadow was what she came to describe as 'the show' she unconsciously put on for her parents – the incredibly successful daughter who could manage it all. For the first time she made a link between her constant preoccupation with work, which was almost like an addiction, and her desire to impress her parents. Making this connection was quite a revelation for Ella. She became more aware of the anger she had developed towards her parents for failing to support her in her studies, the insecurity she felt because of their lack of recognition or nurturing of her talents, and the need to out-shine her brothers. Being able to make those connections helped Ella to look at her work with different eyes and acknowledge the cost of feeling she had constantly to prove herself. She also had to face that her craving for parental recognition was unlikely ever to be satisfied, however hard she worked. Recognising the shadow that motivated her compulsion enabled her to start letting go of it and to make choices based on her own priorities rather than on impressing her parents.

I can't move on

Julian, now in his sixties, had, for many years, been running a highly successful set of financial services businesses, and had developed a loyal and high-performing staff group. Still in good health, he had decided it was time to retire and enjoy the fruits of his hard work whilst he could. Preparing for this, he had spent a substantial amount of money on a refurbished cabin cruiser which he loved and planned to take on long trips 'one day'.

His intention had long been to sell the companies to the senior staff group whom he had nurtured, once he was satisfied that they could sustain them. But that day never seemed to come. Having always prided himself on his clarity of direction and ability to make decisions, he now seemed to find it impossible to move forward with his plan. He could recite the evidence to himself, but yet it felt as if it was never quite the time to let go. His retirement plans were perpetually postponed and the prospect of ever retiring began to feel unreal.

Throughout his early career, Julian had repeatedly felt that his bosses did not work as hard as he did and that he had less and less to learn from them. He had relished the opportunity of using a redundancy package to set up on his own and had enjoyed being the boss. He had developed his staff, designed their training programmes and he had plans for them all, though he had no time for anyone who didn't work hard or was lacking in ambition.

His father, who had died some years earlier, had been clever but neither ambitious nor hard-working. He had drifted from one job to another, so the family had moved frequently and finances had always felt tight and precarious. His mother had held things together with several part-time jobs.

It was as if Julian had been perpetually making amends for his father's failure to provide, his lack of ambition, and his neglect of his children's future. Julian's own irritation with less-than satisfactory bosses, and his drive to be autonomous and successful were part of his desire to escape from his father's approach, as perhaps was his choosing to work in businesses which enabled people to be financially secure. He also realised that he still felt angry with his mother for having gone along with his father's approach to life rather than pushing him, and because her work to keep the family finances afloat had taken her time and attention away from the children. He realised that he was acting like a 'parent' at work to his chosen staff, pushing them the way his mother had never pushed his father, and paying them the close attention he had never had. All this had served him and others well for many years, bringing him success and pleasure and bringing many benefits to his clients and his staff. But now the patterns were becoming chains, impeding his ability to implement his plans for the next stage of his life.

Shining light on the shadows that were driving him proved to be key. Julian realised that he had spent his working life showing his parents how things ought to be done. He wondered whether he had been avoiding retirement because it would make him too much like his idle father. He also reflected that whilst being like a parent at work for his staff had worked well in the early years, he was now making too many decisions for them, not leaving them much space to decide things for themselves, to 'grow up' and become independent enough to take over.

Now he needed to decide more explicitly what he really wanted for himself, rather than being driven by the shadows of the past – and to begin by enjoying the cabin-cruiser for which he had worked so hard. The purchase turned out to be significant in more ways than one. Julian's father's biggest purchase had been a dilapidated narrow boat which he was always fixing up, but never finishing. As Julian began to take trips in the cabin cruiser, it became a symbol of banishing the shadows. After all, it had not been bought with money he didn't have, and he had every right to enjoy it.

Betrayed by the family

The disentanglement from shadows, and the authorising of oneself in role, often becomes particularly difficult in the arena of family businesses where current as well as past family relationships exist alongside organizational and role relationships.

Lucy, the daughter of a successful entrepreneur, had been promised the top position in her father's retailing company. The eldest of three siblings, she was seen as a potential good leader for the expanding business. Her energy, focus on sales and toughness had been seen as key ingredients for a successful CEO. However, her apparent confidence covered up how dependent she had actually been on her father. After Lucy had made a number of wrong business decisions, he realised she was not as capable as he had thought and decided to sack her. The effect on Lucy was quite devastating. Her work identity and sense of competence were completely entangled with her family role as the eldest child. Her 'authority from within' was weak: she could not see how she could achieve success and recognition outside her father's company and felt very vulnerable.

This pattern is often found in family businesses, where the development of an adult work identity can be particularly complex. The 'family system' and the 'work system' are often not distinctive enough, producing confusion within the individual and within the organization. Collins and Porras (1994) document the particular challenges of creating businesses that remain sustainable after a powerful founder era. In a family business, the children often struggle to achieve the necessary separation from their parents as founders. Their authority from within tends to rely on and get confused with the parent-boss's approval, creating a state like a never-ending adolescence. For Lucy, it proved very important for her to work in another company where she could grow her own competence. As she did so, she discovered that she had earned her father's respect in a different way, and was able to enjoy that without being dependent on it.

Although this dynamic is particularly obvious in family businesses, where the actual parents are also the bosses, we would argue that, to an extent, there is always an element of overlap of family and work systems. Each of us can benefit from understanding how the shadows of our early life influence how we authorise ourselves to take up our roles at work.

Separating out and understanding what belongs where can help. As David, for example, became aware that he was reacting to his boss as if he were one or other of his distant parents, things changed for him and he was able to take up his role more fully. Ella's childhood experiences gave her a strong drive for success, and a desire to be a good parent, but until her shadows became illuminated, she was like an addict whose cravings could never be satisfied, seriously affecting her work–life balance. Julian's shadow was that of his feckless father whose inability to take his financial and parental responsibilities seriously (as Julian saw it) had driven his son to do the opposite. This shadow had resulted in Julian having difficulty in letting his staff develop their full competence, making it hard to let go when his time came to retire. For Lucy, it was important to build a sound work identity in her own right, outside the family business.

Getting practical

Here we offer some practical suggestions for you to consider in your management of your staff, as well as yourself.

Feelings as data

A starting point, and not to be under estimated, is being alert and paying attention to feelings – our own or others' – as 'data', rather than taking things at face value and simply reacting to them. When feelings seem disproportionate, this is often a signal that other forces, including shadows from the past, may be at work. The next chapter explores in more detail how we can work at using these feelings to help us make sense of what is going on below the surface.

Transference

Plato tells us that on the portal of the Academy in ancient Athens was carved 'Know Thyself'. Taking time to develop self-knowledge yields benefits in managing relationships at work. This includes reflecting on how experiences from early life may be influencing present feelings and behaviour. When our reactions to others at work, or their reactions to us, seem out of kilter, it is worth asking 'Who might this person represent for me?' or 'Who might I be for this person?' In other words, what is the transference?

One of the perils of being in a position of authority is that it is likely to evoke emotional reactions in others which have their origins in early relationships with powerful authority figures. These might be negative and damaging, as was the case for David, but it can also be problematic when they are over-positive or idealised. For example, a boss might be treated as if they were an all-knowing authority, at the expense of developing one's own thinking and initiative. In either case, the capacity to be effective is likely to be impaired.

Awareness of transference can help us manage our own reactions more effectively. It can also help us learn to live and work with such reactions from others.

Space to think

It can be valuable to create regular space to reflect on the qualitative 'how' of relationships as well as the 'what' of performance and metrics. This means actively countering the common assumption that 'touchy-feely' or 'soft' stuff is not for real managers and leaders.

The examples in this chapter have illustrated how a coach can help unravel what is going on, bringing to the surface what is at first unconscious and in the shadows – shining a light on the possible early origins of behaviour and response. However, coaching is not the only approach. Many managers find it useful to set up regular co-consultation meetings with a peer, or a 'learning set' with a small group of peers. Each person brings a current work issue to present and hears the reflections of their colleague(s) to help throw light on where patterns of behaviour and strong feelings may come from, and thus what may be going on beneath the surface.[1] People often say that they have discovered that working on someone else's issue throws unexpected light on their own.

This approach can also be used in supervision meetings with direct reports. Without intruding, it is possible for an emotionally intelligent manager to open a space where reports feel able to recognise and name shadows from their past.

Conclusion

Given that early experience can so powerfully impact the way we take up our work roles, then the more fully we understand these processes, the better. The managers in our vignettes began to free themselves from stuck positions once there was illumination of the shadows of their early relationships in their current experience at work, particularly with figures of authority.

We suggest that both for our own development and for fostering the development of others, it is worth giving as much regard to aspects of emotional awareness on the surface and beneath it, as we do to technical skills and knowledge. Noticing patterns in our relationships, and emotional reactions in ourselves and others, especially puzzling ones, and actively seeking to throw light on the shadows from the past they may represent, can help us to make sense of them and thus to manage, lead, follow and co-work more effectively.

As the late Richard Beckhard, one of the pioneers of organizational development, used to say in his management master-classes, 'There's your stuff, there's my stuff, and there's our stuff. Good managers take the time to figure out whose is which!'[2]

It takes time to get there, but working in the light – even if it's dim at first – is usually more productive than living and working amongst un-named shadows.

Notes

1 It is beyond the scope of this chapter to discuss learning sets in detail. There are many approaches, but all involve a shared commitment to learning, with clear boundaries of confidentiality so that trust and collaboration develop.
2 Part of the King's Fund training, 'Top Managers Programme', delivered in London between 1989 and 1993.

20

FEELINGS AS DATA

Kay Trainor

Managers often find themselves under intense pressure to make their organizations work well – to achieve demanding targets, win new business, or beat competitors' performance – the usual stuff of corporate life if you like. It can be a brutal world. So, what have feelings got to do with that?

Well, evidently, we all have them . . . certainly at home, in our private lives, at the opera even, or watching sport, but at work there is often a hidden (or not so hidden) message that 'we don't do that here'. Though now, in addition to 'hard' managerial competencies, managers are supposed to have (or to learn) the skills of 'emotional intelligence' (Goleman 1995) – including self-awareness, self-regulation, empathy and social skills – so as to manage themselves and influence others effectively, and so that feelings can enhance rather than impede performance.

While there is no doubt that these skills are valuable, the way emotional intelligence is understood and developed has some serious limitations:

> We have come to regard emotions as *assets* – precious or toxic as they may be – rather than as *data*. Therefore we focus on *managing* them, which often means trying to exploit, diffuse, or sanitize them, far more than staying with them long enough to discern their *meaning*. And when we do the latter, we usually interpret them as revealing something about their owners alone.
>
> *(Petriglieri 2014 p. 1)*

But what if feelings, far from being perceived as 'personal' or getting in the way of clear decision making and strategy, were considered as data – really important data – about what is really going on below the surface in organizations? What if they had a 'meaning' which, if understood, might help managers and leaders cut to the quick of situations and transform their organizations?

Unconscious communication

The process whereby human beings communicate through making other people feel their own frightening or overwhelming feelings is ubiquitous whenever we are unable to use words to convey our experience. This unconscious process, called *projective identification*, starts when we are infants without access to words, when we feel pain or anxiety and communicate these feelings to our parents/ caretakers, through crying for example. The emotionally available caretaker will not only hear the cry as a sound, but will feel something of what the baby feels and will be able to use this to respond appropriately. Thus, the process of putting one's feelings *into* another person serves not only to get rid of what feels unbearable, but also to get help.

In the earlier parts of this book, there are many examples of how staff 'take in' their clients' most unbearable experiences – the fear of the cancer patient, the rage of the adolescent, or the confusion and memory loss of the drug addict – and 'identify' with them. This can make the work itself too hard to bear, affecting staff, services, and sometimes whole organizations in ways that lead to dysfunction. Where staff have learned to attend to their experience as data for understanding the dynamics in their workplace, it can be very useful.

All very well, you might say, for helpless infants, or patients and clients *in extremis*, but how is this relevant in organizations that sell goods, make cars, design software or offer corporate services? The three following examples seek to illustrate how feelings, once the meaning was understood, led to significant practical changes in the headquarters of a clothing retail company, a growing computer software company and a business academy.

What if my feelings are not just mine?

Management at Xbrand, an international high street brand making clothes for a youth market, had concerns about employee retention at the London headquarters. XBrand is a popular employer choice for young people and they never have trouble recruiting. They consider themselves fair employers and describe a high level of employee satisfaction as measured through regular questionnaires. The fact remained however that they were losing young women employees – particularly from their large HR division, and wanted to understand what was happening as the constant turnover was affecting efficiency at every level of the company. The consultancy team proposed a series of observations[1] as a start to the consultation.

> I was deployed to observe the HR floor. The 30-strong HR team consisted largely of women in their 20s in an open-plan office on the third floor. The walls were covered with huge digital displays of very thin teenage models wearing XBrand clothes. As agreed with the manager, I sat on a chair near the edge of the office. None of the young women took any notice of me. They worked and swapped banter about brands, who was

wearing what, from where – colours, styles, shops. There was a lively and companionable atmosphere.

As time wore on, however, I began to feel strangely isolated. It felt odd that not one of the women had said anything to me, an alienating feeling at odds with the light-hearted, inclusive atmosphere. I knew they had been made aware of the observations taking place and it was possible that they had been given instructions to let me get on with my task and leave me alone. But it felt like much more than that: I felt ignored and invisible. Toward the end of the hour, one of the women left her desk, holding a file, saying that she was delivering it to Nancy. She set off walking straight toward me. It seemed as if she would crash into me and I flinched involuntarily just before, at the last moment, she veered around my chair as if I were simply an object in her way. I felt a fool for flinching and began to feel self-conscious. I became aware of my age, of feeling old (though only in my mid-30s at the time) and self-critical of what I was wearing, all very uncomfortable feelings.

In discussion with the consultancy team later it was the contrast between my own experience and the apparent light-heartedness and jollity of the HR team which seemed significant, as if 'unwanted' feelings may have been 'put into' me while 'above the surface' the jollity and companionable atmosphere continued. We decided to investigate this hunch, holding discussions with small groups of the HR team to discuss their experience and aspirations.

What emerged proved significant. Not surprisingly, many of them had come to the company with aspirations to work at the more glamorous end of the fashion industry, to be models or designers themselves. Finding themselves instead in a role in HR, many of them felt doubly demoralised: not only had they not achieved their goals of becoming models or designers themselves, but they also found themselves constantly reminded by the omnipresent digital displays of models of the world from which they were excluded. They had 'given' me a powerful experience of how ignored, inadequate and unsuccessful they felt (already 'old').

When themes from these discussions were shared with the management team, they made two decisions. They re-organized the layout of their headquarters, splitting the HR department over two floors, each of which also housed the merchandising and design departments. This had the effect of physically connecting different parts of the business and giving HR direct contact with the designers. They also introduced a pairing scheme where employees from different departments met in cross-department pairs to discuss their work. The consultancy team revisited the HR department after six months, again convening a series of discussion groups, and found some significant changes. Although some HR staff had left (including two who had won places to study design), the number was far lower than before. Amongst those who had stayed, there was an enhanced sense of belonging and a lessening pre-occupation with the 'glamorous end' of the business. One young woman commented that the design department was 'not as interesting as I'd imagined'. It seemed that the greater contact between departments had reduced some of the earlier splitting between the (idealised) design function and the (overlooked and under-valued) HR team.

Naming the unnameable

Jon is the managing partner of Ecompute, a computer company he founded with Derek, a close friend from university. They had created the company some ten years before the incidents described here, investing everything they owned including putting up their houses as collateral when the company expanded. Originally, their main activity had been developing their own software ideas, but now they worked increasingly with a wide range of designers and entrepreneurs in an area which was becoming a mini 'Silicon Valley' around the large city where they were based. Jon now led on the design-implementation side while Derek led on the commissioning process.

> Jon had asked for consultancy as the company had just received a large government grant to set up a creative hub for business development in the computer software field. This was likely to quadruple their activity and involve having bigger premises and more employees. Jon valued what he called the 'family vibe' of the company and was concerned not to lose the friendly open spirit of the original enterprise as they expanded.
>
> In the second of two introductory meetings with Jon to discuss how we might support the wider organization to prepare for the process of expansion, Jon was describing to me one of their most successful innovations, a complex piece of software which allowed for 'big data' sharing. He spoke passionately about the software and described it in detail, using technical words I had never heard of and referring to mathematical concepts of which I had no idea. As he warmed to his subject, I began to feel increasingly out of my depth, but there was an unstoppable feeling to the 'lecture' (which is what it became): he was quite carried away by his product.
>
> My contact with Jon so far had given me the impression he was someone open to ideas, so I decided to share my experience with him, of feeling rather intimidated by his intelligence and knowledge. 'Oh no!' he replied, 'really? That's what the designers all say about us.' He went on to describe meetings with designers, held in upmarket screening rooms where Encompute's products were 'shown off' on large intimidating screens, as if to say 'Beat that'. The company was increasingly being experienced as rather full of itself and unable to connect with young designers on the ground, a connection which would become even more important as they developed the new hub. Jon had been shocked to realise that he had behaved in his conversation with me in just the way the company was behaving with outsiders, and was concerned about the impact this was having. Now he wanted to understand why.
>
> The theme of intimidation turned out to be significant for both partners. As the company had grown, Derek's technical capacities had proved

inadequate to the demands of the expanding company. Aware of the level of commitment Derek had made to the company, Jon had been reluctant to take up his authority as managing partner either to make sure Derek was adequately skilled or to find someone else who was. Instead he had taken on more and more of the responsibilities himself. It transpired, during a painful conversation where the partners were eventually able to speak honestly, that Derek felt intimidated by his multi-talented friend and felt his own limitations keenly. It seemed that he had passed on the intimidation he felt (but could not face) by creating an ever more impressive but potentially alienating commissioning process. In this conversation, Jon too was able to admit his own sense of intimidation in the face of the new expansion. He had felt isolated and overwhelmed with the new responsibilities.

The sense of intimidation and incompetence, first openly acknowledged by the consultant, turned out to pervade all levels in the organization. It had been an important communication and unravelling it led in due course to the partners' deciding to employ a deputy chief operating officer to support Jon in managing the challenges of the expansion.

Consulting to oneself

In both the examples just given, it was the consultant who first named the experience that was being 'put into' them – acting as a sort of lightning rod to receive the difficult feelings and then working with the client to understand what they might mean. Consultants can be very useful in this process, but managers and leaders can also learn to hone these skills and take up a 'consultancy stance' themselves or internal consultant in relation to their work, developing the capacity to notice their own feelings and creating a space in which to try and understand what they might mean. Over time, it may become possible to create this space even whilst in the thick of things, as in the example which follows.

Leila works at what she sometimes describes as a 'swanky' business academy offering a range of trainings to corporate clients. She is the head of the leadership development section and manages a team of 14 tutors who work in pairs to design and deliver the programmes.

One day, she found herself in the canteen queue with one of her tutors, Tim, who asked her, seemingly in passing, whether his co-tutor, Kathy, had spoken to Leila about the final day of their current programme. When Leila said she hadn't heard from Kathy, Tim explained that Kathy had made a mistake with her diary and had double-booked herself for the last day of the programme. 'I felt you should know,' he said, adding that Kathy had already shared with the client that she had a problem with the final day of the programme and needed to re-arrange it.

Leila was furious. Unable to get hold of Kathy, she wrote a strongly worded email demanding that Kathy come to speak with her immediately and expressing concern that her actions would damage the reputation of the programme. To Leila's amazement, Kathy's response, which came via text, was not apologetic, merely saying that she could not help the mistake that had been made and was negotiating with the client group to find the best solution.

This further inflamed Leila, who began to write a very angry response. It was at this point that she managed to pause and wonder what was going on. Why was she so angry, she asked herself? Kathy and Tim were excellent tutors and very professional. This mistake was unusual and she knew Kathy would have done her best to resolve the issue. She went back over what had happened in her mind, reviewing how she had heard the news – the conversation in the canteen with Tim. Why had he told her, and why in such a casual way? It was not so much the double-booking itself, she realised, but the experience of how it was communicated to her, that had had such a powerful effect.

This was an important realisation. A relatively ordinary occurrence had had an unusually strong impact on her. Why? Her first thought was that Tim must be angry with Kathy for being careless with her diary (which he was) and that he had passed this difficult feeling on to Leila through telling her about it in a way which made her angry too. This seemed plausible – but it also felt bigger than this. She began to wonder if the anger she felt might have deeper relevance. Her calm restored, she arranged to meet with Tim and Kathy together to discuss the situation.

During the conversation, it emerged that several of the participants on the programme had not had a choice about signing up but had been sent by their managers, as a sort of corrective, because they were considered 'difficult' at work. Understandably angry, they had lived up to this reputation on the programme and both Kathy and Tim had struggled to work effectively with the group. As they spoke, it became possible to think about the anger both the tutors and Leila had experienced in a different way. Considering it as 'data', it could be understood as part of a communication about anger, a kind of a distress signal from the participants which needed attention.

This shifted the focus from the diary issue to how best to handle the final day of the programme (whatever the date). They decided to have an open discussion with participants in which their feelings about being 'sent' on the programme might be explored. They also discussed what they might do differently in future. One decision was to change how they contracted with participants. They also agreed to have what came to be known as 'Stress meetings' for department staff to explore difficult feelings arising during programme delivery.

The key to this positive outcome was Leila's capacity, as the manager, to 'push the pause button' before acting, making time to think how her anger might be telling her something about the system she was working in and not just a personal response to what had happened. The 'signal' that such a pause was needed was her noticing that her anger seemed both disproportionate and not typical of her. What would have happened if she had not paid attention to this? It is easy to imagine the cycle of recrimination and resentment which might have ensued had she merely acted on her anger rather than considered it as data.

Feeling, thinking, doing

In the human body, pain is sometimes experienced at a location other than where it originates. This 'referred' pain is the result of the interconnection of sensory nerves in different parts of the body. Similarly, systemic thinking is based on a recognition of the interconnections within and between systems. For example, at the academy, the original locus of distress was in the clients. Their anger was communicated to the group, then to the tutors, and then on to Leila. The distress in the system might have continued to ricochet from one part to another, as often happens in organizational life, but Leila was able to be stop herself from immediate (re)action and to 'listen' to it as a communication. This made it possible to change something for the better both for her staff and for the academy's clients.

It is worth noting that just as referred pain can contribute to a diagnosis or can confuse and mislead, so our feelings can be 'referred' data about other parts of the system, but they can also be (more) about us. Usually there is a mix of both. We need to be aware of how we are prone to being 'used' by others as a conduit. Bion (1961) used the term of 'valency' – the affinity of particular atoms to combine with others to form molecules – to describe our capacity for 'instantaneous combination' with others. However, individuals vary with regard to which particular kinds of projections they are most likely to identify with, and a degree of self-awareness about this is essential for using feelings as data accurately. For example, the consultant in the first two case studies showed a particular affinity for identifying with projections of experiences around inferiority and inadequacy, while the manager in the third example may have had an affinity for picking up rage in the system.

For the manager who is (at least partially) convinced that feelings may be important data about the organizational systems of which he or she is part, how can this become useful in practice?

In each of the case studies, there was a three-part process that made it possible for something to shift. These three parts were, with equal weighting, *feeling*, *thinking* and *doing*. One could depict these as a triangle, as in Figure 20.1.

At XBrand, the consultant *felt* ignored, invisible and aware of her age. First the consultant team, and then the management team, were able to *think* about what these feelings might be saying about the system, rather than leaving them to reside in the consultant as (just) a personal experience. They were then able to *do* something which led to an improvement in retention. At Ecompute, the consultant *felt* intimidated by Jon's passionate but overly technical lecture about his product. Sharing the experience with Jon as possible data, rather than holding it as her own, made it possible for him to start to *think* about the parallels with the designers' experience of the company. And putting a name to the feelings opened up a new conversation between the partners so that they were able to *do* something about the huge challenges ahead, employing a COO. At the academy, Leila *felt* furious. She then stopped

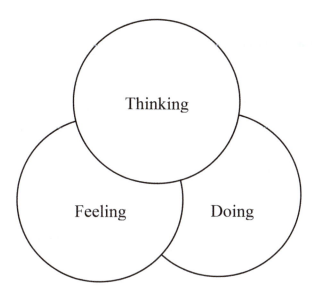

FIGURE 20.1   Thinking, feeling, doing triangle

herself from a knee-jerk response to *think* about this feeling and what sort of communication it might be. As at Encompute, this made possible new conversations, in this case with her staff, which led to implementing various changes (the *doing*).

In each case, the three parts of the process were essential and interdependent. At the Academy, for example, Leila would not have found out about the important experience of the leadership programme participants had their anger not been communicated to and *felt* by her. She would not have been able to make sense of the *feeling* had she not been able to stop and *think* about what it meant. And both *feeling* and *thinking* would be of no use had she not gone on, with her team, to *do* something.

Conclusion

The diagram in Figure 20.1 can serve as a prompt. When we are (too) busy *doing*, can we pause to notice what we are *feeling*? When we are too full of feeling, can we also *think* about it rather than ignore or act on it without thinking? It is probably not possible to do all three simultaneously. What we can do is learn to move a bit more fluidly from one part of the triangle to another, paying attention to what we may be overlooking.

One could argue that in all three case studies, people could have simply talked directly about their frustrations and anxieties, moving directly into collaborative problem-solving. However, they did not. HR staff at XBrand 'spoke with their feet'; the founding partners of Encompute were too fearful of the repercussions of naming their concerns to speak openly with each other; the academy clients may have been inhibited by shame at having been sent on a course to sort out their difficult behaviour. Yet it is precisely at such moments, when our experiences cannot be communicated in words, that we are most likely to push them out of awareness and 'into' others to feel on our behalf, and that we most need someone able to make themselves available – present and mindful – to 'hear' the communication and work with it.

Effective action depends on accurate sense-making. Alongside all the other kinds of information managers have at their disposal, using feelings as data can add valuable information that may not be available in any other way.

Note

1 The kind of observation used in the 'Tavistock approach' grew out of the practice of infant observation in psychotherapy training. It places as much importance on what the observer *feels* during the observation as on what they see. The observer makes themselves 'available' (open) to absorb what others may be feeling and trying to make sense of these feelings as unconscious communications, as well as to more explicitly observed activities and processes. In clinical practice, this is an aspect of what is sometimes called 'listening with the third ear'.

21

THE MYTH OF RATIONALITY

Why change efforts so often fail

James Krantz and Kay Trainor

Upheaval has become the norm for our organizations – relentless social, technological and economic change. Hyper-competitive global environments, the emerging role of networked organizations, and geopolitical instability all pressure our organizations to constantly evolve and adapt. Steering organizations through these turbulent waters, and managing change, have become an essential part of any leader's role today. And yet many change efforts fail. The question we ask here is: 'why?'.

Managers have extraordinarily powerful tools at their disposal for achieving change. Vast amounts of information are at their fingertips. Sophisticated techniques for managing finance, marketing, operations, human resources and product development are readily accessible. Many distinguished journals make the latest knowledge and best practices a click away. Yet no matter how rational or sensible the plans produced from these tools, something else often happens. While sophisticated planning and analytic methods are essential to effective change, they are not enough. It seems that something is missing from the standard repertoire.

We propose that the 'myth of rationality' often steers managers away from anticipating and addressing the emotional 'undertow' of change efforts, as if the deep underlying emotions stirred up by change – and the 'irrational' reactions and behaviour they evoke – were merely an unwanted side-effect or sign of failure rather than inherent and inevitable. In this chapter, we explore two dimensions of this emotional undertow, both of which require attention for change efforts to be effective and sustainable:

1 emotional disturbance caused by loss;
2 heightened anxiety caused by the dismantling of 'social defence systems' during change processes.

Change and loss

Micro was a very successful small company developing customised educational software for large publishing companies. The young workforce was bright and talented, taking great pride in the sophistication of their products and dedicated to the company's educational mission.

When a large software company, called Emblem here, purchased Micro, Micro's senior managers (who had become wealthy) were faced with transforming it into a division of a much bigger company with very different educational software development practices aimed at the retail market. Emblem's executives were eager to bring Micro into alignment with their priorities and ways of working. In particular, they viewed Micro's cherished underlying software engine as just one more delivery system and had no interest in maintaining an expensive proprietary platform.

Micro's former owners faced the prospect of adjusting from being leaders of an elite entrepreneurial firm into being middle managers of a mass market software company. The emphasis shifted from cutting-edge development to market appeal, speed of development and efficiency. Of the many new practices, among the most resented was the expectation that Micro programmers and developers would methodically account for their time. Whereas before they flexibly managed their own time, now they were expected to bill at least 40 hours/week on active contracts. Rather than being celebrated for their craftsmanship, they were now rewarded for productivity.

In announcing this, Micro's managers took no responsibility for what they were doing, in effect telling the staff: 'Emblem is making us do this awful thing to you.' Unable to acknowledge the painful loss of identity, the Micro managers engaged in what could be regarded as defensive splitting, which cast the new Emblem leadership as mean spirited and uncaring while they themselves were compassionate and loyal, though hapless, victims of Emblem. This served to maintain a surface solidarity with 'their' staff, who were becoming increasingly disturbed and resentful, but got in the way of Micro integrating into Emblem. Staff distress was labelled as a problem of 'morale', rather than being recognised as a dynamic revealing important information about underlying cultural clashes and structural issues that needed to be sorted out.

This reached crisis point at an angry and confrontational meeting with Micro's major client which led to calling in external consultants (with 'staff morale' still being the identified problem). What emerged through the consultation was a recognition that the unacknowledged disagreements between the Emblem and Micro approaches had been brought into the meeting with the client, where each had tried to win over the other by getting the client to ally with their position.

They also came to realise that the Micro division was being held back by 'deadness' in the chain of command arising from emotional withdrawal of the former Micro executives. The former owners were disturbed by what was unfolding and guilty for having benefited while the staff suffered so dramatically. Framing the dysfunction as if the disquiet and withdrawal resided in the staff alone served to deny and defend against their own loss.

Splitting off and denying painful feelings – and locating them in others – is very common for managers in difficult situations. Instead of acknowledging loss, the 'winners' (in this case Micro's former executives who had gained financially from the change) attributed, or projected,[1] their unacknowledged grief into the 'losers' (here, the staff who were being forced to give up cherished values and working practices). The complex reality – that change involves both gains and losses – is avoided, and the psychic work of grieving the past so as to be able to invest in the future is blocked.

Roberts (2005) draws a useful parallel with what happens when a bereavement occurs during pregnancy. The juxtaposition of these two major life events presents the nearly impossible task of preparing for birth and mourning simultaneously. Research indicates that in most cases, the bereaved woman 'opts for her live baby and mourning is postponed'; often the mourning is never resumed, with long-term consequences for both mother and child (Lewis and Casement 1986 p. 45). In organizational change, the contradictory and competing psychological demands of birth and death tend to get split apart, so that some people focus more or less exclusively on 'birth' (the benefits of the change) and may denigrate the past, while others focus on loss and may idealise the past.

Much of the psychic pain of grieving has to do with ambivalence towards what has been lost. We tend either to idealise or to demonize the lost person or situation, rather than recognising that one has both positive and negative feeling towards them. While this splitting reduces inner conflict, failure to face and manage the mixed feelings interferes with the healthy management of the mourning process (Freud 1917; Klein 1940).

Marris (1986) suggests that in organizations the internal conflict evoked by ambivalence is often externalised and may get played out between individuals or sub-groups. 'Tribes' form – those in favour and those opposing the change process – relieving psychic tension, reducing confusion, and bolstering a sense of identity and belonging, now defined in terms of being 'for' or 'against' the change process. This is a familiar picture. Where grief is suppressed rather than externalised, there may be withdrawal and apathy instead of a fight, or a long, drawn-out low-grade rumbling often called 'resistance'. Denigration of the past by the 'pro-change tribe' can lead to others feeling too alienated to engage with the new organization.

Marris identifies an essential element of grieving as the reconstructing of meaning: detaching one's sense of purpose from the past and reformulating it so that there can be a sense of continuity of identity and meaning. In the case of Micro, many of its former executives were unable to do this in the new company. Instead, they joined a former client organization where they felt more able to create an environment with the same values and orientation as Micro had before it was acquired. Those who stayed, and most of the staff, were able to seek out a meaningful role within Emblem.

This kind of 'natural attrition' is common at times of major change. However, when the psychological demands of reconstructing meaning and identity feel too great, there may not even be a capacity to wait for this kind of process to evolve, as in the next case study.

> A large hospitality brand agency, Parent Company, opted to acquire one of their largest clients, International Hotel (IH), when the opportunity arose. Parent Company had no direct experience of hotel management but the acquisition was seen as a good fit. For Parent Company, it was a route to other hotel clients; for IH, it meant joining the agency that had helped build their reputation and would continue to do so. Preliminary discussions focused both on the goodness of fit and the competitive strength arising from combining their resources.
>
> However, when the leadership of Parent Company started working with the management team of their newly acquired company, they felt that their ambitions were met with 'too many complexities' as they put it. Rather than struggling with these complexities to find ways to combine the talent from both companies, they fired the entire management of IH, replacing it with their own internal team of people, who had little or no hotel management experience.
>
> How could the senior management team of Parent Company have persuaded themselves that this disastrous decision was a good one? Strategically and financially, the acquisition of IH made sense, but something got in the way once the prospect of working together became a reality. The senior management team of Parent Company had known all along that they lacked expertise in hotel management and that they would need to integrate with the IH team in order to be most effective. What they had not anticipated was how much change real integration of a new company would involve, and the level of anxiety this would generate. In order to push forward with the desired acquisition, they had developed a fantasy that none of them would need to learn anything to take up their new roles, and that none of them would lose anything. While this made it easier to proceed with the negotiations and for the acquisition to take place, when it came to actually working together and creating a new top team, they were confronted with a more challenging reality than they were prepared for. Rather than engaging with the complexities of genuine integration, they took the disastrous decision to sack the hotel team, and the potential flowering of a new enterprise was lost.

Typically, those being acquired are the ones most likely to feel the sense of loss, although in fact there is loss on both sides, acknowledged or not. There is also potential benefit for both sides, which those carrying the sense of loss may not be able to see. One of the particular challenges facing managers trying to merge two organizations is that everyone needs to expand and change their idea of 'colleagues-in-the-mind' so that the new people no longer have the status of 'outsiders' (into whom negative emotions are often projected). While a polarized them-and-us image may help people cope with uncertainty and vulnerability, it inevitably compromises the ability to make best use of available talent and expertise and damages the integration effort.

Anxieties and defences in organizations

Anxiety is an inevitable part of the human condition, stemming back to infancy when we are utterly dependent on others for survival, to feel safe and to develop our first coping mechanisms or defences (see Chapter 1). As we grow older, the ways we shield ourselves from anxiety – our defences – become more sophisticated, although defences from the earliest months of life, such as splitting and projection, may re-emerge at times of heightened anxiety. Some defences are individual, such as striving to be top of the class or persuading ourselves that another's opinion is of no importance. Others are shared, as when a friendship group at school disparages another group as 'geeks' or 'jocks' to affirm their own status. Some of these defences promote development, enabling us to engage with challenging situations; others can inhibit it, such as blaming others for our disappointments and failures.

We carry these anxieties and coping mechanisms with us into the workplace, and our organizations also provide us with new sources of 'containment' for our anxieties that help us cope with anxieties in a mature way. For example, close-knit teams, achievable targets or bonuses, clear areas of responsibility and lines of accountability and predictable routines can all serve to help us manage anxieties around belonging and worth. However, we also encounter new sources of anxiety at work: doubts about our competence, the demands of managing hierarchical and peer relationships, and less conscious anxieties related to the nature of the work itself (see Chapter 24).

Organizations develop structures and practices that serve defensive purposes (often referred to as social defence systems). Menzies (1960), in her classic study of hospital nursing, showed how impersonal elements of organizations such as protocols, technologies, systems for allocating tasks and responsibilities, and even organizational design (see next chapter for examples), while set up to facilitate work, can also come to be utilised for the additional purpose of helping people manage anxiety. For example, the hospital's approach to scheduling, decision-making and work assignment created a depersonalised and fragmented pattern of care that served to shield nurses from the painful anxieties stimulated by close contact with illness and death. At the same time, it depleted their ability to mobilise their competence and reduced work satisfaction, impacting negatively on patient care and on staff retention.

In modern corporate environments, systems which serve both task-related and defensive aims abound. Accounting is used to bring order and manage risk but can also be used to bolster a sense of predictability. HR protocols, targets and reward systems are designed to ensure objectivity and fairness but can become prescriptive and constraining. Restructuring to improve performance can become a panacea that takes the place of paying attention to significant underlying issues.

The paradox of change

An important starting point for planning change efforts is to recognise that massive anxiety will inevitably be stimulated when individual and organizational equilibrium is disrupted. Old psychological contracts are broken, loyalties and informal networks are undermined, the support that comes from familiarity and predictability is lost, and the complex web of political and social arrangements must be renegotiated. On the surface level, change brings anxieties about job security, change of status, or fears about one's competence in the new conditions. At an unconscious level, there are often powerful destabilising anxieties about loss of identity, primitive fears of being swallowed up and utterly lost, or of being attacked by malign forces.

Furthermore, significant change is likely to involve the dismantling of existing social defence systems, so that on top of the new anxieties evoked by the change itself, old anxieties which had previously been contained by the old arrangements are likely to resurface. So it is no surprise that people often become (at least temporarily) less able to think effectively. Thus, change generates a paradox: it undermines the very qualities which are needed to keep us from being overwhelmed by anxiety so that the change can succeed.

Sometimes change is managed in a way that promotes a more integrated, mature and sophisticated approach to coping with the emotional challenges: the organization's leaders find ways to 'contain' the heightened anxiety. But since the leaders themselves are likely to be prey to high levels of anxiety, their capacity to attend to that of others is often diminished just when it is most needed. As anxiety swirls around the organization and reflective capacities are submerged, we often see counter-productive defensive behaviours. Distrust upwards and downwards, scapegoating and withdrawal can surface, as the next vignette illustrates.

> Eaton, a global trading firm, depended on its information technology (IT) division for its profitability. Considered one of the most sophisticated IT operations on Wall Street, the division had an annual budget exceeding $1billion and employed over two thousand people worldwide. Despite its impressive accomplishments, the division was under increasing pressure to undertake large-scale innovation so as to be more responsive to the needs of the business units, to keep up with accelerating changes in technology, and to be less costly. Eaton saw the division as bloated, and its response to their demands as listless. To move things forward, they put Ted, one their most successful young traders, in charge, with the idea that this would make the IT division more attuned to the needs of the firm's core business. Although

he had neither management nor IT experience, Ted was a brilliant trader and had received much acclaim.

True to his remit, Ted set out to transform the division, using ideas gleaned from 'best practice' at other leading-edge companies to develop a 'vision' which was both prescriptive and faddish. Given his lack of deep understanding of the actual work of the IT division, his vision of the future was neither compelling nor plausible to the division's staff. Further, as the senior team he had brought together began to implement the plan, they fundamentally changed the working arrangements in the division and stripped out 'unneeded layers'.

Ted and his team were intensely frustrated by the difficulty in getting others to join their ideas and regarded the staff's lack of comprehension and disengagement as backward thinking, resistance and sabotage. As the sense of estrangement and conflict intensified, meetings became ritualistic and empty of substance. Outside of the meetings, the division's managers derided the change efforts: Ted's tendency to come in on Mondays excited about the book he'd read over the weekend and how it illuminated aspects of his 'model' became a standing joke.

Not surprisingly, the effort fell apart. First the division fragmented into two groups – those aligned with Ted and his team, and those who were opposed. Ted became increasingly enraged, resorting to threats and tantrums. At one point he lashed out at a mid-level staff member, publicly reducing his pay significantly. The dream of creating an environment of empowerment, creativity and collaborative innovation ended up producing a punitive environment of suspicion, persecutory feelings, and contemptuous sabotage.

The anxiety here started at the top: Eaton depended on the IT division and feared it was not keeping abreast of technological innovations, putting the whole company at risk. Rather than taking the time needed to diagnose the root causes of IT's problems, Eaton reached for an 'instant' magic solution, enrolling Ted to bring about transformation. Ted dealt with the impossible demands placed on him with further quick magical solutions of his own. Because the considerable anxieties of IT staff were not contained, collaborative problem-solving was impossible. The drastic and impulsive changes introduced by Ted's team further fuelled anxiety, and splitting and disarray ensued.

Paying attention to the 'emotional undertow' of change

The kind of over-hasty and unthought-through approach in the Eaton story is very common when companies feel under pressure to respond quickly to perceived risks. Indeed, one of the main reasons for not taking people's feelings of loss and anxiety into account is the fear that doing so will slow down the necessary change process to a dangerous extent, putting the company at even greater risk. However, while there may well be a temporary slowing down, in the longer term making space to hear and work with difficult feelings gives change efforts a much greater chance of succeeding.

> Mixbox was a company supplying both fiction and non-fiction content for TV broadcasters. They had an excellent reputation and many production companies were loyal to their brand and approach. However, their context was changing dramatically: traditional approaches were giving way to more interactive programmes and viewer-generated content, and the digital revolution in the sector was challenging every aspect of their work, particularly in the non-fiction part of the company.
>
> A new CEO, aware of the risks Mixbox faced, was determined to make sure the company continued to thrive in this fast-changing marketplace and decided to merge the two teams commissioning non-fiction – the 'single broadcast' or SB team, and the 'multiple broadcast' or MB team – as the content each team produced now overlapped significantly. Terry, the lead commissioner in the MB team, who had experience of working in both teams and had been a member of Mixbox's 'Digital Future' group since its inception ten years previously, was promoted to the new role of head of non-fiction and tasked with achieving the joining of the two teams.
>
> Working separately, the two teams had been able to defend against certain dilemmas. The SB team focused on quality and had been responsible for many of the award-winning productions on which the reputation of Mixbox had been built, but their single-broadcast documentaries brought in relatively little revenue. The MB team, producing content which was more popular and broadcast many times, generated much higher profit. In effect, the CEO was asking Terry to bring quality and profit together.
>
> The implementation of the CEO's plan was beset with difficulties from the outset. People arrived late to meetings and ignored agendas. When the former MB team 'imported' the electronic graph they had been using to track income hour by hour, the former SB team were appalled. One of its senior members, Theresa, stormed out of a meeting, accusing Terry of reducing the whole enterprise to its lowest common denominator and offering her resignation. The CEO encouraged Terry to accept it. Instead, Terry chose to hold fire and try to make sense of what was happening. Thinking about the situation as a whole, rather than jumping at the chance to get rid of a 'difficult' individual, he came to understand Theresa's behaviour not as wilful undermining but as an expression of grief in the system. Instead of simply pushing through the implementation of the change process, trumpeting its advantages, he made space for the teams to explore and give voice to what each had lost through the merger.
>
> There were dozens of such occurrences. Containing the impulse to react in the heat of the moment was not easy. Progress towards a joined-up team seemed slow for a long time. When a break-through eventually came, in the form of a jointly commissioned piece of work which brought together the

best from both teams, it was quickly followed by a resurgence of hostility. In the longer-term, however, the merger proved a success, with a 20% increase in revenue over the first two years.

Each team was dealing with the loss of their previous identity as a self-contained unit with particular achievements they were proud of, and particular working practices that had contributed to their successes. The merger also brought to the surface the long-standing latent competition between the teams, and their fears about losing status. The SB team's leader left the company, leaving his team not only mourning his loss, but also feeling vulnerable to having MB impose its culture and working practices on them.

Furthermore, as long as they had remained separate, neither team had had to face the inherent tensions between profit and quality. When the structure changed, each team had to engage with the dilemmas of competing priorities. While this presented a significant new challenge, it also presented each team with new opportunities, notably for a more mature engagement with core issues previously held at bay.

Loss and anxiety are experienced by both groups involved in mergers, consciously or unconsciously. For example, Terry understood that the extreme reaction to the proposal to impose the graph on the combined team was not just about 'resistance' and anxiety in the SB team, but also a defence against uncertainty in the MB team when faced in meeting after meeting with proposals from their SB colleagues for commissions that seemed likely to prove unprofitable. His response was to 'press the pause button' and arrange for the whole combined team to meet together with the CEO to understand better the rationale for the proposed merger.

Terry had the skills and knowledge needed to design the change process, but he always maintained that it was paying attention to the emotional data – using it to understand what was needed at each stage – that made the process successful. Many change efforts and mergers fail or end up as reports on the shelves of CEOs. Taking time to pay attention to the emotional 'undertow' of change efforts can reap rewards, not only easing the emotional difficulty of change, but also making it more sustainable.

However, this approach involved risks for Terry, notably in resisting pressure from the CEO to move the process forward quickly, not getting caught up in anxiety that taking time to attend to the 'emotional undertow' would prevent the necessary changes from happening. Terry also had to live with not knowing whether his reading of the situation was right, and therefore if his actions would actually further or hinder the process. The capacity to tolerate not-knowing, or 'negative capability'[2], has been described as a crucial element of creative leadership by French and colleagues (2009 p. 197).

> Creative leadership is called for at the edge between certainty and uncertainty, both a necessary and a difficult place to work in the current context of organizational life. Whereas positive capabilities direct leaders and followers

toward particular forms of action rooted in knowing, negative capability is the ability to resist dispersing into inappropriate action.

They argue that the emphasis in leadership training on action and decisiveness ('positive capabilities') is often at the expense of developing the ability to be fully present to what is actually going on, rather than what is 'meant' to happen. Change, which by definition is about a future which has yet to emerge, requires working with limited knowledge, limited control, and a degree of humility. This is the opposite of what Gabriel (1998) calls 'the hubris of management', the fantasy that everything can be predicted and planned. Furthermore, when leaders are able to tolerate ambiguity and uncertainty without undue anxiety, this helps others to manage their own anxieties and to develop their own capacity for reflective thought before jumping into actions driven by the need to avoid not-knowing and complexity.

Conclusion

The myth of rationality is enduring, resilient, and dangerous to those undertaking organizational change efforts. It is reinforced by and reinforces the view that emotional responses to change are merely undesirable 'side effects' of organizational life, a matter of individual vulnerability or an expression of 'resistance' to what is unfamiliar or challenging. Seeing 'irrationality' in this way prevents seeing the important part these dynamics play in the success or failure of change efforts, and building in ways to attend to them. Listening to those 'resisting' change not only contains difficult feelings so that they are less likely to be acted out in ways that undermine the change process, but can also bring valuable information into view. As described in Chapter 6, it is important that leaders are able to ask themselves the question about the resister: 'How are they right?' (Shapiro 2001), particularly when 'they' seem most wrong. Objections to the change process often hold at least a grain of truth, for example drawing attention to aspects of the new design which have been overlooked and which – if given attention – can prevent things from derailing later.

Central to 'the Tavistock approach' is the idea that organizations are 'socio-technical systems' (see Introduction). The myth of rationality reinforces the tendency to over-emphasise the formal aspects of organization (the 'technical system') and to under-emphasise the human element (the 'social system'). Paying attention to both is crucial to success. Alongside the advanced tools and analytic methods developed to support change, other tools are needed that can make the underlying emotional processes more intelligible and provide help in steering the process so that the social system can work hand in hand with the new structures and practices that comprise the technical system.

In mature and contained environments, hopeful views of the future are tempered by a sober appreciation of the challenges involved. The disarray, confusion, and uncertainty that change inevitably evokes become more manageable where there is a positive but realistic image of the future. But when the emotional impact of change feels too difficult to pay attention to, a split image of the future may prevail, with some parts of the organization holding an idealised (perhaps even utopian) picture, while others experience cynicism, deadening despair, and a lack of confidence in the leadership.

In this more 'primitive'[3] kind of environment, there is often strong pressure to voice unquestioning support for the idealised future image. Doubt or criticism is treated as disloyal, and ambivalence cannot be tolerated. Fearfulness and other feelings associated with the difficulties the future may hold are likely to be projected into particular individuals or sub-groups who then become increasingly 'resistant' and may express or act out the doubts in extreme ways that contribute to their being ignored or scapegoated. Finding ways to address the emotional impact of change, alongside the technical, structural aspects of change efforts, offers a way forward that increases the likelihood of successful outcomes.

Notes

1   Projection is an unconscious defence whereby feelings which we cannot acknowledge as our own are attributed to others. See for example Chapter 1, pp 14–15. For the related process of projective identification, see Chapters 1, 2 and 20.
2   'Negative capability' was first used by Keats in a letter to his brother in 1817, where he defined it as: 'when man is capable of being in uncertainties, mysteries, doubts, without any irritable reaching after fact & reason'.
3   The word 'primitive' is used to indicate that the defence mechanisms in use come from the earliest period of life. Under stress, human beings tend to 'regress' to these earlier ways of coping unless the organization can provide sufficient containment to make the stress more bearable.

22

NAVIGATING ROLES IN COMPLEX SYSTEMS

Vega Zagier Roberts

Traditional bureaucratic hierarchical structures with well-defined departments are increasingly giving way to matrix organizations, temporary cross-functional project systems, and other structures that support speedy flexible responses to rapidly shifting demands from the wider environment. All of this places new and complex demands on managers, who often have to reinvent or rediscover how to take up their roles.

Much of what is required to work effectively in organizations, especially at senior levels, cannot be contained in a job description: roles need to be 'found' by the person in the job. To some extent, this has always been the case, but it is more than ever the case now. Reed and Bazalgette (2006) describe an iterative process, organizational role analysis, comprising three elements: *finding* the role (finding the system where the role is located and locating it within the multiple other systems in play); *making* the role (sense-making through developing one's understanding of the internal and external requirements of these different systems and of the wider context); and *taking* the role (making decisions and taking actions based on the first two stages). In this chapter we shall focus mainly on the *finding* stage, as a crucial first step in managing oneself to be effective in role.

A key challenge in this process is that all managers are part of more than one system and therefore have more than one role.

Open systems thinking[1]

In the 1960s, The Tavistock Institute of Human Relations developed open systems theory (OST) as a way of thinking about organizational structures and roles. Organizations were described as systems, 'a set of activities within a boundary' designed to achieve the task of the system (Miller and Rice 1967). While boundaries serve to demarcate what is inside from what is outside the system, they are most usefully thought of as semi-permeable membranes which need to be managed so as to enable and regulate the exchanges with the environment (including other systems or between sub-systems) necessary to achieve their aims. For the reader's convenience, we re-cap some of the main elements of OST here; a fuller description is available in Chapter 4.

At its most simplistic, one could depict a system as in Figure 22.1:

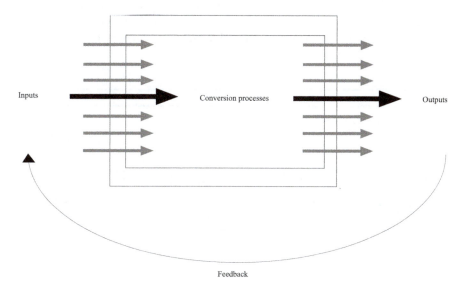

FIGURE 22.1 The primary task

Inputs might for example include raw materials or human resources or information, to be converted into outputs such as saleable products, services, trained personnel, or business plans. As shown in Figure 22.1, among these different input-conversion-output processes, at any particular moment, one is dominant: this is called the *primary task*, that is, the task that the system must perform in order to survive, and which the other conversion processes support. A shoe factory not only takes in leather to turn into shoes, but also information from the environment to produce business plans and strategies, untrained personnel to become skilled workers, etc. but if it ceases to produce shoes, it is no longer a shoe factory. As circumstances change, the primary task may change, either temporarily (as when an acute emergency arises) or permanently. There are many well-known examples, from Nokia to Virgin, of companies whose dominant throughput – and hence their primary task – changed over time. This can throw up huge challenges as old identities and roles disappear, so that the question 'what are we here to do *now*?' becomes more crucial than ever.

Miller and Rice (1967) described the primary task as 'a heuristic concept, which allows us to explore the ordering of multiple activities . . . [and] makes it possible to construct and compare different organizational models' (p. 25). Thus, the ideas which follow are not offered as rules or models: they have value only to the extent that the reader discovers them to be useful in making sense of their situations. Specifically, the notion of the primary task offers a starting point for studying the relations between parts and wholes, and 'finding' one's role in each of the systems of which one is a part.

An organization can be represented as an ensemble of a number of sub-systems such as teams or departments. Some of these may be sequential, as in the assembly of automobiles, with the outputs of one sub-system becoming the inputs for the next (Figure 22.2). In other cases, sub-systems are not sequential but operate in parallel, for example marketing, research, human resources and the assembly line of a factory (Figure 22.3).

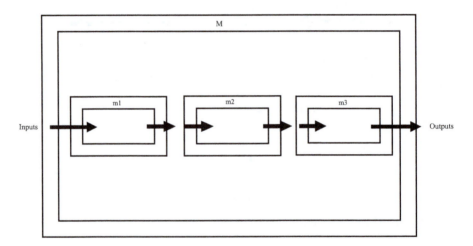

FIGURE 22.2 Sequential sub-systems

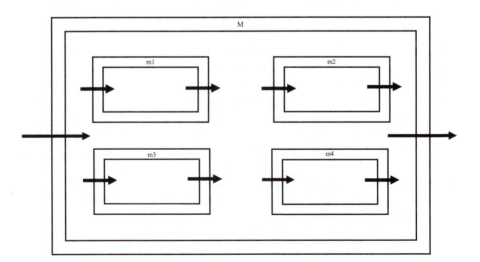

FIGURE 22.3 Non-sequential sub-systems

Each sub-system has its own task, and together their outputs contribute to the primary task of the organization as a whole. And each system needs to be managed: the flow of resources (skills, raw materials, information, etc.) needs to be regulated so that they are sufficient to achieve its particular task. The management function is located at the boundary of each system as it involves regulating exchanges across the boundary. At each higher level, the management function involves the coordination of the sub-systems within it, shown in Figures 22.2 and 22.3 as M for the management of the larger system, and m for the management of a sub-system. In traditional hierarchies, M is the manager of all the m's in his or her system.

Managing oneself in multiple systems

Every person in an organization is part of a number of systems both inside and outside the workplace. In order to take up one's role effectively, one needs to identify which system the role is in and what the primary task of that system is, i.e. to which task one is contributing.

Let us start with a very simple example: a sales rep meeting with a potential customer. We could think of this meeting as a system 'managed' by the rep in order to achieve the desired output of a sale, and at this level, this may be the only output that matters. However, the rep is likely to be part of a higher-order system such as a sales team or department. In his or her role as a member of a team, it might be as important – or even more important – than making an immediate sale that the output of the meeting is a potential customer with a positive feeling about the company and its products, making future sales (possibly by a colleague) more likely. Holding this in mind will influence how the rep manages the encounter.

Managing competing priorities within an organization

The more senior one is, the more likely one is to be part of a number of different systems with different – and sometimes competing or conflicting – aims.

> Carmen was the head of risk control of an investment bank, tasked with monitoring the deals traders made to ensure both that they complied with regulation and that they did not expose either the bank or its clients to undue risk. External regulations had multiplied exponentially since the 2008 crisis, and Carmen's department was treated by traders as if they were at best a necessary nuisance, at worst as the enemy, hampering them from achieving all they were capable of.
>
> One could think of the bank as having three key tasks: investment (profit); compliance; and restoring and maintaining public trust in the banking system. Carmen's department was located at the crossroads of these competing tasks and accountabilities and she herself was deeply vested in contributing to the bank's success though developing ethical investment practice. However, in meetings with traders, she and her team were treated as if they were

external controllers restricting investors' freedom, rather than colleagues with the bank's interests at heart. Consultants observing a meeting of risk control officers and traders noticed that Carmen's team did in fact have a heavy-handed critical approach, as if they had identified with the traders' views of them as 'police'.

One might hypothesise that the three tasks identified were experienced as competing, if not contradictory. To manage this tension, the traders kept only the first in view, while Carmen and her team focused on the other two. Interactions between the traders and the risk control department could then feel more like an encounter between competitors than between colleagues with a shared over-arching purpose. Each needed to move between their roles 'at the boundary' of their own department and their roles in the 'system' of directors of the bank as a whole. From this latter position, it might have been easier to develop a stronger sense of shared identity and purpose, with all departments coming to act more congruently with the bank's espoused values.

Heifetz and his colleagues at Harvard's John F. Kennedy School of Government identify a core leadership skill as 'getting on the balcony' so as to see the patterns which cannot be seen while 'on the dance floor' (Heifetz, Grashow and Linsky 2009). From a balcony position, Carmen might have been more able to understand the systemic drivers to her situation, and perhaps have found a way to put the knock-on effects of the bank's competing tasks on the agenda at meetings with directors, rather than feeling left to fight things out in confrontations with traders.

Task and sentient boundaries

Miller and Rice define task boundaries as those which are designed to facilitate task achievement, i.e. the conversion of inputs into the required outputs, whereas sentient systems are those which receive loyalty and commitment from its members, i.e. where there are emotional bonds promoting a sense of belonging. The degree to which these two kinds of systems coincide, overlap or remain separate vary with the type of organization and task, often appropriately so, and sometimes not.

Natural coincidence of task and sentient boundaries

Here the work-task system originates in members' sentience (feelings, beliefs, loyalties). For example, a group of people in a company come together out of a shared concern that lack of access to affordable childcare is limiting opportunities for female staff. Their aim is to set up a crèche. Members share attitudes and values from the outset, but then need to develop roles and role-relationships in order to produce the desired output (the crèche).

A trade-union is another example of a situation where task and sentient boundaries naturally coincide.

Partial or non-coincidence of task and sentient boundaries

As people join a task system at work, they bring with them their affiliations with other groups and systems such as their profession or their commitment to certain aims and values. This sentience may find expression in the objectives of the task system they have joined, but often it does not. In that case, they are likely to look for other outlets.

Where these are found outside the task system, they may not cause any difficulty. However, in some situations people create outlets within the task system through the formation of sub-groups whose priorities may not be aligned with those of the task system. Rice (1969) identifies a key element of group task leadership as managing group sentience, 'to harness group emotions and feelings in favour of group task performance' (p. 276).

Contrived coincidence

Here work is organized deliberately to increase the sentience within work groups in order to enhance task performance, for example organizing the workforce into small close-knit teams that foster loyalty among members *and* also shared commitment to the task. Team-building retreats may also be used to foster a sense of shared identity and emotional commitment to the work system, thus increasing the extent to which task and sentient boundaries coincide.

Contrived non-coincidence

At times work is organized deliberately to minimize sentience that could interfere with task performance. For example, in their study of an airline, Miller and Rice (1967) found that flight crews were constantly changed (sometimes with each flight), lest sentience reduce the vigilance essential to safety.

Inter-group systems

Straddling inside and outside

Tom, an experienced energy specialist, was the director of the sustainability department (SD) of Worrid, a large energy company which, like many of its competitors, was the frequent target of criticism for polluting the environment. His job was to contribute to the development of greener policies and practices within the company, both to enhance its reputation and its market share as consumers increasingly moved their accounts to greener suppliers, and to fulfil its social responsibilities. His time was almost equally divided between meetings with other departments inside Worrid and being part of a network of agencies fighting for a cleaner, more sustainable environment. He often felt marginal and ineffective in both parts of his job: his recommendations to

Worrid directors were largely ignored, while some network members saw Tom as a tokenistic nod to environmental concerns from an anything-for-profit 'enemy' entity.

On one occasion, when discussing a particularly wounding appraisal meeting with his manager, he was invited by his coach to draw a 'system map' to show how he located himself in the two overlapping systems of Worrid and the network. He had great trouble doing this and eventually located himself outside the Worrid system altogether (Figure 22.4(b)). He realised that he had come to identify more and more with the network's views and culture, to the point of feeling he was indeed 'working for the enemy', at which point he left his job for a post in a lobbying organization. While this may well have been the best choice for him personally, he lost the opportunity to influence Worrid's policies and behaviours; he was replaced by someone with more passion for the company's market aims than for its environmental impact, thus confirming external perceptions that Worrid's sustainability department was indeed mainly for show.

One way of thinking about Tom's situation is that his role in the network was as a *representative* of Worrid. A system map of the network could look like Figure 22.4(a), with each member (x) representing their particular 'home' agency or organization.

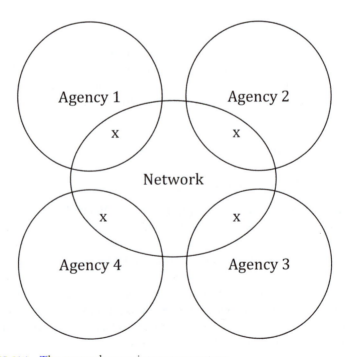

FIGURE 22.4(a)   The network as an intergroup system

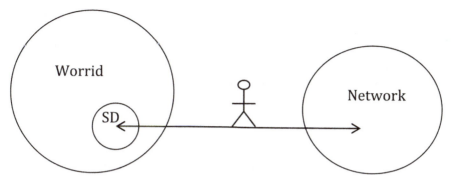

FIGURE 22.4(b) Tom's system map of the network

Tom's system map did not show him as part of either system but rather as travelling between the two (See Figure 22.4(b)). One could say he had 'lost' his representative role, and thus had become unable to take it up to the benefit of both systems. He needed to navigate his roles as a Worrid director *and* as a member of the network. In the end found the tensions too great to manage.

Sentience and inter-group systems

For optimal collaboration and commitment to an enterprise, a degree of sentience is essential, not least because sentience is closely linked to meaning, and a sense of shared meaning within one's task system is an important source of motivation and commitment. However, sentience can also work against task performance. In Tom's role dilemma above, there was a virtually total overlap of task and sentient boundaries in his network role, and very little sentience in his departmental director role, leading to his distancing himself emotionally from the company that employed him.

The consequences of too little or too much overlapping of task and sentient boundaries can often be observed both in temporary intergroup systems like committees and project groups, and in longer-term or permanent systems like multidisciplinary teams. Initially, members may come with a strong sense of 'us' with the department or professional discipline they represent. Their lack of emotional investment in the inter-group system may manifest as they scroll through their emails rather than participating in meetings, or focus on defending the interests of their 'home group' at the expense of the shared enterprise for which the inter-group system was convened. If this persists, optimal collaboration may prove hard to achieve, as each rep holds on to their own expertise, authority, identity and interests. However, not infrequently this sentience to the 'home' group shifts over time as members become more committed to the shared project and develop affective bonds with other members of the new group. Eventually the new group may become so invested in the shared task, or it may become so central to members' identity, that they 'forget' the other half of their dual (representative) role. The very differences – say in expertise or perspective – that led to their being part of the new group can become eroded by the desire to be a strong 'us', with a risk that 'groupthink' takes the place of combining members' expertise. At its most extreme, excessive sentience can lead to groups staying together long after their initial task has been achieved (or abandoned).

The special case of the family business

Here two systems overlap: the family and the business. In a small family business, the two may overlap almost entirely, with most or all members of the business being members of the same family. But even here, people have different roles in the two systems. The mother of the family may be a director, but taking her role as director requires different skills, competencies and activities from taking her role as mother. In a large family business, the overlap may be quite partial, with some family members not participating in the business, and some directors not being members of the family.

Often the two systems get entangled, as already described in Chapter 21. For example, family dynamics can pervade the way business is run (or vice versa). Cardona and Rafaelli (2016) describe a pharmaceutical company owned by the parents, where their four children were on the management board. The two sons had each been appointed managing director at some point, only to be fired in turn for what their father considered poor decisions. One was so wounded by this that he had virtually no contact with the family for several years. All four children felt emotionally deprived by their parents' having always put the business first; vying for their parents' love and attention made for difficulty taking up their organizational roles effectively. The focus of the consultancy to this company was to help them distinguish the two systems and to be clearer what role they were taking up when.

Kets de Vries et al. (2007) describes a very different situation where Jack, the owner of a supermarket, gave his son Kevin a job in the produce department. When the department manager reported that Kevin was not performing adequately, Jack took up his role in the business system and told the manager to treat Kevin like any other employee. When Kevin's performance continued to be poor, Jack fired him. However, in his role as father, he sensed his son's need for support and guidance and invited him to the family's hot-tub to discuss his future and how his father could help him. As De Vries puts it, and in contrast to the previous example, Jack 'had a successful business *and* strong family relationships because he treated the family like a family and the business like a business' (p. 29).

De Vries suggests in family businesses there are in fact three systems involved rather than just two: the family system, the business system, and the ownership system, each with its own values, aims and priorities. This presents particular challenges requiring a multi-faceted approach that pays attention to all three systems.

Finding one's role when the boundaries keep changing

Open systems theory first developed at a time of relatively greater stability both of organizational structures and of their environments. Nowadays, systems 'maps' to show the location of roles and the relations between sub-systems are likely to be temporary, particularly in the corporate sector as it relies increasingly on designs that support flexibility and innovation. Hirschhorn and Gilmore (1992) give many rich examples of the complexity of role-finding in more fluid organizations where 'maps' can no longer be relied upon, and where therefore what the manager has in his mind becomes ever more essential. They propose that she or he needs to be aware of four different kinds of boundaries, each associated with a key question:

- The task boundary: what are we here to do?
- The identity boundary: who is 'us' and who is 'them'?
- The political boundary: how do the interests of different sub-systems compete or align?
- The authority boundary: who makes decisions binding on others, and what authorises them to do so?

But as soon as we rely on what is in our minds, rather than what is formally embodied in organizational charts and structures, we inevitably run into the difficulty that different people are likely to make different assumptions about the questions above, and therefore to interpret boundaries differently. In traditional stable organizational structures, departments or 'silos' are likely to have more or less shared views, but the more that managers simultaneously hold roles in multiple systems (some of which may be new and temporary), the more ripe the field will be for conflicting interpretations of one's own and others' role-boundaries. For example, Hirschhorn and Gilmore describe an interaction between an engineer and a shop-floor worker in a company that was encouraging more collegiate and less hierarchical relations. When the worker asked about the rationale for a design decision made by the engineer, the engineer responded as if the question were an unwarranted criticism. Both then retreated back to the very stereotypes and traditional relations the company was trying to do away with.

> Because neither has an accurate 'map' to figure out the kind of relationship [they are now] in and what boundary they have encountered, the interaction that was intended to make them more effective colleagues only served to separate them. The result is a failed encounter and an unproductive relationship.
>
> (*Hirschhorn and Gilmore 1992 p. 106*)

The company's aim here was to create or strengthen a new boundary that included both engineers and shop floor, in order to facilitate more effective joint problem-solving which was sometimes inhibited by hierarchically based assumptions about who was authorised to make recommendations. We could see this example as involving an aspiration to enlarge all four boundaries described above, strengthening the sense of an interdisciplinary 'us' with a shared investment in making the company's products as successful as possible. What the vignette illustrates all too well is the relative fragility of these wider boundaries in the mind, and how readily they are eroded by a regressive pull that catapults us back to earlier ways of relating with which we are more familiar.

All this can create considerable anxiety, as there is both a fantasied and a real risk of 'getting it wrong'. And when things do 'go wrong', people often retreat back to their silos. For every innovative step forward into new forms of organization and self-organization – be it Scrum or Agile Teams or Holocracy – this is often quickly followed by an outcry about its limitations, and stories across the internet of failed experiments. One could hypothesise that alongside the desire for more flexible forms of organization, with devolved authority, there is a competing desire for predictability, dependency and keeping accountability firmly higher up the hierarchy.

'The ordering of multiple activities': boundaries, organizational design and organization-in-the-mind

In designing an organizational system, one starts – at least at a conscious, rational level – from the perspective of what structural arrangement will best serve the achieving of the task. However, design is also determined by other factors. Colman (1975) proposes that design emerges from the interplay of 'rational' and 'irrational' elements, where the irrational comprises both covert (conscious but unspoken or unacknowledged) and unconscious factors. The design that emerges from this interplay then impacts on how people working in the organization understand what is required of them, and thus on their behaviour and feelings.

As an example: in some companies, where HR is seen as integral to strategy, the director of the HR department is part of the Executive Board; in others, where HR is regarded as a support or 'feminine' function, or as about managing procedures involving personnel (such as hiring, firing, training, employee complaints etc), the HR director is likely to be at a lower level in the hierarchy. While one could make a perfectly cogent argument for either design, it is clear that each will affect both how the HR department is used and contributes to the enterprise, and how its director and members will understand and take up their roles. In some companies, HR can become a locus for procedural compliance and control, and a 'thorn in the side' of those seeking to advance innovation and flexibility. Alternatively, as in the family business described by Cardona and Rafaelli (2016), where the founding couple had assigned operational and strategic work to the father and 'looking after the staff' to the mother (and later to the daughters), the HR department may operate as the 'caring' part of the organization.

All this shapes the *organization-in-the-mind* (OITM), that is, how we perceive and understand 'how activities and relations are organized, structured and connected internally', our 'idea of the organization which, through experiencing and imagining, forms in my inner psychic space and which then influences how I interact with my environment' (Hutton, Bazalgette and Reed 1997 p. 114). It both shapes and is shaped by meanings – processes of sense-making – which are both individual and collective (see Chapter 6 for a more in-depth exploration of OITM).

Where boundaries are placed nearly always facilitates some aspects of task performance while rendering others problematic. For example, Borwick (2006) describes XYZ, a European-wide overnight-delivery company where the transport department had the task of picking up customers' goods and getting them onto evening flights so that they would arrive the next day. In order to achieve the overnight goal, they often did not complete the paperwork required by customs. The company's custom agents then had to complete the paperwork and meeting the overnight target became very stressful. One way of understanding this was that the risk that goods might be delayed at customs was not seen by the transporters as *their* problem: their role ended at the boundary of getting the goods to the airport on time. The design of XYZ meant there was no structural connection between the transport department and the customs control department (except at the very top of the organization) and therefore no way to manage collaboration between the two on the ground.

In situations like this, an 'obvious' solution is to change the organizational structure. For example, XYZ might have dissolved the custom control department and placed customs agents within transport teams, which would have affected not only working practices, but also meaning, identity and relationships. What we often observe is that re-drawing boundaries – while it may solve the presenting problem – brings about new problems as old collaborations are dismantled. Furthermore, organizational restructuring also dismantles existing ways of managing anxiety (see Chapter 21). The design of XYZ served to maintain a level of equilibrium, albeit at the expense of the well-being of their customs agents. Thus, before deciding on a new structure, it is important to consider where the new pressure points are likely to arise, and what might be put in place to mitigate the adverse consequences of the change.

Conclusion: Managing and leading contemporary organizations

In this chapter we have offered a number of tools that can be useful to managers:

- *Getting on the balcony.* Here one shifts one's perspective to a higher-order boundary, for example from director of one's own department to the boundary around all one's fellow directors and their departments. This enables one to focus on how the challenges in one part impact on and are impacted by the requirements of the larger system.
- *System-mapping.* One can start by mapping a specific role, identifying the system in which it is located and then adding the other systems in which one also has roles. However, sometimes it is useful to start by drawing the organization as a whole and then locating oneself with the different systems in which one has roles. For each system, one can identify the primary task and then consider

how parts relate to other parts and to the whole. As a second step, it may be useful to add the sentient systems to the task systems on the map.

- *Organization-in-the-mind*. Drawing one's system map often also brings into view something about the picture that has formed in one's inner world of one's organization and one's place in it. For example, when Tom drew his system map (Figure 22.4(b)), it brought into view his sense of not feeling part of Worrid. The relative size or shape or colour of the systems on one's map may say more about one's inner relatedness to different parts of the organization than about how parts and wholes relate 'in reality'. Alongside a system map, where one seeks to depict structural relationships as they are intended, as accurately as possible, it can be illuminating to draw an organization-in-the-mind picture (see Chapter 6, p. 65).

All of these are tools for managing oneself in multiple roles, that is, managing one's contribution to the primary task of the systems where each role is located.

Leadership requires something more. As discussed in Chapter 6 and further developed in Chapter 24, management focuses on the 'what' (primary task) and the 'how' (ensuring that the necessary resources are available). Leadership, on the other hand, is about the 'why'. This requires thinking about what is going on from a position beyond the boundary of the organization: thinking both about what the outside world needs *from* the organization, and what impact the organization is having/wants to have *on* the world.

This may well throw up some fundamental contradictions, dilemmas and hard choices, as was the case both for Tom and Carmen. Heifetz of the John F. Kennedy School of Government at Harvard University (1994) has identified a core leadership task as enabling people to recognise and face these hard choices, but *at a pace they can stand*, thus mitigating against the tendency to split up dilemmas so that each is held in particular sub-systems, with a dispersing not only of accountability but of a shared sense of meaning, of 'who we are and what we are here for'.

When leaders are able to 'discover the link to society' (Shapiro 2001) and articulate it in a way that has meaning for others, they are more likely to be able to harness sentience in ways that further task performance.

Note

1 Some of the theory in this section has already been described in earlier in this book, notably in Chapters 4, 6 and 17. We have chosen to recap essential points here for the benefit of readers using this chapter on its own.

23

BEYOND THE INDIVIDUAL

Reframing blame and responsibility for 'rogue' behaviour in the financial services industry[1]

Ajit Menon

The financial services (FS) industry was impacted badly by the crash of 2008. What followed was a strong negative public feeling against the industry, as taxpayers were forced to pay exorbitant sums to bail out some of the large institutions affected, with far-reaching consequences which continue to affect public spending and debt. Hypotheses abound as to why and how the crash happened, including bankers' unrestrained greed, individual traders driven to impress by the size of the success they achieved, inadequate accounting and auditing practices, and inadequate regulation that fostered corrupt behaviours.

In most of these analyses, it is as if the industry exists in a vacuum in the glass towers of big cities. While society at large continues to be angry at 'the bankers' for having put them in the current difficult position, and at governments for the ensuing austerity measures, there has been relatively little discussion or acknowledgement of the societal forces, including the culture and collective behaviours that contributed to creating the conditions that led to the crisis. Much of the writing and media coverage on the subject has focused blame for what happened on the greed and corruption of individuals such as the UBS trader Kweku Adoboli, or on revelations about 'corrupt' organizations such as some of the big banks, or on the impact of deregulation. Whilst the unmasking of individual and organizational behaviour may make for good stories, this approach is limited in terms of shedding light on what went on, or on what might be done differently in the future by whom.

This chapter will analyse the interplay of individual, organizational and – crucially – societal dynamics before and after the crash of 2008, and the impact of these dynamics on behaviour in the FS industry. In the process, the notion of what blame means, and where responsibility lies in this context, will be re-framed. Whilst we are aware that there are many different business activities that fall under the FS industry, from banking to insurance, in this chapter we have used examples of traders and trading to analyse the system.

All accounts of events are sourced from material available in the public record.

Rogue individuals?

Since the crash, a number of organizations have been subject to sanctions from the regulators or have been put under what is known as a 'skilled person's review' (a form of extra scrutiny), but it was the arrest and high-profile prosecution of a number of individuals which particularly caught the public imagination.

Let us first introduce some of the 'villains':

* The dubious accolade of the original rogue trader belongs to Nick Leeson who lost nearly $1 billion and caused the collapse of Barings Bank in 1995. He was sentenced to six and a half years in prison.
* In 2008, the French trader Jérôme Kerviel was convicted for a breach of trust, forgery and unauthorised use of Société Générale's computers resulting in a loss of €4.9 billion. He was sentenced to three years in prison.
* Kweku Adoboli, a trader in UBS's global synthetic equities division, booked fictitious hedging trades in order to hide the fact that he was exceeding his risk limits. This exposed the bank to much more chance of loss than it could see. He was sentenced to seven years in prison in 2012 for fraud, having lost $2.3 billion of the Swiss bank's money.
* Tom Hayes was a trader for UBS and Citigroup who dishonestly drove manipulation of the Libor (London Interbank Offered Rate), a bank reported interest rate, to enhance his trading results. In August 2015, he was sentenced to 14 years in prison.

No doubt these individuals committed punishable crimes, but did they deserve the intense coverage and blame provoked by their trials? What was it about them which led to their 'applying', as it were, for the role of rogue of 'rogue trader', and to being selected for the role?[2] How did they come to do what they did, in the way that they did it, and what might they have in common?

The four 'rogue' traders mentioned above were all 'outsiders', as were many others (Gapper 2011). Nick Leeson, for example, was – untypically for the milieu – the son of a plasterer and hairdresser; Jérôme Kerviel's father was a blacksmith from Brittany. Kweku Adoboli was an outsider in a number of ways, from his Ghanaian roots to his non-elitist education, and because he came into the trading environment via the back office, rather than coming directly to the trading floor. He nevertheless rose from a job as a summer intern in 2002 to be a director with a salary of £110,000 by 2010. Tom Hayes also had a modest education. Furthermore, his aloofness and awkwardness (explained later by a diagnosis of Asperger's syndrome) made him stick out: his colleagues nicknamed him 'Rain Man' (after Dustin Hoffman's 1998 autistic film character) or 'Tommy Chocolate' because of his habit of ordering hot chocolate when he went drinking with them. He too was extremely successful and generated a profit of £170m for the bank in three years.

We all need to belong and feel accepted. Having so many points of difference with others on the trading floor, these 'outsiders' may have been driven to take higher risks, and to work outside the law, in order to prove themselves worthy of group membership. Their reckless behaviour was often rewarded by their being singled out as star performers. Although this never actually made them insiders, it may have helped them to deal with their exclusion, and also with the anxiety endemic in the FS industry of losing one's position if one does not generate enough profit, thus fueling ever increasing risk-taking in order to hold on to their positions as stars.

To cast them (merely) as 'rotten apples' is to attend only to part of their stories. For example, in the case of Adoboli, accounts reveal that he sought community wherever he went and did what he could to create it. A university friend said 'He would take the weight of the student union on his shoulders, and he did the exact same thing at UBS . . . He wanted to help, he wanted to do well and that, in the end, got him into trouble'. He recalled an instance when a senior manager came to Adoboli and said they'd forgotten to book a client trade two weeks earlier and were facing a $1.5 million loss. 'And he's like, what can we do, is there anything you can do to fix it? OK, leave it with me, I'll try to trade around it and make back some of the loss'. As Adoboli said at his trial:

> I was found guilty under criminal law, so according to the law I was wrong. I don't want to cause pain to anyone. In fact, that's the tragedy of all this. The pain was the result of trying really hard not to cause the pain.
>
> *(Fortado 2015)*

He wept as he spoke of his sense of betrayal by an employer to whom he had been so dedicated, saying, 'UBS was my family and every single thing I did . . . was for the benefit of the bank' (Fortado 2015).

The judge took Adoboli's defence into account and passed a reduced sentence. However, in his sentencing remarks, the judge at his trial noted,

> The fact is that you are profoundly unselfconscious of your own failings. There is the strong streak of the gambler in you, borne out by your personal trading. You were arrogant enough to think that the bank's rules for traders did not apply to you. And you denied that you were a rogue trader, claiming that at all times you were acting in the bank's interests, while conveniently ignoring that the real characteristic of the rogue trader is that he ignores the rules designed to manage risk.
>
> *(Judiciary of England and Wales 2012)*

Rogue organizations?

So far, we have focused on the characteristics of individuals who engaged in rogue behaviour. In this section, we will consider some of the characteristics of the organizations involved (and others which have not been 'outed') which created the conditions in which this behaviour could flourish.

Elitism and lack of diversity

The experience of traders such as Adoboli and Hayes, who climbed the ranks despite their non-elitist backgrounds, race or ability to fit into groups, could indicate a meritocracy. The reality was otherwise: in fact, the industry was (and is) notorious for creating barriers to entry. As recently as 2016, the UK government's Social Mobility Commission found that most investment banks still favoured young people from middle and higher income families and from the country's top universities, with 'a tendency to recruit for familiarity and similarity, and focus on perceived "fit"' (Social Mobility Commission 2016 p. ii). They described a highly normative system where even the type of shoes worn could lead the wearer to being included or excluded. Similarly, in France, the top derivative traders at Société Générale were recruited from the elite French engineering and mathematical schools. It is precisely in these kinds of intensely 'normative' settings that groupthink is most likely to flourish and go unquestioned.

Extreme environments

This insider/outsider dynamic was reinforced by particular organizational policies. Many corporate environments shape the behavior of their staff with carrots and sticks, and nowhere is this more true than in the finance sector where performance is so clearly linked to profits achieved, with the performance of employees constantly rated by comparing it to that of others. As we have seen, the rewards can be enormous, with mouth-watering bonuses, but the 'sticks' are also huge, with some banks operating an annual 'cull', routinely firing a significant number of their least profitable staff.

Trading floors are extreme work environments, characterised by Hirschhorn and Horowitz (2014) as settings where the stakes are high, the velocity of decisions and their consequences great, and bad decisions are often irreversible. The trading floors of the FS industry of the early 2000s had all these ingredients. Traders spent their days in a frenzy in front of computer screens, screaming down headsets at brokers with little respite. A typical day for Hayes was described as:

> . . . utterly immersive. There are no meetings during the day and no lunch break. The only reprieve is a five-minute run to the toilet or the bank's in-house coffee bar. His pulse is elevated. His pupils dilate . . . A billion dollars changes hands with seven keystrokes.
>
> *(Vaughan and Finch 2017 p. 19)*

Even after the markets closed, traders had many hours of paperwork to complete before their day ended. Adoboli described being obsessed with the markets, following the news around the clock, getting only three broken hours of sleep a night, and losing the capacity to think rationally.

> There was no energy left. And you end up going into autopilot when you're that tired, and of course autopilot means that you make mistakes, you don't recognize warning signs when they're all around you, and it snowballs from there.
>
> *(Fortado 2015)*

While these adrenaline-charged environments might well appall many people, they are intensely attractive to others, not only for their high rewards but because of the speed, pressure and excitement in themselves. If, in addition, one's successes alleviate the pains of social exclusion, joining the organizational culture can become irresistible to outsiders like Hayes, Adoboli, and the others, with much to prove. Furthermore, the adulation they received had an almost 'gladiatorial' quality. There are accounts of employees being encouraged by senior management to crowd around glass barriers and observe the super-traders at work so as to become more like them.

Turning a blind eye

It is hard to believe that the organizations in question were unaware of the malpractice of their super-traders, and yet they continued to ignore and reward it as long as they could. For example, in Hayes' case,

> The revelation that one of their top traders was trying to rig Libor doesn't appear to have rung any bells with UBS's senior managers who seemed more interested in Hayes's trading prowess. Hayes was promised another multimillion dollar bonus and received a series of fawning call from executives.
>
> *(Vaughan and Finch 2017 pp. 82–83)*

At his trial, his defence argued that influencing Libor was so common in the industry that it had become widely accepted practice, and therefore Hayes could not have realised that what he was doing was wrong.

Perhaps the most spectacular example is that of Leeson and Barings Bank. Stein (2000) postulates that the Big Bang stirred up great anxiety at the aristocratic and arch-conservative Barings Bank, bankers to the royal family for over a century, that their conservatism could lead to their annihilation in the new context. In 1984, they set up Baring Securities without any of the usual management controls or even a financial director, and over the next decade, Baring Securities grew exponentially, run first by Heath, a wild gambler, and later by Nick Leeson, a man without prior experience of derivatives trading or knowledge of relevant mathematical models, but already known for his lies, outrageous behaviour and risk-taking. However, his excesses were overlooked as Baring Securities generated such enormous profits as to dwarf the parent company. Leeson was regarded as a miracle-worker. Even when he began to lose significant sums, and was leaving a trail of evidence – perhaps in a desperate unconscious cry to be stopped, Barings repeatedly decided not to investigate his activities. Stein outlines numerous breaks with the bank's own rules, including doing away with the accountability hierarchy that enables self-regulation. He proposes that the banks' senior executives' concerns about the risks of their own conservatism 'led them to select as "savior" an opposite or "shadow" to themselves, an extreme risk taker' (p. 1223) on whom they then felt totally dependent. This dependence made it unbearable to 'see' what was in plain sight. Just ten days before the bank's final collapse, the CEO visited Leeson, invited him to dinner and appeared to still be considering awarding him a £450,000 bonus.

Similar anxieties about failure and the need for a saviour can be seen in the case of UBS, where both Adoboli and Hayes worked. UBS had avoided bankruptcy following the crash because the Swiss government had bailed them out, but had nevertheless lost billions of dollars and thousands of jobs. Following the crisis, Adoboli's gains on the trading floor were of great benefit to the bank which may well have felt dependent on the likes of Adoboli to save them from annihilation. Certainly, he always maintained that the bank turned a blind eye as long as he brought in the profits, and there was evidence at his trial that the bank had in fact uncovered at least three other instances of unlawful trading.

Perverse organizations and their accomplices

Long (2008) describes this turning a blind eye as characteristic of perverse organizations, where 'certain organizational character traits inform the actions taken by organizational leaders and members' (Long 2008 p. 3). She proposes that perverse structures, where one's own benefit is at the expense of a more general good, tend to develop in contexts where relations are predominantly instrumental, as is the case in the FS. In order to achieve this benefit, organizations engage 'accomplices'. Adoboli, Hayes and other rogue traders could be seen as having 'applied' for the role of accomplice because they could thereby meet their own unconscious needs to belong and shine, thus making for a perfect fit between their needs and those of their organizations.

Furthermore, Long notes that 'perversion begets perversion' (p. 15). Thus the rogue traders, perhaps initially 'recruited' as accomplices based on a certain valency[3] they had for this role, were then caught up in a cycle where the more they broke rules and laws, the higher the profits they generated; the better they were rewarded, and the more the reality of what was going on had to be denied by everyone involved. Despite organizational collusion appearing (with hindsight) to have been so blatant, the denouement in most cases was that once the 'rogue' practices were revealed, the organizations absolved themselves from any accountability by placing the blame on the individuals involved.

At times of great flux, and the intense anxiety that comes with uncertainty, organizations develop cultures and leadership designed to manage the anxiety rather than to manage the challenges of the real situation that cannot be faced. Lawrence hypothesises that in these situations, the phantasy world takes over from the rational, diminishing leaders' (and others') capacity to think. As a result,

> role holders at all levels become less able to relate to the external environment . . . [and] become entrapped in the inner, political environment of the institution, in a life of action and reaction, doing not being. The preoccupation is with survival which is essentially narcissistic . . . And so crises, particularly financial ones, repeat themselves till they reach such magnitude that the enterprise fails.
>
> *(Lawrence 1998 p. 56)*

A rogue society?

It would be easy to stop there, with the blame held somewhere between the organizations involved and the profiles of the outsiders they drew into the fray. But we would argue that what happened needs also to be understood in relation to the wider context within which it took place.

A culture of mania

The Great Depression of the 1930s was arguably the worst economic downturn in recent history. In a determined spirit of 'never-again', legislation was put in place to regulate the financial sector. However, in the 1980s and 1990s, this was deemed to be impeding growth and a process of deregulation ensued across the world. In the UK, for example, London was falling behind other financial centres; and a change in stock market rules in 1986 (Financial Services Act 1986) under the Thatcher government led to the Big Bang; a dramatic increase in market activity due to the changes in the industry's structure. This strengthened London's position as the leader of financial services once again.

Stein (2011) describes an incubation period for the 2008 crisis over the preceding two to three decades, a period characterised by 'a culture of mania'. Drawing on Klein (1935), he notes four features of mania observable during this incubation period: denial (of vulnerability), omnipotence, triumphalism (a sense of superiority and winning out over others), and over-activity to dispel concerns about risk and vulnerability. During this time, there were a number of serious financial crises in other parts of the world that could have served as warning signs but were not. For example, the precipitants of the catastrophic 1991 crisis in Japan, when inflated land and stock prices collapsed and led to the country's 'lost decade', bore many similarities to what was going on in the West.

Over the same period, the FS industry had been developing innovative techniques and new products that (ostensibly) offered higher returns for ordinary rates of risk. Although this runs counter to what is generally known about the relationship between profit and risk (Tuckett 2011), for a time it seemed to work. Between 2003 and 2008 bonuses in the City rose from £3.3 billion to £11.6 billion (Vaughan and Finch 2017). This good performance allowed banks to carry on issuing debt.

The new products were based on new mathematical models of risk which were meant to make risk controllable, models which most people in the FS (let alone their clients) did not understand but wanted to believe in. As one regulator later reflected, 'We were prepared to be convinced [by the mathematical geniuses] . . . The longer things seemed to be going well, the more inclined we were to believe . . . Mortgage holders, credit card users, bankers and markets – all shared the unconscious fantasy' (Gill and Sher 2011 p. 68).

This 'magic-think' extended beyond the FS into most households, as easy credit seemed to make it possible to buy goods and own homes almost without money. Household debt reached unprecedented levels. Housing loans in the United States were being issued against almost negligible collateral, with risk no longer appropriately priced, while in the United Kingdom, customers were able to self-certify their income in order to obtain mortgages irrespective of their actual ability to repay the loan. The inevitable eventually happened and the crisis ensued by a sort of domino effect: house owners could not repay their loans; banks realised their own vulnerability and were no longer willing to lend money to each other; the money markets collapsed; bank shares and asset values fell; big financial institutions lost liquidity and failed; world trade and the 'real economy' suffered huge losses; investors withdrew due to anticipated reduced assets and further collapses ensued (Tuckett 2011).

Ambivalence towards regulation

Governments use regulatory bodies as mechanisms to control and safeguard the system. After the early years of the crash, public sentiment around the FS industry was strongly negative: there was outrage that the government has not controlled the 'greedy bankers'. Fred Goodwin, the former CEO of the Royal Bank of Scotland (RBS), was stripped of his title after RBS was nationalised, sending a strong message to the public of governmental support. New regulations were put in place to oblige the industry to follow safe(r) practices. The Financial Conduct Authority (FCA) and its then CEO, Martin Wheatley, were ruthless about the need to regulate culture and behaviour, and a number of firms were fined for poor conduct.

However, the greater regulation that followed the government bail-out of the banks brought with it significant hardship, both to individuals and to financial institutions. It became difficult to obtain mortgages, particularly for first-time buyers, and banks such as HSBC threatened to leave the UK. This led to a push to soften regulations.

The FS industry's ambivalence towards regulation is well known: regulation threatens profits and competitive advantage. But the industry is not alone in this.

We are all ambivalent about regulation. On the one hand, we want to be protected and kept safe (well regulated); on the other hand, we want to be free to make our own choices, be it in what we eat and drink, or how fast we drive, or how we raise our children. We want our money kept safe *and* we want easy credit and high returns on our investments. In the halcyon, pre-crash days, this dilemma seemed to disappear for a while, but with the increased regulation after the crisis, it is back. As memories of the crisis recede, there has been a strengthening of the protest against regulation. The government, dependent on the public for re-election, has now openly reneged on promises and reversed many commitments made in the wake of the crash. For example, Wheatley was removed in 2015, and shortly afterward the regulator announced that the planned inquiry into banking practices was being shelved. Meanwhile, household debt is again rising rapidly, with a record £31.6 billion in 2016 of car loan debt alone in the UK (Collinson 2017). Analysts are predicting that subprime car loans will be the trigger for the next financial crash.

All this is fairly conscious. However, there are also perhaps societal factors which are less conscious but which nonetheless play a significant part. For example, the UK has a deeply rooted class system with a long history of class conflict. The growing proportion of young people unable to buy their own homes is contributing to ever-greater inequalities in society. Wealth is an important factor in maintaining the class system, and the ambivalence toward regulation – and even towards the downfall of companies like Enron may be an expression of ambivalence not only towards control but also towards equality.

Unconscious demands on organizations: what do we really want from the FS industry?

Earlier in this chapter, we looked at how organizations unconsciously enroll or recruit individuals to carry out certain functions on their behalf. Extending this systemic perspective, we could think of 'rogue' organizations as enrolled or recruited by their contexts to meet some need that is neither acknowledged nor recognised.

Enron is a particularly dramatic example of determined efforts to thwart control. Stein (2007) suggests that business leaders tend to regard regulation as fettering growth in order to protect people outside the company – a 'conflict of interest' perspective. While not denying that there are conflicting interests, both within companies and between companies and external parties, he argues that there is an important and often denied 'mutuality of interest' (p. 1406). Circumventing the regulators appeared initially to protect the company's interests. In fact, Enron's leaders brought about great harm to the company. Not only did thousands lose their jobs and pensions, but the share-holders lost the entire value of their holdings and the company went bankrupt.

But what if Enron's actions were not just their own but partly driven unconsciously by the FS industry's hatred of regulation, which Enron tested and – for a long time – triumphed over? (It is worth remembering here omnipotence and triumphalism are features of a manic culture). And beyond the industry, there were elements in the wider context that also played a part, not least a rising societal and political trend towards putting self-interest ahead of the common good, which Long has identified as a key feature of perverse organizations. Hoggett takes Long's ideas further, arguing that recent social changes 'may have generated a perverse culture in contemporary capitalist societies . . . [characterized by] inversion and distortion, whereby selfishness becomes generosity, enslavement to credit and consumption becomes freedom, public accountability becomes totalitarianism . . . [and by] the spread of collusion and organized self-deception' (Hoggett 2010 pp. 57–58).

Finally, let us consider what purpose the rogue behaviour of particular individuals and organizations might have served on behalf of us all. As a society we create a fantasy around the concept of the banker in our minds. This identity of wealth and power self-perpetuate leading individuals to enact our greed, hubris, excess and hedonism that we do not wish to acknowledge in ourselves. The myth that the streets of the City of London are paved with gold, where anyone can make their fortune, has been around for a long time. When the industry fails to bring this about, it becomes a receptacle into which we can export our anger, shame and denial.

In the next chapter, Daum explores the impact of societal fantasies and desires in three other sectors (insurance, energy production and the pharmaceutical industry). He suggests, for example, that big pharmaceutical companies are our shamans to whom we attribute the power to cure all our ailments (and whom we then excoriate because they fail to do so). Might we, in a similar vein, look to the finance 'wizards' to be our Rumpelstiltskins, with the power to turn the straw of our limited resources into gold?

Conclusion: some considerations for systemic interventions

In the aftermath of the crash, the focus has mainly been on the actions of particular organizations and on individuals who were 'caught' in the act. However, it is evident that punishing wrong-doing and putting tighter regulations in place, although necessary, are not enough to bring about lasting change. Rather, we need interventions that attend to all levels – individual, organizational and societal – and to the complex interplay of the dynamics between them.

As we have seen, individual circumstances, background, identity and unconscious needs play a significant part. Having to deal with anxieties about group membership in a very elite club, coupled with anxieties about keeping one's job and meeting the demands of extreme environments, makes certain individuals particularly vulnerable to engaging in rogue behaviour. Self-awareness on the part of employees regarding their own vulnerability to being 'used' by the system in particular ways can help, but managers and leaders also need to be aware of these vulnerabilities in the people they hire and manage, and to be alive to how the culture of their organizations – the unwritten rules and norms, and reward systems, both formal and informal – can 'induct' people into behaving in particular ways.

The industry also needs to break down the barriers to entry. With a more diverse workforce, there is less group-think and more challenge. Whilst globalisation seems to be reducing these barriers on the surface, there are still many tiers of status and groups within banks. Despite the experience of Adoboli, Hayes and others of successfully climbing the ranks despite their non-elitist education, race or ability to fit into group norms, their status as outsiders would have had an impact for them at an unconscious level.

We also need to intervene at the level of the consumer, recognising the industry's vulnerability to societal demands, both conscious and unconscious. A capitalistic mindset, where demand determines supply, will not create a robust and fair system. It will only serve to exploit societal fantasies around what is possible. Rather, the FS industry can contribute through information and education, so that consumers better understand the risks they take and the consequences of their choices both for themselves and for the overall system.

It is heartening to see signs that this kind of whole-system approach is coming into mainstream thinking in the FS sector. In the introduction to a recent collection of essays published by the Financial Conduct Authority (2018), they underline the need for:

> a shift from linear thinking about culture and conduct to a dynamic, systems perspective. Whereas linear thinking diagnoses one cause to one effect, a systems perspective acknowledges the whole system around the individual and the interactions and inter-dependencies between each part in the system.
> *(FCA 2018 p. 18)*

In addition, they emphasise the importance for organizations to foster a culture where it is safe to speak up and learn, rather than merely comply.

How can we all – individuals, organizations, and society more broadly – avoid getting caught up in groupthink and find the capacity to 'swim upstream' when necessary? Of course, many people did in fact try to do just this before the crisis, issuing warnings which were ignored, or whistle-blowing and getting fired. Throughout this chapter, we have seen the force of the pressures to collude in denying reality. Unless we can change this, the stage is set for participating in the next crisis: by those of us in society who want to own what we cannot really afford, by the organizations which appear to offer products to satisfy these unrealistic desires, and for the Kweku Adobolis waiting, as it were, in the wings.

Dramas – stories of heroes and villains, and of crime and punishment – are exciting for onlookers. This chapter is an invitation to avoid being seduced by this excitement, to understand the links between the three perspectives, and to recognise the part we all play in creating the conditions which produce the rogue behaviours.

Notes

1 Parts of this chapter have been previously published by the author under the title 'Denial of reality: an exploration of some of the unconscious forces at work in Financial Services', in the FCA Discussion Paper 18/2 *Transforming Culture in the Financial Services*, and are included here by permission.
2 See the section 'Selecting a trouble-maker' in Chapter 15, p. 150, which explores the hypothesis that organizations unconsciously 'recruit' particular kinds of individuals to perform certain functions on behalf of others as well as themselves.
3 'Valency' was described by Bion (1961) as a person's innate capacity for 'instantaneous combination' with particular kinds of projections. This can influence their choice of profession or work-setting (see Chapters 3 and 13) as well as how they are 'used' by their organizations to take up roles such as that of accomplice.

24

FROM MANAGING TO LEADING ORGANIZATIONS IN THEIR CONTEXTS

Matthieu Daum

Should a manager approach problematic behaviours and dynamics such as under-performance, low morale, or conflict in the same way regardless of whether they take place in a factory, or a bank, or a prestigious business school? If one sees these phenomena as stemming from 'problem' individuals, then the answer is likely to be 'yes'. Through that prism, the nature of the business, its history and culture, do not matter. All that is needed is appropriate performance tools, development pro-grammes, or coaching. Alternatively, as described in the previous chapter, or after development interventions fail, individuals are punished or sacked.

Focusing on individuals misses an essential point: a team or an organization is a system, not just a collection of individual parts. And what the systemic sciences have shown is that some properties exist at a systemic level which do not exist in its parts. For example, in the human body, temperature regulation or immunity are not properties of particular cells, or organs, but emerge at the level of the whole body as it organizes itself as a living system. Just as we need to consider the underlying causes of symptoms before prescribing a treatment, so will the manager of a problematic individual or team need to search out what might be going on systemically that is contributing to the behaviours that are causing concern.

This chapter will focus on two elements that can have a profound impact on organizational behaviour but are often overlooked:

1   *The impact of the nature of the work itself.* Providing or selling insurance, produc-ing or distributing energy, developing or manufacturing pharmaceuticals: each set of activities evokes different experience, including different anxieties, both conscious and unconscious. Working practices and cultures develop that influ-ence how people take up their roles, including that of leader or manager.[1]
2   *The symbolic place a company or sector holds for society.* This can include shared hopes, fears, or shared images and stereotypes, as was illustrated in the

previous chapter with regard to the financial services sector. The impact of what is projected onto the industry or company will affect the people working there and can even end up perverting the very purpose for which they were set up.

The case studies which follow explore some of the effects of these two elements in three very different kinds of organizations, and illustrate how attending to them can open up new leverage points and options for intervention for leaders and managers seeking long-lasting improved performance.

A life without risk: working, managing and leading in the insurance industry

The insurance industry has a particular relationship to time: it deals with the future. Where most businesses deliver their products and services in the present, insurers offer us a future guaranteed free of unpleasant consequences to whatever life may bring our way. Indeed, at the core of their value proposition, the future is necessarily a persecutory one, full of missed flights, car breakdowns, burglaries and illnesses, but one from which we can be shielded. At a conscious level, we are buying protection from the financial consequences of negative life events. Unconsciously, we may be buying an illusion that insurance will prevent their happening at all. Paradoxically, when the 'promise' of protection falls short, a common response – after the first shock and outrage – is to buy even more insurance to plug the gaps in our original policy.

The insurance industry can only prosper through fragmenting reality. The message we hear and need to believe is that there is no link between the individual and the whole, or between actions and their consequences. As a society, we contribute to creating the conditions which produce the risks – say, crime or fire and flood – against which we then seek to insure ourselves. But we let ourselves be persuaded that, whatever happens to the whole, the insurance industry undertakes that I, an individual not connected to the whole (apparently), will be kept safe from the negative impacts. Developing a joined up picture would put profit at risk, and expose us to anxiety which has been kept at bay by taking out insurance.

Profit also depends on predicting and quantifying risk. Actuarial science uses statistics and mathematical models to make the calculations on which the cost of insurance premiums are based. One could say that it is in the business of making the unpredictable predictable. This can of course never be fully achieved: however sophisticated the methods used, some risks cannot be foreseen or measured in advance.

What is the impact of all this on how people in the insurance field carry out their work?

One is that the 'nitty-gritty' of the business always seems very difficult to understand for anybody new, whether internal (it can take staff a year or more to understand their activities), or external, like suppliers or consultants. The way people present their work seems designed to amplify its complexity, so that it takes on almost mystical proportions. This, in turn, can serve at least two functions: one is to limit the kind of information one has to share ('oh, it's too complicated to explain'), and the other is to prevent anyone from being able to develop an adequate picture of the whole. Alternatively, staff may do just the opposite, giving a wealth of technical detail to illustrate each phase of the delivery of their service in a way that tends to obscure the essence of what it is they are doing. This makes it hard for people across teams, and sometimes even within teams, to understand each other. Might this verbal outpour serve to hide useful but potentially disturbing information from others? Or to convey a sense of expertise?

These behaviours create an obstacle for the exercise of leadership. A leader in any organization has to deal with some level of what cannot be known such as fluctuation in the market, innovation in competitors, change in consumers' needs and trends, etc. In order to best work with this unknowable, (s)he needs to have access to all that *can* be known. Both the fragmenting and the withholding of information within the insurance industry make it difficult to get hold of this knowledge, and in that way contributes to increasing the level of risk in decision-making, although here there is no possibility to be insured! This increased risk affects how authority and delegation are exercised. Decision-taking tends to be shifted laterally, or upwards, or both, so that it can be hard to pinpoint who took the final decision and can be held accountable for it.

Thus, we see the interplay of two illusions: the illusion that insurance will prevent (rather than merely reduce) the consequences of life's mishaps, and the illusion that risk can (always) be predicted accurately by actuarial science. In the face of impossible demands for guarantees and certainties from both customers and shareholders, stepping back from clear authorship of the work produced and the decisions taken provides some protection for the individuals concerned in the short-term. In the long-term, it stands in the way of effective leadership and management.

Dangers real and imagined: the struggle to transform the culture of an electricity-distributing organization

The Ruritania Electricity Network (REN) is a nation-wide company whose task is to bring electricity from the place of production to the end-users. Its industrial assets are set up as a network, and being a network is indeed inscribed in its very name. Formerly a state company, it had for decades been operating as a top-down, command-and-control bureaucracy. Over the last few years, however, it has been trying to transform its management culture into a more agile, collaborative and responsive one. It has been proving hard to implement this change, despite most people agreeing it would be beneficial not only for efficiency but also for increasing employee satisfaction.

The company directors have located the resistance to transformation at the level of individuals. Interventions have focused on managing these 'difficult' people: moving them into dead-end roles or early retirement, providing incentives for adopting desired behaviours, and coaching. However, despite these interventions, the resistance kept repeating even when the personnel had changed: a clue that something more systemic was probably going on. What then could be possessing this human system in such a way that it has been unable to bridge the gap between intention and action? What might be the underlying investment for this organization not to change?

To begin to answer these kinds of systemic question, it is often useful to consider historical background. On the one hand, from its state-controlled origins, one could anticipate that a bureaucratic approach to management culture would be deeply ingrained and hard to shake off. But in addition, one element has shaped this organizational culture over the last few decades: the choice the country made to go predominantly nuclear. This means that distributing electricity involves connecting the cables to nuclear power stations, a highly productive way of generating electricity, but also one engendering considerable anxiety about risk.

In practice, achieving the high level of safety required for the business to operate required a highly structured set of processes, with a clear chain of command and authorising mechanisms. In other words, the nature of the business itself (given that it is built around nuclear power stations), and also the expectations from society regarding guarantees of safety, consciously and unconsciously shaped the organizational culture. It was as if the human organization needed to provide the same solid, containing capacity as would a nuclear reactor.

This, of course, is a fantasy, an example of the nature of the work unconsciously shaping the mental model through which the organization comes to life. The organizational structure and culture do not, in reality, have to contain highly toxic, radioactive and explosive material that could contaminate an entire region if it leaked or exploded. Rather, like any other organization, it needs to contain human dynamics in order to enable people to engage with each other to achieve the task. Therefore, there was no reason 'in reality' to prevent its moving to a more agile, collaborative, network mode of functioning. But in order to do so, it would first need to recognise and face this 'elephant in the unconscious', i.e. the fear of nuclear/nuclear-like disaster that was populating the collective unconscious, both within the organization and in society more broadly. If at a rational level this organization exists in order to distribute electricity across the country, at a psychic level it (still) exists to contain the collective fears and anxieties of a nuclear accident.

Bringing this issue fully into awareness, to be talked about and thought about, could make it possible to differentiate between those activities that are about necessary risk management (which are few) from those which are about fantasised danger (most of them), and to begin the culture transformation process with the latter, perhaps through some pilot projects. Once these show that it is safe to work differently, then the organizational transformation process could be spread wider, and eventually enable even those parts which do deal primarily with real-risk containment activities to do so in a reinvented way.

A cure for every ailment: the danger of perverting purpose in a pharmaceuticals company

In the two preceding case studies, we have seen how projections of societal fears can contribute to shaping how organizations operate. Sometimes these projections are so strong, or so difficult to contain, that they can threaten to pervert the very purpose for which an organization was set up. This is the case for Bayastrofil, a pharmaceutical company, and of Michael, a man destined for a wonderful career there but who felt he had no choice but to leave an organization whose purpose he considered had been perverted.

Michael was in his 40s, a top graduate of one of the world's elite universities, who had chosen a career in the pharmaceutical industry amongst the many offers that he had received. He opted for Bayastrofil, a global pharmaceuticals company, because the overall mission of the company caught his altruistic self: contributing to people's well-being and solving some of the world's greatest health challenges seemed a quest worth embarking on.

After a rapid rise to senior manager level, he found himself increasingly unable to reconcile the company's strategy with his own values and sense of purpose, and decided to quit. Rather than moving to another company in the same sector which might present similar issues, he launched his own company with the clear objective of bringing high-quality, affordable, natural health products to the many.

Michael's decision came about following a series of insights he had on the pharmaceutical industry and on the impact it had in the world. Amongst such insights was the realisation that the production and the over-use of antibiotics were actually contributing to the rise of antibiotic resistant microbes; that of all the drugs produced by all pharmaceuticals companies, a significant proportion were no more effective than placebos; and that the business model of the industry needed people to be ill in order to stay afloat and grow: people in good health were actually bad for business. This became evident when, as marketing director for his unit, he was invited to a meeting with the R&D team who had found an interesting molecule, but could not see an existing recorded pathology for which it could be commercialised. The meeting then proceeded with the aim of finding broadly linked non-pathological behaviours that they could then package as a syndrome, in order, later on, to frame it as an illness. As he put it, 'We entered the meeting with a molecule, and we left with an illness'.

How does an organization whose purpose is to bring more health to the world end up creating more ill-health through the side-effects of its products, or even inventing illnesses so that it can sell new products? Surely it must take perverse decision-makers to drive such behaviour. But where does the perversion come from? It would be quite easy to locate it in particular individuals, perhaps senior executives or the CEO. But is that enough to explain what remains, after all, a collective behaviour? What about the chairman, the shareholders, the teams on the ground, and all those with leadership and managerial responsibilities? Are they all inherently perverse? We suggest that, rather than being perverse individuals, these role-holders are caught up in a web of projections that they internalize,[2] which then leads to losing touch with the company's purpose.

One driver of this kind of situation is the idea that a corporation must exist in order to make money, rather than that it must make money in order to continue to fulfil its purpose. If making money becomes the only purpose, then everything else gives way to this. Bayastrofil's stated mission was 'to solve the world's greatest health challenges', but this was lost in the drive to sell as much as possible, even when this involved inventing illnesses or encouraging medics to over-prescribe. Of course shareholders expected Bayastrofil to make a profit, and higher profits attract more investment. This would enable further growth, research, development and employment. But what made it possible to swap so easily the original purpose (bringing health to the world) for what should be a mere consequence (making money)? What might have been operating at a less conscious level that led to so many people to engage with this distortion of the company mission?

Our hypothesis is that the symbolic place held by the pharmaceutical industry in society's collective psyche (i.e. society's projections onto it) fuels collusion in a collective, unconscious process. It is as if this industry has the knowledge about healing drugs and the power to rid us of illness, pain, perhaps even death. They are our organizational equivalent, at an unconscious level, of the shaman or witch doctor. So, through this very primitive mental model, we hand over to them a huge amount of fantasised power, a projected omnipotence to heal or to deny healing. Vilifying the industry, for example for withholding life-saving drugs from the poor or for duping people into using vaccines that cause harm, obscures the part we all play in this projective process.

It is this projected power, introjected without being processed, that leads to perversion. When so much fantasised power is handed over to a particular group, without the checks and balances that generally accompany power in the external world and which could ensure that such an industry does indeed work for the good of all, the way is clear for perversion to set in. It is too easy to ascribe this to (others') greed. We suggest that it is not greed per se that leads to perversion. Rather, it is our collective, unconscious surrendering of power to organizations that embody our primitive need for an all powerful healer that creates the conditions in which greed can take over.

Towards transformation

How can we reduce the blind spots and defensive behaviours generated by the nature of the work itself, or avoid identifying with the intensity of society's projections onto our businesses?

Bringing the bigger picture into view

On a housing estate in the US, where houses were more or less identical, the electricity consumption was 30 per cent lower in one particular block, compared to the surrounding blocks. The only difference was that in this block the electricity meter was in the entrance hall, whereas in the others it was in the basement. As one passed in front of the meter, one could therefore notice if it was going faster than usual, identify what was causing this, and switch off this or that appliance. The positioning of the meter made information available that brought about changes in behaviour (Meadows 2008).

Today, we all have access to information that we never had before, including constant evidence of the interconnections between what we do inside our organizations and the impact it has elsewhere. This flood of information can drive more denial and defensive splitting of effects from causes, or it can open the way for transformation.

One thing that the three organizational examples above have in common is the issue of the 'bigger picture'. Focusing solely on individual behaviours means we are bound to miss fundamental, underlying drivers such as the collective strategies that have evolved to deal with the impossibility of insuring against the consequences of our decisions, or the nuclear reactor-like tightness of a particular organizational culture, or projections of shaman-like omnipotence. Bringing this bigger picture more clearly into view makes it possible to think about previously hidden causes and effects, and to begin to address these.

This requires challenging ourselves to explore *both* the impact that we and our organiation are having on the world around us, and also the impact of that world on us. Our argument here is that in order to achieve real transformation, leaders and managers need to develop a greater awareness of those (often psychic) products of the external world that we introject to a degree that affects our organizational functioning.

Management and leadership

Another way to think about this is to distinguish between *task* and *purpose*, and between management and leadership. The primary task, a core concept throughout this book (see for example Chapters 4 and 23), is defined in terms of the outputs or products of the organization. Purpose, on the other hand, is about what difference an organization makes in the world (Bazalgette, Quine and Irvine 2009). As the bigger picture becomes clearer to us, we can work at clarifying the purpose of our organization, asking 'Why does this organization exist? What transformation is it meant to produce in its context? And what is the gap we are experiencing between this stated purpose and the one we are actually enacting?' What then becomes available is a new way of taking up our organizational roles which we could call 'leadership through purpose', mobilising the system we work in to produce the impact in the world which we believe the organization exists to produce – rather than merely responding to our own and societal anxieties about the future, a nuclear accident or powerlessness in the face of death.

This is the work of leadership. If management is about the 'what' and the 'how' of achieving the primary task, making the best use of available resources within current constraints, leadership is about the 'why' (Sinek 2009). Or to put it a bit differently, one could say that management takes its cues from the cards that reality has already dealt, whereas leadership shuffles the cards and deals a new hand to play with.

Owning our part

'You are not stuck in traffic – you are traffic!' A sat-nav company using this in their advertising was, accidentally or intentionally, bringing to awareness an interesting insight: there isn't 'a world out there' that we go in and out of; we are not *apart from* the world, but rather *a part of* the world. Our actions and our reactions are at the same time a response to our experience in the world and also co-create this very world we are experiencing.

But there are reasons why, even when we 'know' (or could know) something, we do not allow this knowledge to penetrate enough into our awareness to drive transformative action. Recognising the part one has played in co-creating the world we live in is daunting because it risks stirring up feelings of guilt and shame. Providing containment – that is, making it more bearable to face these feelings – is an essential part of effective leadership. Without it, people are at risk of retreating back to using blame, projection and 'turning a blind eye', all ways to locate responsibility elsewhere in order to defend against the emotional cost of 'seeing'.

Alternatively, they may leave, as was the case with Michael. One of the earliest studies (Menzies Lyth 1960) contributing to the systems-psychodynamics approach was of a teaching hospital where the presenting problem was the high dropout rate among student nurses, particularly the most gifted ones. For them, the way the organization's practices and culture were used to defend against anxiety also drained their work of meaning and worked against the purpose for which they had entered their profession. It is not unusual for high-potentials like Michael to reach a point of crisis in mid-career where they can no longer bear to collude. They are likely to see no choice but to leave, a serious loss to their organizations since they are often the very people who have the insight and ability to lead the kinds of transformations we have been discussing.

Conclusion

Individual behaviour is the tip of the iceberg, a symptom rather than *the* problem. Real transformation means diving deeper, beyond individual explanations for the current dysfunction, to explore both what is going on under the surface in ourselves and our organizations, and what is going on in the wider context: in other words, how the inside is getting out and the outside getting in.

Exploring what is collective is likely to work best as a collective exploration. This requires fostering conditions that help people feel safe enough to join in such exploration. To do this, leaders need an inner disposition of curiosity rather than blame. And to accept both that our actions do impact the world beyond what we might initially have intended, and that the world does impact on us beyond what our Cartesian understanding of free-will might have taught us to believe.

Notes

1 Part IIa of this book explores this in a range of health, social care and education settings.
2 The psychoanalytic term for this process is 'projective identification': the 'recipients' of projections unconsciously identify with the projected feelings in ways that can affect their behaviour (see Chapters 1 and 2).

AFTERWORD

Consulting to oneself

Vega Zagier Roberts

Throughout this book, we have been addressing two themes. The first we might call 'emotional intelligence' (Goleman 1995): the capacity to be in touch with our own and others' emotions, and to contain these so that they derail us less. The second is sense-making, taking into account multiple levels of meaning: our inner world, the nature of the work we are engaged in, organizational dynamics, and what is going on in the wider context.

Although the case studies are written from the perspective of the external consultant, the aim of this book has been to offer tools – concepts and practices – which readers can use for themselves to make sense in new ways of the situations they find themselves in. The external consultant has, of course, the advantage of being external, which can make it easier to avoid getting caught up in assumptions, shared blind-spots and familiar stories to explain what is happening. However, anyone working in organizations can develop the capacity to consult to themselves, 'helicoptering above' situations so as to develop a deeper and richer view.

Extending the scope of what we pay attention to

Sense-making starts with attending to data: this is the evidence on which we base our hypotheses, which in turn determine the actions we take. The better our hypotheses, the more likely our actions are to be effective. However, as described in Chapter 6, our neurological response to new information can be experienced as unpleasant, leading to repressing what disrupts the stories we have been using to make sense of our lives and our organizations. Thus, even as we seek better solutions, we may also screen out data that does not fit with our existing schemas: we are more likely to pay attention to evidence that fits with what we already think, a phenomenon known as confirmatory bias (Chater and Loewenstein 2015).

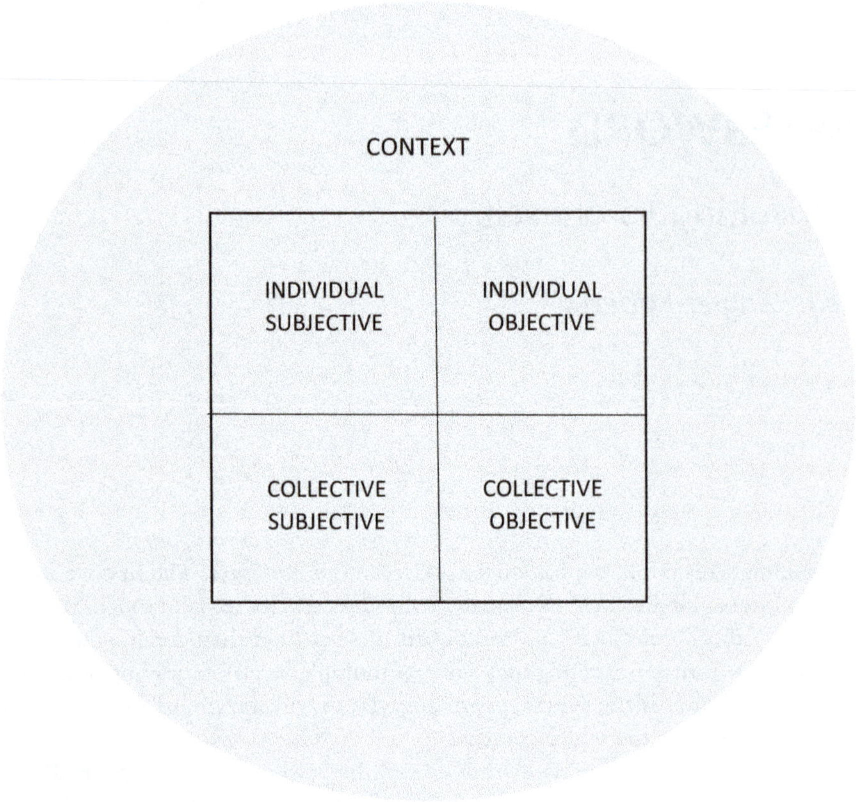

CONTEXT

INDIVIDUAL SUBJECTIVE	INDIVIDUAL OBJECTIVE
COLLECTIVE SUBJECTIVE	COLLECTIVE OBJECTIVE

FIGURE A1 Integrating multiple perspectives

In consulting to ourselves, we often need to enlarge the range of evidence beyond what we have paid attention before. A useful tool for doing this is provided in Figure A1, adapted from the Integral Approach developed by Wilber (1996). He proposes four quadrants or domains of attention (see Figure A1), and argues the importance of integrating all of them. To his four quadrants, we add a fifth perspective, (the wider) context. Each of us is likely to have a 'default' way of making sense of what we find perplexing or troubling, tending to focus on evidence from one or two of these five perspectives: the diagram can serve as a prompt to remind ourselves to pay attention to what we may be overlooking.

- *Individual subjective*: personality, 'shadows of the past' (see Chapter 19), mental maps, personal values and aspirations.
- *Individual objective*: knowledge, skills and behaviours that can be observed.
- *Collective subjective*: culture, including shared beliefs and assumptions, unwritten rules ('the way we do things around here'), informal systems of rewards and sanction, and informal hierarchies.

- *Collective objective*: structures, protocols, reporting lines, policies and rules, formal systems of rewards and sanctions, and formal decision-making processes.
- *Context*: societal attitudes and anxieties, recent public events and media reporting, economic changes, political leadership.

Mapping our hypotheses onto the diagram can help us to become more aware of our 'favourite' perspectives, and to develop the discipline of systematically paying attention to the ones we tend to overlook. Chapters 22 and 23 illustrate the pitfalls of limiting one's sense-making to one or two domains, and how paying attention to all five can help us develop more productive interventions.

Problem-solving in teams

The schema just given can also be useful in team problem-solving and strategising. So often, when our first solutions fail, we tweak and then repeat them. When a leadership development programme fails to deliver, we try another programme to change people's behaviour. When restructuring does not bring about the desired change, we restructure again. One of the drivers to this pattern is that a team tends to listen more to some voices than to others, often stifling the voices of those who deviate from the prevailing view. As discussed in Chapter 21, one of the most useful questions we can ask ourselves is 'How are they right?' especially when 'they' seem to be obviously wrong (Shapiro 2001). This of course does not imply that it is 'they' who are right, and we who are wrong, but rather that there is likely to be at least a grain of truth in even the most unlikely views.

One way to use the integral approach in group settings is to start by inviting each person to develop an initial hypothesis about what is driving the situation that needs to be addressed, and to map these onto the diagram. This can reveal a pattern, and indicate shared blind spots. Sometimes everyone's first hypothesis is in the same part of the diagram. For example, 'the problem may be attributed to Mary's personality (upper left quadrant) or to a culture of conflict-avoidance (lower left) or to impossible targets (lower right). At other times, there may be a small number of 'outliers' whose initial sense-making is in another part of the diagram from the majority. With luck, the group will include people with different default ways of making sense of the situation. Even when this is not the case at the outset, by systematically pushing themselves to consider all five perspectives, group members will come up with an ever-wider range of hypotheses. By definition, none of these are likely to be complete, and none are entirely wrong: each brings something new into view. Thus, this approach can facilitate the group's moving from an either-or to a both-and-also state of mind where complexity becomes more bearable, opening up new possibilities.

Some questions that can serve as life-rafts when one is all at sea

Caught in the maelstrom of complex – often very unpleasant – events, and under pressure to act, we may well struggle to think. Overleaf are some questions that can be useful. They are implicit throughout this book; where they are a focus of a particular chapter, the chapter number is given in brackets.

- What if my feelings are not just mine? (Chapters 2 and 20)
- What if the story I have been telling myself is not the only story? (Chapter 6)
- What if this awful moment is a gift, bringing into view something I have been overlooking? (See, for example, explorations of resistance to change in Chapter 21.)
- What might be coming up from the client group we work with, or from the nature of the core work of this organization? (Chapters 2, 11 and 24 among others)
- What if the 'dysfunction' is serving a purpose that benefits the system in some way, and what might this be? (Chapter 15)
- What kind of management/leadership am I being pulled into, and why does the system need this from me at this moment?
- What is my organization-in-the-mind right now and what might it be telling me? (Chapter 6)

A spirit of enquiry

As set out in the preface and foreword, this book has been about honing our spirit of enquiry – our willingness to let go of old certainties in order to play with new ways of seeing and thinking. In the Afterword of the First Edition, Obholzer said that his favourite definition of consultancy was 'licensed stupidity', that is, not-knowing and asking 'naïve questions'. Consulting to oneself is about standing back and looking at our own situations with fresh eyes: to question the 'obvious', and to dare not to know.

APPENDIX

The genealogy of systems-psychodynamics

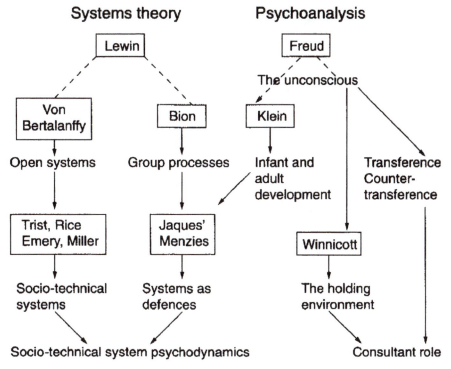

FIGURE A2 Genealogy of systems psychodynamics

Figure reused with permission from Taylor & Francis, LLC. Originally appeared as Figure 10.1, 'Genealogy of systems psychodynamics', in Miller, E. J. (1997) 'Effecting organizational change in large complex systems: a collaborative consultancy approach' in Neumann, J. E, Kellner, K. and Dawson-Shepherd, A. (eds) *Developing Organisational Consultancy,* Abingdon: Routledge, p. 188.

BIBLIOGRAPHY

Adams, A. and Crawford, N. (1992) *Bullying at Work*, London: Virago.

Anderson, R. (1992) (ed.) *Clinical Lectures on Klein and Bion*, London/New York: Tavistock/Routledge.

Armstrong, D. (1991) 'Thoughts bounded and thoughts free'. Paper presented to the Department of Psychotherapy, Cambridge.

——(1992) 'Names, thoughts and lies: the relevance of Bion's later writings for understanding experiences in groups', *Free Associations*, 3.26: 261–282.

——(2005) *Organization in the Mind*, London: Karnac.

Bazalgette, J., Quine, C. and Irvine, B. (2009) 'The purpose of meaning and the meaning of purpose: a container for our atomized yet globalized world'. Paper presented to the International Society for the Psychoanalytic Study of Organisations, Toledo, Spain.

Bion, W. (1961) *Experiences in Groups*, New York: Basic Books (see 'Selections from: Experiences in Groups', in A. D. Colman and W. H. Bexton (1975) (eds) *Group Relations Reader 1*, Washington, D.C.: A. K. Rice Institute Series).

——(1967) 'Attacks on linking', in *Second Thoughts: Selected Papers on Psychoanalysis*, London: Heinemann Medical (reprinted London: Maresfield Reprints, 1984).

——(1977) *Seven Servants*, New York: Jason Aronson.

Borwick, I. (2006) 'Organizational role analysis: managing strategic change in business settings', in Newton, J., Long, S. and Sievers, B. (eds) *Coaching in Depth: The Organizational Role Analysis Approach*, London: Karnac.

Cardona, F. and Rafaelli, D. (2016) 'Turbulent family and organisational dynamics in the context of succession in a family business', *Organisational and Social Dynamics* 16.2: 245–254.

Chater, N. and Loewenstein, G. (2015) 'The under-appreciated drive for sense-making', *Journal of Economic Behavior & Organization*. Online at: http://dx.doi.org/10.2139/ssrn.2596897

Clay-Williams, R., Ludlow, K., Testa, L. et al. (2017) 'Medical leadership, a systematic narrative review: do hospitals and healthcare organisations perform better when led by doctors?', *BMJ Open*. Online at: https://bmjopen.bmj.com/content/7/9/e014474

Collins, J. and Porras, J. (1994) *Built to Last*, New York: Harper Collins.

Collinson, P. (2017) 'Sub-prime cars: are car loans driving us towards the next financial crash?', *The Guardian*, 10 February.

Colman, A. D. (1975) 'Irrational aspects of design', in Colman, A. D. and Bexton, W. H. (eds) *Group Relations Reader 1*, Washington, D.C.: A. K. Rice Institute Series.

Dicks, H. (1970) *Fifty Years of the Tavistock Clinic*, London: Routledge & Kegan Paul.

Financial Conduct Authority (2018) DP18/2: *Transforming Culture in Financial Services*. Discussion paper, first published 12 March.

Fortado, L. (2015) 'A rogue trader's tale', *The Financial Times*, 22 October.

French, R., Simpson, P. and Harvey, C. (2009) 'Negative capability: a contribution to the understanding of creative leadership', in Sievers, B., Brunning, H., De Gooijer, J. and Gould, L. (eds) *Psychoanalytic Studies of Organizations: Contributions from the International Society for the Psychoanalytic Study of Organizations*, London: Karnac.

Freud, S. (1917) 'Mourning and melancholia', in *Collected Papers*, Vol. 4, London: Hogarth Press, 1925.

——(1921) *Group Psychology and the Analysis of the Ego*, Penguin Freud Library, Vol. 12, Harmondsworth: Penguin Books, 1984.

——(1924) 'Recommendations to physicians practising psychoanalysis', in *Standard Edition*, Vol. 12, London: Hogarth Press, 1958.

Gabriel, Y. (1998) 'The hubris of management', *Administrative Theory and Praxis*, 20.3: 257–273.

Gapper, J. (2011) *How to be a Rogue Trader*, London: Penguin.

Gill, A. and Sher, M. (2011) 'Inside the minds of the money minders: deciphering reflections on money, behaviour and leadership in the financial crisis of 2007–2010', in Sievers, B. and Long, S. (eds) *Towards a Socioanalysis of Money, Finance and Capitalism: Beneath the Surface of the Financial Industry*, Abingdon: Routledge.

Goleman, D. (1995) *Emotional Intelligence*, New York: Bantam Books.

—— (1998) *Working with Emotional Intelligence*, New York: Bantam Books.

Griffiths, R. (1988) *Community Care: Agenda for Action*, London: HMSO.

Grubb Institute (1991) 'Professional management'. Notes prepared by the Grubb Institute on concepts relating to professional management.

Gustafson, J. P. (1976) 'The pseudomutual small group or institution', *Human Relations*, 29: 989–997.

Gutmann, D., Ternier-David, J. and Verrier, C. (1999) 'From envy to desire: witnessing the transformation', in French, R. and Vince, R. (eds) *Group Relations, Management, and Organization*, New York: Oxford University Press.

Heifetz, R. (1994) *Leadership Without Easy Answers*, Cambridge, MA: Harvard University Press.

Heifetz, R., Grashow, A. and Linsky, M. (2009) *The Practice of Adaptive Leadership: Tools and Tactics for Changing Your Organization and the World*, Cambridge, MA: Harvard University Press.

Hirschhorn, L. and Gilmore, T. (1992) 'The new boundaries of the "boundaryless" company', *Harvard Business Review*, May–June: 104–115.

Hirschhorn, L. and Horowitz, S. (2014) 'Extreme work environments: beyond anxiety and social defence', in Armstrong, D. and Rustin, M. (eds) *Social Defences Against Anxiety: Explorations in a Paradigm*, London: Karnac, pp. 189–212.

Hoggett, P. (2010) 'Perverse social structures', *Journal of Psycho-Social Studies*, 4.1: 57–64.

Hutton, J., Bazalgette, J. and Reed, B. (1997) 'Organisation-in-the-mind', in Neumann, J., Kellner, K. and Dawson-Shepherd, A. (eds) *Developing Organisational Consultancy*, London: Routledge.

Isaacs, W. N. (1993) 'Taking flight: dialogue, collective thinking and organizational learning', *Organizational Dynamics* 22.2: 24–39.

Jaques, E. (1951) *The Changing Culture of a Factory*, London: Tavistock Publications (see 'Working-through industrial conflict: the service department at the Glacier Metal Company', in Trist, E. and Murray, H. (eds) *The Social Engagement of Social Science, Volume 1: The Socio-Psychological Perspective*, London: Free Association Books, 1990).

——(1953) 'On the dynamics of social structure: a contribution to the psychoanalytical study of social phenomena deriving from the views of Melanie Klein', in Trist, E. and Murray, H. (eds) *The Social Engagement of Social Science, Volume 1: The Socio-Psychological Perspective*, London: Free Association Books, 1990.

——(1965) 'Death and the mid-life crisis', in Spillius, E. B. (ed.) *Melanie Klein Today, Volume 2: Mainly Practice*, London: Routledge, 1990.

Judiciary of England and Wales (2012) Sentencing remarks of Mr. Justice Keith in *R v Kweku Adoboli*, 20 November. Online at: www.judiciary.uk/wp-content/uploads/JCO/Documents/Judgments/kweku-adoboli-sentencing-remarks-20112012.pdf

Keats, J. (1817) *Letters of John Keats: A Selection Edited by Robert Gittings*, Oxford: Oxford University Press, 1987.

Kets de Vries, M. F. R. and Carlock, R. S., with Florent-Treacy, E. (2007) *Family Business on the Couch: A Psychological Perspective*, Chichester: John Wiley and Sons.

Klein, M. (1940) 'Mourning and its relations to manic depressive states', in *Love, Guilt and Reparation and Other Works 1921–1945*, London: Hogarth Press and Institute of Psychoanalysis, 1975.

——(1959) 'Our adult world and its roots in infancy', in Colman, A. D. and Geller, M. H. (eds) *Group Relations Reader 2*, Washington, D.C.: A. K. Rice Institute Series, 1985.

Lawrence, G. (1977) 'Management development . . . some ideals, images and realities', in Colman, A. D. and Geller, M. H. (eds) *Group Relations Reader 2*, Washington, D.C.: A. K. Rice Institute Series, 1985.

——(1995) 'The presence of totalitarian states-of-mind in institutions'. Paper presented at the inaugural conference on 'Group Relations' of the Institute of Human Relations, Sofia, Bulgaria, 1995. Online at: www.psychoanalysis-and-therapy.com/human_nature/free-associations/lawren.html

——(1998) 'Unconscious social pressures on leaders', in Klein, E., Gabelnick F. and Herr, P. (eds) *The Psychodynamics of Leadership*, Madison, CT: Psychosocial Press.

Lerner, M. (1986) *Surplus Powerlessness*, Atlantic Highlands, NJ: Humanities Press International.

Lewin, K. (1947) 'Frontiers in group dynamics, Parts I and II', *Human Relations*, 1: 5–41; 2: 143–153.

Lewis, E. and Casement, P. (1986) 'Inhibition of mourning by pregnancy: a case study', *Psychoanalytic Psychotherapy*, 2.1: 45–52.

Long, S. (2008) *The Perverse Organisation and its Deadly Sins*, London: Karnac.

Main, T. (1968) 'The ailment', in Barnes, E. (ed.) *Psychosocial Nursing: Studies from the Cassel Hospital*, London: Tavistock Publications.

Marris, P. (1986) *Loss and Change*, London: Routledge.

Meadows, D. (2008) *Thinking in Systems: A Primer*, White River Junction, VT: Chelsea Green Publishing.

Meltzer, D. (1978) *The Kleinian Development*, Perthshire: Clunie Press.

Menzies, I. E. P. (1960) 'Social systems as a defence against anxiety: an empirical study of the nursing service of a general hospital', in Trist, E. and Murray, H. (eds) *The Social Engagement of Social Science, Volume 1: The Socio-Psychological Perspective*, London: Free Association Books, 1990.

Menzies Lyth, I. E. P. (1979) 'Staff support systems: task and anti-task in adolescent institutions', in *Containing Anxiety in Institutions: Selected Essays*, London: Free Association Books, 1988.
——(1983) 'Bion's contribution to thinking about groups', in Grotstein, J. S. (ed.) *Do I Dare Disturb the Universe?*, London: Maresfield Library.
——(1990) 'A psychoanalytical perspective on social institutions', in Trist, E. and Murray, H. (eds) *The Social Engagement of Social Science, Volume I: The Socio-Psychological Perspective*, London: Free Association Books.
Millar, D. and Zagier Roberts, V. (1986) 'Elderly patients in "continuing care": a consultation concerning the quality of life', *Group Analysis*, 19: 45–59.
Miller, E. J. (1990a) 'Experiential learning in groups I: the development of the Leicester model', in Trist, E. and Murray, H. (eds) *The Social Engagement of Social Science, Volume 1: The Socio-Psychological Perspective*, London: Free Association Books.
——(1990b) 'Experiential learning in groups II: recent developments in dissemination and application', in Trist, E. and Murray, H. (eds) *The Social Engagement of Social Science, Volume 1: The Socio-Psychological Perspective*, London: Free Association Books.
Miller, E. J. and Gwynne, G. (1972) *A Life Apart*, London: Tavistock Publications.
Miller, E. J. and Rice, A. K. (1967) *Systems of Organization: The Control of Task and Sentient Boundaries*, London: Tavistock Publications (reprinted London: Routledge, 2001) (see 'Selections from: *Systems of Organization*', in Colman, A. D. and Bexton, W. H. (eds) *Group Relations Reader 1*, Washington, D.C.: A. K. Rice Institute Series, 1975; see also 'Task and sentient systems and their boundary controls', in Trist, E. and Murray, H. (eds) *The Social Engagement of Social Science, Volume 1: The Socio-Psychological Perspective*, London: Free Association Books, 1990).
Obholzer, A. (1987) 'Institutional dynamics and resistance to change', *Psychoanalytic Psychotherapy*, 2.3: 201–205.
Petriglieri, G. (2014) 'Emotions are data, too', *Harvard Business Review*, May. Online at: https://hbr.org/2014/05/emotions-are-data-too?autocomplete=true
Quine, C. (2006) 'Discovering purpose: exploring organisational meaning', London: Grubb Institute: unpublished working note.
Reed, B. and Bazalgette, J. (2006) 'Organizational role analysis at the Grubb Institute of Behavioural Studies: origins and development', in Newton, J., Long, S. and Sievers, B. (eds) *Coaching in Depth: The Organizational Role Analysis Approach*, London: Karnac.
Rice, A. K. (1963) *The Enterprise and Its Environment*, London: Tavistock Publications.
——(1965) *Learning for Leadership*, London: Tavistock Publications (see 'Selections from: *Learning for Leadership*', in Colman, A. D. and Bexton, W. H. (eds) *Group Relations Reader 1*, Washington, D.C.: A. K. Rice Institute Series, 1975.
——(1969) 'Individual, group and inter-group processes', in Trist, E. and Murray, H. (eds) *The Social Engagement of Social Science, Volume 1: The Socio-Psychological Perspective*, London: Free Association Books, 1990.
Roberts, V. Z. (2005) 'Birth and bereavement: the emotional impact of organisational change'. Keynote paper given at New Directions Conference 'Psychoanalysis and Group Process', Washington D.C., 11–13 February.
Rock, D. and Schwartz, J. (2006) 'The neuroscience of leadership', *strategy+business*, 43. Online at: www.strategy-business.com/article/06207
Santayana, G. (1905) *The Life of Reason, Volume 1* (reprinted New York: Dover, 1980).
Segal, H. (1986) 'Manic reparation', in *The Work of Hanna Segal: a Kleinian Approach to Clinical Practice*, London: Free Association Books/Maresfield Library, 1986.
Shapiro, E. R. (2000) 'The changing role of the CEO', *Organisational and Social Dynamics*, 1: 130–142.

——(2001) 'Institutional learning as chief executive', in Gould, L., Stapley, L. and Stein, M. (eds) *The Systems Psychodynamics of Organizations*, London: Karnac.

Sinek, S. (2009) *Start with Why: How Great Leaders Inspire Everyone to Take Action*, New York: Portfolio (a member of the Penguin Group USA).

Social Mobility Commission (2016) 'Socio-economic diversity in life sciences and investment banking: research on the barriers for under-privileged young people wanting to work in life sciences or investment banking'. Report published 1 September.

Spielberg, S. (2017) *The Post* [film].

Stein, M. (2000) 'The risk taker as shadow: a psychoanalytic view of the collapse of Barings Bank', *Journal of Management Studies*, 37.8: 1215–1229.

——(2007) 'Oedipus Rex at Enron: leadership, Oedipal struggles and organisational collapse', *Human Relations*, 60.9: 1387–1410.

——(2011) 'A culture of mania: a psychoanalytic view of the incubation of the 2008 credit crisis', *Organization*, 18.2: 173–186.

Symington, N. (1986) *The Analytic Experience: Lectures from the Tavistock*, London: Free Association Books.

Trist, E., Higgin, G., Murray, H. and Pollock, A. (1963) *Organizational Choice*, London: Tavistock Publications (see shortened version 'The assumption of ordinariness as a denial mechanism: innovation and conflict in a coal mine', in Trist, E. and Murray, H. (eds) *The Social Engagement of Social Science, Volume 1: The Socio-Psychological Perspective*, London: Free Association Books, 1990).

Tuckett, D. (2011) (ed.) *Minding the Markets: An Emotional Finance View of Financial Instability*, London: Palgrave Macmillan, pp. 1–25.

Turquet, P. (1974) 'Leadership: the individual and the group', in Colman, A. D. and Geller, M. H. (eds) *Group Relations Reader 2*, Washington, D.C.: A. K. Rice Institute Series, 1985.

Vaughan, L. and Finch, G. (2017) *The Fix: How Bankers Lied, Cheated and Colluded to Rig the World's Most Important Number*, Chichester: John Wiley & Sons.

Wells, L. (1985) 'The group-as-a-whole perspective and its theoretical roots', in Colman, A. D. and Geller, M. H. (eds) *Group Relations Reader 2*, Washington, D.C.: A. K. Rice Institute Series.

Wilber, K. (1996) *A Brief History of Everything*. Boston, MA and London: Shambhala.

Winnicott, D. W. (1947) 'Hate in the countertransference', in *Collected Papers: Through Paediatrics to Psycho-analysis*, London: Hogarth Press and the Institute of Psychoanalysis, 1958.

——(1971) *Playing and Reality*, London: Tavistock Publications (reprinted Harmondsworth: Penguin Books 1980).

INDEX

Note: *italic* page numbers refer to figures; numbers preceded by n are chapter endnote numbers.